60p

JOURNEY TOWARDS MUSIC

VICTOR GOLLANCZ

JOURNEY TOWARDS MUSIC

A memoir

LONDON
14 HENRIETTA STREET COVENT GARDEN
1964

Published by Victor Gollancz Limited
and printed in Great Britain by
The Camelot Press Limited of London
and Southampton

For my beloved companion
in concert-halls and opera-houses
over a period of
close on forty years

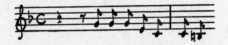

and for Peter Heyworth

And a new music there
It hears, music that wells
Undying and all other kinds excels.
—LUIS DE LEON (see page 63)

FOREWORD

IT IS PROPER that people should feel passionate about music, and perhaps natural that the expression of any opinions on the subject contrary to their own should wound or even anger them: indeed a lady very dear to me who was good enough to have a look in manuscript at my remarks about a certain composer didn't love or even like me any more for a good couple of days afterwards, and if her distaste hadn't suddenly vanished I should unhesitatingly have abandoned publication. Ought I then to point out that all criticism, of any art but perhaps particularly of music, is to some degree subjective, a matter of upbringing, environment, physical constitution, intellectual and spiritual proclivities, type of emotional responsiveness, even trivial and transitory moods; and that Cecilian writings should be objected to only when based, as I fear a good deal of this memoir may be based, on sheer ignorance?

There are several men and women whom I wish to thank. First my wife, who endured for seven weeks, with extraordinary patience, my withdrawal from her and the world except for a little bridge; my late father; my daughter Livia, for assuring me that the script was devoid of musical howlers, and I only hope that she is right; Colonel Moses, for placing his unrivalled knowledge at my disposal—he has been everywhere and heard and seen everything; Harold Rosenthal, that master of operatic history, for saving me from some Homeric errors; Neville Cardus, Ernest Bean and Frank Hollins, for invaluable suggestions; Sheila Bush, unique among proof-readers in respect of care, acuteness and generosity; Alec Robertson, for some material about Verdi; William Mann, for settling over the telephone a point half a dozen others had failed to settle (and one had settled wrongly) in a week; several critics, whose talk during otherwise boring intervals at the Festival Hall or Covent Garden has enlightened me on this point or that, and so has helped me, substantially if indirectly, in the writing of this memoir; my secretary Susan Davies, who is as efficient as she is beautiful—so beautiful that it would be a mistake to set her to music (see page 34); Diana Odling, for the spirit in which she copied out the music; my wife again, for letting me reproduce two of her paintings; and myself and my firm, for so kindly permitting me to borrow a few passages from 'My Dear Timothy'.

I have failed to track down the copyright-owners, if any, of a photograph or two. I apologise for any offence thereby committed; and if the hypothetical persons so involved would care, upon material-ising, to write to me, I should of course happily agree to any financial arrangement they might kindly suggest.

V. G.

Bottom House,
  April 12th, 1964.

CONTENTS

PAGE

PROLOGUE: An interview   17

CHAPTER I: Preliminaries—fat years and lean years—gramophone on Campden Hill Square—Stravinsky at the Langham Hotel—the birds in Rome—'modern' music—spirit in music—Benjamin Britten's War Requiem—words and music—inevitability in music—Berlioz' *Romeo and Juliet*—love-music—Berlioz' *Damnation*—his *Symphonie Fantastique* —his *L'Enfance du Christ*—the pifferari in Rome.   26

CHAPTER II: Production—*Manon* and Massenet—Rossini—*Count Ory, Il Barbiere, La Pietra del Paragone*—Wieland Wagner's *Fidelio*—prisoners' chorus in Düsseldorf—the music-camp—the Frankfurt *Fidelio*—lighting.   43

CHAPTER III: Operatic nostalgia—outmoded elegances—studying libretti—opera in English—historic performances—sacramental beauty—'remembering'.   51

CHAPTER IV: First opera nights—my mother's music—Chopin —my father.   64

CHAPTER V: Struggle for me by Verdi and Wagner—the Verdi-Wagner climate in my gallery days—the Art Work of the Future — *Aida* — *Tristan* — *Rigoletto* — Tetrazzini — Maria Ivogün—Joseph Schwarz—*Ballo*—*Trovatore*—Donizetti—Bellini—the Verdi renaissance—*Falstaff*—*Otello*.   68

CHAPTER VI: *Tannhäuser*—*Lohengrin*—*Parsifal*—*The Ring*— performances of *The Ring* before 1915—Leitmotifs—what I enjoyed in *The Ring*—'spotting' motifs—*The Ring* as an occasion.   77

PAGE

CHAPTER VII: Wagner performances in the twenties and thirties
—the splendour of 1927—Frida Leider—Flagstad—Melchior
—Olczewska—*Samson and Delilah*—Bruno Walter—Verdi
performances in the twenties and thirties—Claudia Muzio
and Toscanini in Milan—various Otellos—Joan Cross—
Sadler's Wells—the Old Vic—Charles Corri—Elisabeth
Rethberg—a performance in Siena—Rosa Ponselle—a
Falstaff in Charlottenburg.   87

CHAPTER VIII: Growing doubts about *The Ring*—length—
music-drama—Giovanni de' Bardi—the ideal opera—
leitmotifs again—Wagner's music—'too-muchness'—final
feelings about *Tristan*—the morality of *The Ring*—music
and personal life—the conflict between Wagner and Verdi
decided.   97

CHAPTER IX: Gluck's *Orfeo*—*Mignon*—Zélie de Lussan—
Hänsel and Gretel—music-halls as halls of semi-music—
Marie Brema—purity in music—Monteverdi's *Orfeo*—
Pelléas—Maggie Teyte—Maeterlinck—*Elektra*—Thomas
Beecham — *Salome* — *Rosenkavalier* — Lotte Lehmann—
Elisabeth Schumann—Strauss at the Tivoli—Strauss at
Walterspiel's—*Ariadne*—*Arabella*—*Capriccio*—*Die Fleder-
mauss*.   113

INTERLUDE: Zeffirelli's *Tosca*—opera in devastated Hamburg—
Jülich—Callas's *Tosca*—Zeffirelli's *Rigoletto*.   136

CHAPTER X: Beethoven.   141

CHAPTER XI: *Idomeneo*—Puccini—Destinn—*La Fanciulla del
West*—Queen Mary—*Turandot*—a hideous evening at the
Opéra-comique—singing—plays and opera—*Faust*.   152

CHAPTER XII: The Hammerstein season—*Four Saints in Three
Acts*—the Chaliapin season—the Russian Ballet—memories
of Chaliapin.   164

CHAPTER XIII: Salzburg—open-air meals—open-air music—a
visitation—Meran—cigars—casual music—*musique contrète*
—Salzburg personalities—music at eleven in the morning—
the Edinburgh festival—*Die Meistersinger*—Salzburg per-
formances—Mozart.   173

PART II: The Edgware Road—the Albert Hall—Verdi's Requiem
—religious music—the old proms—Bach—Brahms—Sir
Henry Wood—prom programmes—the White City—the
gramophone—Pachmann—Paderewski—Elena Gerhardt—
Julia Culp—Lotte Lehmann and Elisabeth Schumann in
Lieder—the Bechstein Hall—Ysaÿe and Pugno—Yehudi
Menuhin—Cortot, Thibaud, Casals—the Busch and Lener
Quartets—James Bradshaw—*Perséphone*—*Das Lied von der
Erde*—Berlioz—Schnabel—Klemperer.   191

APPENDIX: A proposed opera season.   227

INDEX   229

ILLUSTRATIONS

IN COLOUR:

Facing page

Probusgasse 6 · painting in oils by Ruth Gollancz   146

Salzburg from the Österreichischer Hof · painting in oils by Ruth
Gollancz   184

IN BLACK AND WHITE:

Facing page

Some bars of *L'Oiseau de Feu* inscribed by Stravinsky   28

Contemporary portrait of Stravinsky by Théodore Stravinsky   29

A savage listening to Mozart   30

'Voici des roses'   38

The Botticelli Venus   39

Berlioz conducting · by Gustave Doré   40

Instruments from the Abruzzi   41

Water-entrance to the Fenice   50

Traviata at the Fenice, 1854   51

Mario and Grisi singing 'Parigi o Cara' · drawing by George du
Maurier   54

Covent Garden in 1858   55

Wagner looking pensive   86

Verdi looking wry   87

Programme of *Aida*, July 28th 1914   92

Destinn   93

Richard Strauss at the Tivoli music-hall   132

Facing page

Programme of *Rosenkavalier* at Salzburg, 1930   133

Set for *Traviata* in ruined Hamburg   136

Set for *Figaro* in the same   137

Hotel-Restaurant Kaiserhof, Jülich   138

Living six to a room, Jülich   139

Beethoven's death mask   150

Schnabel playing Beethoven · by Edmund Kapp   151

Programme of the first night of *Boris*   166

Programme of the first night of *Khovantchina*   167

Drawing of himself · by Chaliapin   170

Another drawing by Chaliapin   171

A gift from Robert Nichols   176

A serenade at Salzburg   177

Yehudi Menuhin   212

The music-camp   213

The Libreria Vecchia   222

Otto Klemperer   223

IN THE TEXT

Page

The opera-box · drawing by George du Maurier   55

The mammoth · drawing by George du Maurier   57

PROLOGUE

AN INTERVIEW WITH
PETER HEYWORTH IN THE OBSERVER

HEYWORTH: You were reported the other day as saying that the trouble with contemporary performances of opera was production. What did you mean?

GOLLANCZ: Simply that the current enthusiasm for elaborate production tends to divert attention from the paramount necessity of providing the essentials—namely, first, great or at any rate good singing, and, as close seconds, fine orchestral playing finely directed and a satisfactory ensemble.

HEYWORTH: But surely there's nothing irreconcilable between the visual and the musical side of opera?

GOLLANCZ: Of course not. It's a question, rather, of priorities: your heart, over the field as a whole, will be where your treasure is. But I must add that certain kinds of fashionably elaborate production do fight with the musical-dramatic genius of the work in question.

HEYWORTH: Examples?

GOLLANCZ: Contrast Visconti and Zeffirelli. Visconti's *Don Carlo* is in total harmony with the genius of that masterpiece—even positively adds something to the embodiment of Verdi's greatness. But Zeffirelli's *Falstaff*! Among the minor exquisitenesses of the work is Dame Quickly's 'Reverenza', with her curtsy as part and parcel of the musical phrase; and she had to do it, if you please, on a narrow step half-way down a great staircase—simply because the staircase was scenically effective!

That was only one of many details: but what really horrified me was the closing scene in Windsor Park. The inwardness of that marvel, something far deeper in it than the superficial ragging, is a sort of quiet: the quiet of an 80-year-old musician who can smilingly accept the follies of life as he looks out in hushed wonder at the beauty of the world. If the stage is to emphasise anything, it should emphasise that. But what did Zeffirelli give us? A distracting over-elaboration, a sort of noisy, brazen fussiness. I soon closed my eyes.

HEYWORTH: I'm certainly with you over *Don Carlo*, but disagree

completely about Zeffirelli. To my mind the 'artificiality' of a
theatre in Windsor Park brilliantly solves the perennial problem of
all that activity and bustle. For once everyone isn't falling over
everyone else. But if for you the essence of all this eerie scene with
its cruel baiting of an old man is its 'quietness', I can quite see why
you don't like the production.

But let's take another example. Do you remember the melancholy
watery October light in Act 3, Scene 1 where Falstaff reflects on his
misfortunes? Surely that adds to the music. But perhaps you'd
closed your eyes by then!

GOLLANCZ: Probably. But I must insist that quiet *is* the essence of that
closing scene. The fairy music, the wedding march, the exquisite
snatches of love-song, *mezza notte*—these are what set the tone.
And, really you know, 'cruel baiting'! Does 'Pizzica, pizzica' *sound*
cruel?[1] . . . Then take *Don Giovanni*. The problem here, from the
musical-dramatic point of view, is to reduce as drastically as possible
the pauses between the various scenes: but Zeffirelli had to have his
elaborate sets, and the first great finale was broken into, with ruin
to the music, by a pause of, I'll swear, a full quarter of an hour. Or so
it seemed, the night I was there.

HEYWORTH: I gather that the whole thing now runs much more
smoothly and quickly than it did on the first night. But do you really
mean that the only problem of producing *Don Giovanni* is to make
the pauses as short as possible? Wouldn't you agree that it is in some
sense a double-headed work—at once classical and romantic—and
that Zeffirelli's production underlines its romanticism in a way that
no other production has done for years?

I'm not saying that this is the only way to produce it, or that there
aren't miscalculations in Zeffirelli's production. But, apart from

---

[1] A few days before this interview appeared in The Observer, I was delighted
to read the following in The Times of January 31st, for I had begun to fear
that my opinion of Zeffirelli might be tiresomely wrongheaded, so gently
pitying did some of my friends seem about it. I ought to add however that, as I
have since been told, musical politics may largely explain the Roman reaction:

"The new season has now been officially inaugurated with Verdi's *Falstaff*.
Mr. Franco Zeffirelli, producing an opera for the first time in Rome, was
responsible for sets, costumes and production, all of which followed the lines of
performances he had already staged in England, Holland and Israel and at
Palermo. . . . The Rome critics, led by the composer, Mr. Renzo Rossellini, in
the pages of Il Messagero, have not been too kind to Mr. Zeffirelli, accusing
him of submerging Verdi in too much production. But the Roman opera-goers
have given his work their unconditional approval. . . ."

providing an absolutely lovely series of sets (something that's not all that common at Covent Garden), surely he also threw light on the score? I wouldn't by any means defend everything he's done—his *Alcina* seemed to me a grossly anti-musical affair, simply because he didn't believe in the work's dramatic validity. But surely his production of *Cavalleria Rusticana* is a case of an opera being reborn through his visual imagination?

GOLLANCZ: Ah, that's quite another matter! Here were utterly delightful stage pictures, accompanied by third-rate music adequately performed. If people had broken into the music to applaud the sets, who would have cared? They probably did—I don't remember. If you must have *Cav.* and *Pag.*—if they must be reborn, God forbid —I couldn't imagine a better way of doing them.

As to the *Don*, I don't recall the production well enough to say yea or nay to you about the romanticism: I remember it only as terribly over-ornate, like an *antiquità* crammed with heavy, dubious furniture. And while it's of course true that the achievement of continuity is not the only problem, it's the crucial one. That's why, I suppose, far and away the most satisfactory performance I've ever seen was done with curtains only. It's astonishing what you can do with hardly any scenery at all: one of the most moving performances of *Fidelio* I've ever attended was also scenically, it happens, the most primitive.

HEYWORTH: Where was that?

GOLLANCZ: In an old barn, at the music-camp near Hermitage. And that reminds me! The most perverse of all *Fidelio* productions must surely have been Wieland Wagner's. *Fidelio* is a hymn to the unconditional sacredness of individual personality—of every 'single, separate' human being. And what did Wieland Wagner give us in the prisoners' chorus, the central expression of this theme? The stylised movement of an undifferentiated mass. Better a thousand times Zeffirelli's realism (marred, by the way, even as realism by the incontinent elevation of Hearn's oak in full view of the audience) than that sort of 'highbrow' preposterousness!

HEYWORTH: But surely men can be oppressed to a point where they do lose identity? That happened in the concentration camps, and the whole point of Wieland Wagner's Stuttgart production was that he made us experience *Fidelio* in the light of recent history. A partial view of an 'eternal' masterpiece, you may say. But surely a relevant one?

GOLLANCZ: No—listen to the music of that chorus!

HEYWORTH: Well, let's get back to where we started. You put great singing first—before the orchestra and ensemble as well as before production . . .

GOLLANCZ: . . . in most opera, yes. Certainly in Italian and Italianate opera. I'm not sure about Wagner, or certain operas, for instance, of the French school.

HEYWORTH: Well, you make some pretty large exceptions, but let's stick to the Italian field, and where that is concerned I certainly wouldn't disagree with you. But isn't the main point that we are living in a period of decline where vocal standards (among other things) are concerned? You must have as long an experience of opera as almost all the board of Covent Garden put together. What do you feel about this?

GOLLANCZ: Of course I agree with you—enthusiastically. And I sometimes wonder if there is not a tie-up between this decline in singing and the attention that's given to production today.

HEYWORTH: Calling in a new world to redress the deficiencies of an old one. But tell me how you came by your love of singing.

GOLLANCZ: It is a matter, I suppose, of early environment. My grandfather, Samuel Marcus Gollancz, was a *chazan*—a synagogue cantor —and the family legend was that he was one of the greatest tenors of the nineteenth century. As he sang only in synagogues, there could be no critical evaluation of this claim: but I vividly remember my father telling me—apropos of the old man's singing of 'Celeste Aida' in our drawing room at a great age and with the merest remnant of a voice—"He sang the last note correctly: he took it *pianissimo*, as few tenors nowadays care to do."

Certainly Jenny Lind thought very highly of him: she once wrote him out a free pass for any performance anywhere in which she might be singing, but whether from admiration of his vocal or of his artistic powers—he turned out miniature *objets d'art* with fine craftsmanship—I am not sure. Incidentally, there is a charming passage in his modest little autobiography, somewhat to the following effect: "I have heard and admired all the great singers of my time, but only three have moved me to both tears and astonishment: Madame Adelina Patti, Madame Jenny Lind and Herr Nachtigall, the *chazan* of a small synagogue in Poland. These three alone seemed to me to be able to play with their voices untiringly and with ease, just as children play with their toys."

Anyhow, that was the atmosphere I was brought up in: the talk was all of Patti, Jenny Lind, Alboni, Mario, Grisi, Pasta, Christine

Nillson, Trebelli, Tamagno, and the rest. On top of that, my father would go about singing the old arias, and although he was always abominably out of tune I got the general hang of them. I was a wonderfully lucky boy.

HEYWORTH: I envy you. Ever since I came across you stamping out of a Sutherland performance and booming "God, she's as dull as Melba" I've realised that you have rather different standards from most people! But what was actually your first real operatic experience?

GOLLANCZ: As a matter of fact it was *Traviata* with Melba; and though I was to think other sopranos far finer, that first *Traviata* committed me to a delight in fine singing that is as fresh and keen today as on that early summer evening more than half a century ago. Soon I was saving up not only my small pocket money but my lunch money too for my summer season in the Covent Garden gallery; and eventually I was going almost every night.

HEYWORTH: You were still at school?

GOLLANCZ: Yes—my heyday was from 1909 to 1912, when I went to Oxford: this deprived me of part of the season. School was over at ten to five: I would rush across to Baron's Court Station, take the tube to Covent Garden, run as fast as I could round the corner into Floral Street, and take up my stand for the happy waiting.

There was always great excitement, as one rounded the corner, in estimating the length of the queue. If its tail stretched beyond the stage entrance, everything depended on how much head it had to it. This you couldn't tell till you'd continued your run to the gallery door; because the practice was to open this door, and let people up the long staircase to a point a little short of the pay-box, some varying time before the pay-box itself was unbarred. So if the queue stretched beyond the stage entrance, and one also found that 'the people had gone up', the position was painfully critical. It happened, however, that I never failed to get in, though once I very nearly failed, and the uncertainty was agonising—I was the last to squeeze through at the première of *Electra* in 1910. (I must spare a second here to celebrate little Harris, a greasy-hatted barber-tobacconist from round the corner in Bow Street who used to hang about the gallery queue with tickets for the amphitheatre stalls, in the hope that he could tempt us if we couldn't get into the gallery. He added only about a shilling to the price, and did his scalping more from a Jewish love of opera—he hated the idea that anyone should miss a performance—than from a Jewish-Gentile love of gain.)

I always sat in the same seat, B49: the regulars used to leave it free for me until it was certain I shouldn't be coming. The only 'honour' I've ever really wanted is a little steel plaque on it!

HEYWORTH: Are there any performances you recall with particular vividness?

GOLLANCZ: The apogee, I suppose, was the Nile scene in *Aida*, interpreted by Destinn, Caruso and Dinh Gilly. No young opera-goer of today could possibly realise what it was like: all the beauty and drama came to life for us in those incomparable voices, not as an occasional rarity, but in note after note and phrase after phrase, and throughout the whole long series of arias and duets and ensembles.

Who could ever forget Caruso in that act, from the overwhelming exaltation of his 'Pur ti riveggo, mia dolce Aida' as he burst in on us, to his equally tremendous 'Sacerdote, io resto a te' as he strode across the stage to surrender? My God, how we leapt to our feet to applaud him as the curtain came down! Or who could ever forget, either, Emmy Destinn's 'O patria mia', with its glorious combination of vocal purity and passion?

I adored Destinn: we used to say that her twiddly bit in the first act of *Tosca* was alone worth our whole half-crown 'and then some', and she accomplished the change of register in 'Vissi d'arte' with almost inconceivable mastery. But best of all were her soft high notes. They were like exquisitely rounded pearls, suddenly appearing, perfectly poised, out of nowhere: and were specially breath-taking when they opened a phrase, as with 'Un bel di' in *Butterfly*.

Then there was a wonderful *Ugonotti*, with Destinn, Tetrazzini, Scotti, Journet and Zenatello (or Caruso, but I never heard him in that role) all in the same cast; Zenatello's great leaping 'Esultate' at his entry in *Otello*; John McCormack's Don Ottavio; Maggie Teyte's Mélisande; Chaliapin's Boris; Vanni Marcoux, equally fine (perhaps because of his presumably Italo-French origin) in parts as disparate as Arkel and Sparafucile; Gilibert's Father in *Louise*; and Martinelli, whom I heard at his British debut, as Cavarodossi. And I must spare a word for little Zucchi, whom we used to call the pocket Caruso. He specialised at Covent Garden in such tiny roles as Il Messagero and Borsa, but might well have sung Radamès and the Duke in smaller houses—probably indeed did so. (Ah, and I suddenly remember Patti, at a charity concert: singing like a gentle spring morning at close on 70. I was sitting in the cheapest seats, which happened to be not behind but actually *on* the platform, so that I was within a very few yards of her; and I used to brag about this proximity long afterwards, whenever people grew eloquent, in the proprietory sort of way all amateurs have, about their own musical experiences. After many encores at what was supposed to be the end of that concert she had to sing 'Home, sweet home', her regular signal that she had really finished, twice over. Elisabeth Schumann, in her beautiful autumn, sang with just the silvery ease of Patti in old age.)

All this was before the first world war. Later there were Lotte Lehmann's Marschallin, Ponselle's Norma, Maria Ivogün's Zerbinetta, Rethberg's Aida, Richard Mayr's Minister in *Fidelio*, not to mention his Ochs—but I could go on for ever. And the point I want to make is this: it was above all the vocal interpretation that realised, not only what the music had intended, but the dramatic meaning of the whole. And if the scenery was makeshift—well, that was a pity, but by comparison . . .!

HEYWORTH: And what do you think are the marks of really great singing?

GOLLANCZ: Heavens, what a question! I am anything but a technician, and incidentally, like my father, can't sing, hum or whistle even approximately in tune: I hear the exact notes in my head and yet can't reproduce them. But I'll have a shot at answering you so far as operatic singing is concerned. To be in the supreme class, I'd say, he (let's say he for convenience) must have a big, full voice of beautiful quality. (James Joyce once asked me, "Don't you think the most important thing in a tenor is that he should sing *loud*?"— referring to O'Sullivan, the Irish tenor at the Paris Opéra who used to sing in *William Tell* and *La Juive*. That is half the truth. And one of the marvels about Caruso was that, however powerfully he might sing, you always felt he could sing twice as powerfully if he wanted to.)

His—the great singer's—breath control must be perfect: so must his intonation and his phrasing—and he must attack with his consonants in the middle of the note. He must be a master of clean, steady *mezza voce*—a *mezza voce* devoid of mawkishness or sentimentality. His cantilena must be beautifully smooth and even (rather like a little Chippendale drawer going in 'with the air' as you follow it through with your finger); and he must also be able, when occasion demands, to sing with a high sense of drama.

He must be expert in the right kind of vibrato, which enriches

JOURNEY TOWARDS MUSIC

the quality of a note, and be incapable of the wrong kind, which obscures its situation and makes it unclean. There must be a certain authority in his voice and singing. Above all, he must be musical; and he must serve the composer in the single-minded sort of way in which Klemperer serves Beethoven.

I have been talking of singers in the supreme class: but a singer can be pretty great if he possesses, in a high degree, only a considerable number of these qualities.

HEYWORTH: Well, to leave the supreme class on one side, you presumably don't think there are as many great singers nowadays as there were when you were a boy?

GOLLANCZ: Now I must be careful. I don't possess a gramophone, and rarely listen to one. The reason you may think rather peculiar: though I hear a great deal of music, listening to it is always an occasion for me, and I don't want to be able to turn the thing on and off at my whim. Take works one can hear only once every so often, like the Missa Solemnis or *L'Enfance du Christ* or the late Beethoven 'cello sonatas: I like looking forward for weeks or months to hearing them. But not having a gramophone means that there may be many singers, unfamiliar to me except by hearsay, who might truly be called great. Then again I should like to leave *Lieder* singers out of account.

Finally, let me differentiate between Wagner and other forms of opera. I've never heard a really good Wagner tenor, with the possible exception of Melchior: the basses and baritones are as good, I think, as they have ever been in my time (though I've never really enjoyed a Wotan as much as van Rooy): and I am inclined to rank Birgit Nilsson with the very greatest of Wagnerian sopranos.

HEYWORTH: Well, after all these reservations, what's your verdict?

GOLLANCZ: There were many great singers when I was a boy: there is only one today. Don't misunderstand me. We have a number of fine singers, a number it's a delight to listen to, a few that may even be called superb. I think at random of Lisa della Casa, of Christoff, of Ghiaurov, of Victoria de los Angeles, of Rita Gorr. But no one of these is in my opinion great.

Take the basses. Ghiaurov enraptured me the other night in *Don Carlo*; but my mind went back to Chaliapin (for all his musical naughtinesses), and I couldn't help feeling that he had just the last thing that Ghiaurov misses.

HEYWORTH: And who's your exception?

GOLLANCZ: Callas. I shall never forget the first time I heard her, years and years ago, in *Norma*, and how I thought, in a sort of ecstasy, "Here at last it is again!" Nowadays, of course, she often highly displeases one: and then, it may be for a minute or two, it may be for a whole aria, one says, worshipfully, "Yes, she's in the great tradition." Who else, nowadays, could perform that miracle of her entry into 'Dite alla giovane' in the second act of *Traviata*?

HEYWORTH: One last question. May it not be that, throughout our talk, you've been looking at the past through the rosy spectacles of remembered happiness?

GOLLANCZ: I daresay!

CHAPTER I

I DIDN'T DARESAY anything of the kind: I had no doubt, and this remains my opinion, that the present is far inferior to the past in respect of operatic, other than Wagnerian, singing. I simply felt that the question and answer would make an effective ending.

But I enjoyed the interview so much that I cannot resist going on; and I think with delight of trying to remember, at any odd moment, musical experiences I have loved, and occasionally hated, over a period of close on sixty years. But I shall be handicapped by my own carelessness. I ought to have kept all my programmes (how I wish now I had!), but my practice has been very variable: for a year or so I would be obsessive about preserving, and even hiding from cleaners-up, these mementoes of happiness, and then for another year or so I would treat them with a shameful lack of respect or even throw them away. And I was feckless in another way too. The Covent Garden programmes of my boyhood consisted of large four-page folders, with the current performances on the outside and a rich list of forthcoming ones within. Now my father, the only business-man in our family, collected stamps, and being of a tidy disposition used to cut off the perforations and paste the torsos into an album. (I had reason to regret this when, after his death, the album descended to me: there was a penny black or a blue Mauritius or something with a name like that in it.) In the case of some of my operatic programmes I followed his lead: I cut out the current programme, glued it into an exercise-book and threw away the rest. So a great deal that might have reminded me of performances I may have heard but have forgotten has perished.

There will be a lot therefore that I shall fail to remember at all: there will be a lot that I shall think I remember vividly, but be unable to verify: and there will be a lot that I shall indeed think I remember, but in a vague and confused sort of way. Still, I shall rely on such memories as I have, and shall not bother on the whole to look up works of reference and suchlike, for after all this is a personal memoir of no historic importance, and if on occasion I go wrong no great harm will have been done. I may even invent a little, but always in the spirit of truth.

Something else must be borne in mind. There have been periods in my life when I have heard a great deal of music, and periods when I have heard hardly any. The fat years have been from the middle nineteen-hundreds to 1914, from the middle nineteen-twenties to the middle nineteen-thirties, and from about 1948 to the present time: the lean years have been the rest. The leanness is to be explained by a number of factors, mostly disastrous. Before the middle nineteen-hundreds I was handicapped by immaturity. From 1914 to 1919 I was guarding the coast of Northumberland, assisting the headmaster (later Archbishop of Canterbury) at Repton, and garrisoning Singapore, with only occasional intervals in London to refresh me. From 1919 to the middle nineteen-twenties I was trying to make a living for my wife, myself and the beginnings of a family: I was working day and night, could hardly ever spare an evening off, and was at first so poor—I mean as the middle class talks of poverty, not poor as the poor are poor —that the cheaper seats once a fortnight at the local cinema were the best we could manage. (The door-man there was a great favourite of ours: we always consulted him about the quality of the film we thought of seeing, and he always replied 'Not bad . . .' and then, after a little pause, 'Takes some following, mind!') But we did have a gramophone, a rather rickety old one, in those days, with, at first, only about half a dozen records, which we played obsessively day after day, mostly before breakfast. We had Mozart's heavenly dissonance quartet, which I remember thinking, I cannot imagine why, quite unmozartian; Caruso and Geraldine Farrar in the 'Libiamo' from *Traviata*—and how my heart would leap up in that faded William-Morrisy drawing-room on Campden Hill Square as I heard its great soaring phrases!; Zenatello and Destinn in the Nile scene duet from *Aida*, Destinn singing with the rapt urgency, a sort of spiritual urgency, that can never be explained to anyone who hasn't heard her; Caruso in a popular *canzone*, not 'Funiculì Funiculà' but with a similar ring to it; Scotti in *Tosca*; and, best of all, the Beethoven C sharp minor quartet, opus 131. We usually kept that for the evening. A little later we got the fifth symphony, and Livia used to toddle a sort of mime to the scherzo— we called it 'running into the corners'. At two and a half she could already distinguish that particular record: she would pick it out, give it us to put on, stand quite still during the first two movements, then plunge into her performance with a giggle as the scherzo started up.

But we did hear a little 'live' music just before we got married: indeed it was at Covent Garden during what I have always called the Wedding March at the end of *L'Oiseau de Feu* that we practically became engaged. Fourteen years or so later Stravinsky was dining with me at the Langham Hotel before a concert he was giving across the road and I told him about this; whereupon he asked for a piece of note-paper, wrote out a bar or two of the music, and added "*Pour Mme. Ruth et Victor Gollancz, souvenir de Igor Strawinsky, qui était en quelque sorte témoin de leur union matrimoniale. Londres le 26 Nov 34*". You can just see 'Langham Hotel, Portland Place, London W.1.' coming through from the other side of the notepaper. I recollect that Stravinsky eat nothing on that occasion but smoked salmon, of which he had two large helpings.

We heard a little music, too, in Rome shortly after our marriage: we had gone there for a second honeymoon about six months after Livia was born, and had put up at the Quirinale, right down by the station— a dingy place in those days, but we could afford nothing better. There was an entrancing compensation, however: our room backed on to the Costanzi, and every morning we could hear the rehearsals quite clearly, those for *Tristano e Isotta* included. There was a garden between the Quirinale and the Costanzi, and the moment the rehearsal got going the air would come alive with a chorus of chirruping birds. But we could rarely manage tickets for the performances themselves. Wein-gartner conducted: with a single finger of his right hand, as always, and with the other arm down the seam of his trousers in correct military fashion. His prelude to *Carmen* was the most incisive I have ever heard. As you waited for the curtain to go up the ushers shouted at you 'Programma dell' opera! Programma de' grandiosi balli Russi!' At Salzburg, later, it was to be 'Sitzkissen bitte! Einen Schilling!' and in the Verona amphitheatre 'Cioccolata! Caramelle!'

We became regular concert- and opera-goers, as I have said, in 1926. Then from the end of 1936—most overflowing, I think of my musical years, but with the richness of autumn about it: the world's winter was coming on—to say 1948 I had other things than music to think about. At first there was the desperate effort of the Popular Front, with the Left Book Club as one of its spearheads, to check Hitler without war: I was speaking almost every night in the towns and villages of England, and to 'take time off' for more than a very occasional opera or concert could never have occurred to me. (We did go, however, to the Tosca-nini Beethoven cycle in the summer of 1939, when, as everyone knew, the die had already been cast: and I remember the occasion not only for its music but for two disasters it portended. The old Queen's Hall would soon be in ruins; and Jan Masaryk came up to me as the applause was dying down after 'Freude . . . Millionen . . .' and said "I'd love to come to one of your parties". It was to suicide or murder that he was going.) Then there was the National Campaign for Rescue from Nazi

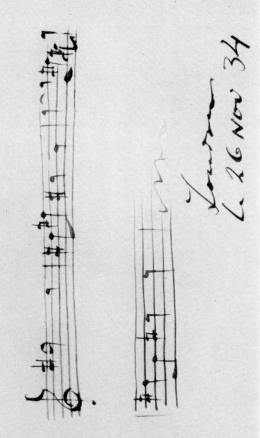

Courtesy of the artist

STRAVINSKY TODAY · BY THÉODORE STRAVINSKY

Terror, and Save Europe Now; and when I got back from Germany in 1946 my publishing affairs were in tatters and I had to repair them. It was not till my return from a first trip to America in 1948 that I could freely hear music again.

§ 2

There is a point I want specially to make in these preliminaries. I am not in the smallest degree a musician. I have had no musical training; in the matter of playing an instrument my highest achievement is to pick out an easy tune on the piano; and though I have read, with eagerness and absorption, quite a number of technical manuals, including one at least on dodecaphony, I have read them, not like a student, but rather as a scientific ignoramus might read about quanta or, if these have been superseded, their modern equivalents. All I know about music I have picked up by the way. I am not indeed an expert in any of the many things I love, such as literature, painting, architecture, bridge and English pottery. I am not even an expert in publishing: the relevant name here is Sir Stanley Unwin.

So what I have to say can be of no possible interest to musicians, many of whom, I rather think, will dislike my whole approach, regarding it as beside the point, based on a misunderstanding and tediously sentimental. I am not blaming them for this or for anything else: I can well understand how maddening outsiders must be to professionals or even to instructed amateurs. And of course I reverence that whole enviable company: what sort of life should I have had without them?

My purpose, then, in these few paragraphs of apologia is simply this: I want to cover myself in advance for any howlers I may be guilty of, and I want to make clear that my only claim to attention is that I 'love music' and that it is for my kin, not for musicians, that I write.

But an important corollary follows. There will be little in the following pages about 'modern' music; just as, if I were writing about my pleasure in art, there would be little about abstracts. The reasons, however, are quite different. With great exceptions—Braque, Klee—I heartily dislike abstracts, and think most of their begetters either talentless or bogus. That is by no means what I feel about 'modern' music. On the contrary: apart altogether from such works as *Wozzeck* and *Lulu*, which I could not hear too often (indeed a few years ago we went specially to Vienna on the sole errand of hearing *Wozzeck*, though we had heard it several times already), I find a good deal of 'modern' music extremely interesting, and comparatively little of it, or at any rate comparatively little of such specimens of it as get to our concert halls, either worthless or *mala fide*. But I must mention in passing Nono's *Hiroshima*. It is not *mala fide* surely, but apart from some fascinating experiments with the voice it is worthless as well as hideous. I was particularly furious when I heard it at a promenade concert last summer, because it apparently put a lot of instruments out of tune for the Mozart that followed.

The reason why in the following pages there will be little about 'modern' music is briefly this. What means most to me in music is spirit (as in the slow variation near the close of the *Eroica*) on the one hand, and sheer physical rapture, often itself spiritual in effect (as in the last movement of Bach's violin concerto in E, or, to name something very different, Verdi's 'Libiamo'), on the other. The purely intellectual content means a lot to me but considerably less. I am speaking of the music itself, not of its interpretation: among interpreters of Beethoven, for example, Schnabel and Klemperer have delighted me more than any others, and above all by reason of their superbly intellectual approach. Now the interest of most 'modern' music is primarily intellectual: and I want this book to be about the spiritual experience and physical rapture that music has given me.

But I do not think that I ought to leave it at that, for I shall surely be asked what I mean by 'spirit'. So let me be a little more explicit:

There are various pleasures to be had from listening to music. There is an intellectual pleasure: the pleasure of following a logical development; of grasping a structure; of noticing ingenuities of harmony and counterpoint, or happy subtleties of ornamentation, or occasional touches of humour, or the like. There is also a sensuous pleasure: the nerves react delightedly, or with horror or excitement or a sensation of lulling tranquillity (and all such reactions are pleasurable), to the drama and passion, the brief silences and gentle beginnings, the whole physical *sound* of the thing. But there are moments, and not only in listening to the works of the few supreme masters, when it is no longer a question of mere pleasure or even of happiness: it is a question of joy inexpressible. Wordsworth has perhaps depicted such moments better than any other writer in English:

> "In such access of mind, in such high hour
>   Of visitation from the living God,
>   Thought was not: in enjoyment it expired.
>   No thanks he breathed, he proffered no request.

From 'The Impossible Adventure' by Alain Gheerbrant (Gollancz)

AN INDIAN OF STONE-AGE CULTURE, IN A FASTNESS BETWEEN
THE ORINOCO AND THE AMAZON, LISTENING TO MOZART ON
A GRAMOPHONE RECORD

> Rapt into still communion that transcends
> The imperfect offices of prayer and praise,
> His mind was a thanksgiving to the power
> That made him; it was blessedness and love."

The expression is exact. Wordsworth, in those last two lines, is by no means saying that he was *giving* thanks, that he *knew* himself blessed, that he *felt* himself loving or loved. He is saying that 'his mind' —namely he, himself, his whole being—*was* a thanksgiving, *was* blessedness, *was* love. He was 'rapt': he was merged: subject and object had become one: or rather, for the moment, the very distinction between subject and object was a falsehood.

(Wordsworth was writing, of course, in the language of his day, when the word "God" came automatically to the lips or pen of a man who was attempting to describe such an experience. Nowadays things are different: to bring 'God' into an argument is immediately to handicap oneself with a majority of the intelligent. So omit 'from the living God' and 'to the power that made him'. The passage can very well stand without them. I am concerned with description, not explanation.)

An experience of the kind, which may fall to the lot of a music-lover not once in a year or a decade but several times a week, and be always fresh and unblunted, cannot by its nature be reflected upon at the moment of its occurrence: it just happens, and that's the end of the matter. But it can be reflected upon subsequently; and the following characteristics then emerge:

(1) The primary note, if single notes can indeed be separated out from the chord, is perhaps one of *rightness* and *inevitability*, or maybe one should say of *inevitable rightness*. This *rightness* is experienced as above beauty, and as above good and evil, though the good and the beautiful (and the evil, as a by-product) partake of it. And to hear this note of rightness is to know that all's well: this is one of the sources of the joy that engulfs one.

(2) To put it in a slightly different way, what is momentarily revealed—not through a glass darkly, but face to face—is *reality*. I do not of course mean that the *nature* of reality is revealed to one, in any way that could be even remotely analysed by, or formulated to, oneself or others. Rather, reality is for a moment *there*. Or more exactly, perhaps, one is for a moment *with* reality. (One responds, so to say, 'that's reality'.) And to be with it is to know again that all's well.

(3) One is not merely *with* it for a moment: one *is* it for a moment. There has been more than a visitation, there is a communion: one is oneself part and parcel of the reality.

(4) The reality experienced must perforce be described as immaterial in the sense that it impinges as being of a totally different order from that of my body, or of the concert-hall, or of the catgut on the fiddlers' violins. Of a *totally* different order: existent in another dimension. And yet, when I reflect upon the experience afterwards, I realise that without my ears and the concert-hall and the catgut—not to mention the food and drink, and the music-paper, and the lodgings, of Beethoven's Viennese existence—no such communion could have been mine.

(5) The whole moment—the reality, myself, and my communion with it, to distinguish what in truth cannot be distinguished—is outside time and place: it is happening everywhere and in eternity. And the reality is *universal*. It includes, or rather it *is*, everything: everything that could possibly happen, everything that could conceivably *be*. But any idea that it is a sum total would, in recollection, be laughable: it is unitary as well as universal.

(6) The communion is also a *recognition*. One *recognises* something with a still but overwhelming delight: one greets it with a "Yes, this is it: this is what I know it to be, must ever know it to be, must ever have known it to be". And what is recognised is also the recogniser.

(7) Certain emotions, one realises later, or perhaps one should say identifications, have accompanied, or rather been bound up with, the moment. One's mind, in Wordsworth's phraseology, has been blessedness and tranquillity, gratitude and—above everything—love. But there has been something else. There has been awe: one has bent the knee.

To repeat, then: I have rarely experienced either the spiritual blessedness I have been attempting to describe, or sensuous rapture, when listening to 'modern' music. But that is not to say that I never shall—so far at least as the spiritual blessedness is concerned. I rather suspect, for instance, that Elizabeth Lutyens' setting of a text by Wittgenstein would give me something of the kind, and I am sorry to have missed its recent performance.

So much by way of preliminaries. Now how to proceed? Chronologically? By subjects? Or by a mixture of the two? What I have provisionally decided is this. I shall use the next chapter to trick out my interview with Peter Heyworth, filling in details that lack of space compelled me to omit, and generally enriching the whole. Then I shall go back to my boyhood; and thereafter shall as far as possible proceed chronologically.

§ 3

But I want to seize the opportunity, straight away, of saying something about the Britten War Requiem, given at the Festival Hall, after several performances elsewhere, this last Thursday, December 12th. I write with a good deal of hesitation: first because my musical limitations are such as I have already explained; secondly because I shall be running counter to many critics I greatly esteem, and to many others who equal me in love, and outweigh me in knowledge, of music; and thirdly because it goes against the grain to criticise in however qualified a manner a work so noble in intent, so powerful in its impact on public opinion, and incidentally so congruous, for anything that this may be worth, with my own most cherished convictions.

I might, moreover, change my opinion in this or that particular after further hearings. Thursday evening's was indeed my fourth, but the first had been over the air and the second and third on a gramophone, and certain passages gripped me on Thursday that had failed to grip me before. And yet I believe that in general my present opinion will stand: namely that this is a fascinatingly interesting and often moving achievement by a great human being, but not, as a whole, the work of specifically musical genius—other than in a loose, journalistic way of speaking—that so many critics have found it.

There are many great beauties in the score. The 'Recordare', for instance, haunts me with the loveliness of its shape: so does the 'Benedictus': and though the 'Libera me' has not moved me on any of the four occasions as much as I had hoped—its jaunty rhythms disturb me —I think it will.

A good deal of the score, on the other hand, seems lacking in purely musical inspiration. The 'Dies Irae' is surely quite ineffective: the reason being, I suspect, that Britten, being what he is, consciously rejects, though I have no warrant for saying so, the traditional idea of a Day of Judgment. Moreover, the reminiscence of a phrase from the march to the scaffold in the *Symphonie Fantastique*—it occurs first immediately after the fanfare—worries me a lot, as reminiscences have worried me before in other works by Benjamin Britten; for while deliberate quotation, or a passing reference to some other composer—

as in Strauss' *Metamorphosen* or Brahms's first symphony—can be highly significant, in the present case the effect can only be to distract the listener's attention by suddenly transporting him to another world. Or perhaps I should say that this is the effect it has on me, for it does not appear to worry others.

What I am chiefly doubtful about, however, is the setting of the verse. There are poems, and passages of poetry, that are far more expressive when heard 'plain', either in the mind or on the platform, then when heard with a musical setting of whatever excellence. In such cases the poetry *is* the music: self-sufficient, the lily requires no gilding and therefore suffers from any attempt to gild it. Could even Shakespeare himself, if he had been among the greatest of musicians as well as among the greatest of poets, have added anything to 'Let me not to the marriage of true minds...'? Or Shelley to 'Pinnacled dim in the intense inane'? Or Keats to 'Of perilous seas, in faery lands forlorn'? Or Coleridge to 'Quietly shining to the quiet Moon'? The thing is there, finally and inevitably complete: anything added is total loss. There is poetry, however, of which this cannot be said. It is true that, except in the case of lyrics definitely written to be sung, any arrangement of language, if properly describable as poetry at all, must suffer *something* from being set to music, *as* poetry and as a whole: but the gain may be such that, in total result, the poetry-and-music is more expressive than the poetry by itself. The general mood, for example, and the content of particular phrases and words may be significantly enhanced: this is a major element in our enjoyment of *Lieder*.

Now Wilfred Owen's poems, whether great or not (and they at any rate approach greatness), are wholly self-sufficient: if they are to make their full impact, which can be overwhelming, they must come to the ear exactly as the poet wrote them: and I am persuaded, given their crucial importance in the whole scheme of the Requiem, that a recitation of them, as plain and simple—as matter-of-fact, almost —as could be, would be more moving, and more effective for Britten's own purpose, than the procedure he has chosen. And if it be objected that a sort of hybrid would result, lacking in unity, then the reply must be that the *Singspiel* is just such a hybrid, but that *Fidelio*, a *Singspiel*, is also a supreme work of art, the greatest, perhaps, ever written.

But there is something else. I spoke earlier of the rightness, or inevitability, or inevitable rightness that great music communicates. I meant an inevitable rightness at the heart of things. But the idea of rightness or inevitability can be applied to great music in a different sense too, though the two senses are involved with one another: in respect, I mean, not of the sum of things, but of the music itself. In other words: one of the criteria of great music is whether you can say of it "He couldn't possibly have expressed what he wanted to express in any other way", or, when the setting of a poem is in question, "He set the poem thus, and could not have set it otherwise."

But I find nothing inevitable in Britten's settings of the Wilfred Owen poems: I never found myself giving a gasp of delighted surprise. This is not to deny that some of them are very beautiful, such as, in part, 'So Abram rose', and, best of all, 'One ever hangs where shelled roads part', with the intermingling Agnus Dei. As to the close of the work, this could hardly be more moving. But with the possible exception of the quasi-recitative 'It seemed that out of battle I escaped', with its lovely orchestral accompaniment, I felt that other settings would have done equally well; and I was disturbed on occasion by a certain obviousness (something as different as could be from inevitability), as in the use of drums to underline 'the drums of Time' in 'After the blast of lightning'. Moreover I found the repetition of words, particularly in 'Move him into the sun', detrimental to the poetry.

I hope I am wrong about all this, for there is a good deal of Britten that I greatly enjoy: some of the Michelangelo sonnets, for instance; Billy's awakening by the Novice; 'Abram and Isaac', flawless from beginning to end; and, most of all, the fairy music in *A Midsummer Night's Dream*. There is something new, I think, in the magic of this: and though it may not quite achieve the clean loveliness of Verdi in Windsor Park, which one can be certain will never cloy, some comparison between the two is not unreasonable. Moreover, I greatly revere Britten the man, if I may say so without impertinence. There are few composers, if any, of whom it can be said, as it can be said of him, that their composing is intensely bound up, not merely with their own inner life, but with the life of the world and their hopes for its salvation.

§ 4

My purpose in bringing up the War Requiem was twofold. I had been provoked by the remarks of a few critics, which would have been extravagant if applied to Verdi's masterpiece or the St. Matthew Passion; and I wanted to comment on a heartbreaking statistical comparison. The Festival Hall had been sold out an hour or two after the Requiem was announced, and could probably have been sold out two or three times over; on the evening before, Berlioz' *Romeo and Juliet* had been performed in the same hall, and no more than about a third of the seats had been bought and paid for. (The hall had looked even barer on another comparable occasion—when Giulini conducted the Four Sacred Pieces of Verdi. But there was a ready explanation then. It was either the eve or the close of the Day of Atonement, and all the Jews in London except me were either beginning or ending their fast.)

Now it is true that Thursday evening was a by no means exclusively musical affair. The performance was in honour of Benjamin Britten's fiftieth birthday, he was conducting the work himself, and he has for many years now been the object of an affection more commonly given to musical executants than to composers. Other recipients of it in my time have been Henry Wood and Yehudi Menuhin: but the parallel with Menuhin's case is closer than with Wood's, love for Menuhin and Britten stemming more, and love for Wood stemming less, from reactions to character or personality than from gratitude in the purely musical sphere. But in another way Britten's case is closer to Verdi's, national sentiments being involved in both. For the fact is that Britten has become in some sense symbolic of this country, as well as of the anti-war feeling that has begun increasingly to flow through it, if so far in a rather vague sort of way and implying little if any personal commitment: just as he himself is at once intensely English and intensely internationalist. It was entirely appropriate that his War Requiem should have been prefaced last Thursday by his own setting of the National Anthem.

(And yet I am conscious that a good deal more might be said to explain the personal adoration a lot of people justly feel for Benjamin Britten. I should like to quote from a letter sent to me by a friend after she had read the last few pages: "When I came back from five years in America in 1945, having barely heard of Britten, and not caring for any music after Debussy: also being desperately unhappy for personal reasons and because this country was in such a low state, I happened to turn on the wireless. Pure, thrilling, rather unearthly music came to my ears, in a 'modern' idiom. I was rapt. What could it be? It was the 'Ceremony of Carols'. When I heard it was by Benjamin Britten I felt the world was not utterly black, the present day not entirely without hope if it could produce this. To a lesser degree Britten has done this for me on subsequent occasions. No other contemporary composer has.")

So a huge house was guaranteed for the Britten Requiem from the start. Now if nothing more were involved than the relative size of the audiences for the Requiem and *Romeo and Juliet* respectively there would be little, given the circumstances, to complain of; but far more is involved, for what I have just been describing is no more than a particular case of a general phenomenon. To put it in a word, the Britten Requiem was an 'event': and people will flock to 'events' but stay at home, perhaps with their gramophones or radio sets on, for mere music. They will pack the hall for Klemperer (and nothing could delight me more) and for Artur Rubinstein and a few others: but they will buy, on an average, up to no more than forty per cent[1] of the seats for 'ordinary' evenings, 'ordinary' meaning, among other things, fine performances of exciting works rarely heard. And let us remember what, in precise statistics, we are talking about. The population of London is more than eight million: the seating capacity of the Festival Hall is less than three thousand. Moreover: it is the dearer seats that are half empty on 'ordinary' nights (you can predict with almost perfect accuracy when you will be seeing 'personalities' and when you will not): the cheaper seats are much better filled.

I have no solution to offer: my only purpose has been to have my fling about a situation that infuriates me. And I shall seize the opportunity of paying a warm tribute to my friend Ernest Bean, who has handled what must often have been a heartbreaking situation with magnificent aplomb.

The leanness of the audience last Wednesday was the more deplorable, in that the complete version of *Romeo and Juliet* can be heard only about once a decade: I have myself heard it four times only since I started going to concerts—on Wednesday evening; over the air in 1934; at Queen's Hall in 1935; and superbly done at the Carnegie Hall four or five years ago, directed by someone who had led the 'cellos in the N.B.C. orchestra under Toscanini. Moreover the conductor was Colin Davis, surpassed among living Berliozians by no one and equalled only by Pierre Monteux himself. Finally, the work is a masterpiece. A 'flawed' one, it is often said. This may be so, indeed it is so; but is there no trace of a flaw, then, in some admitted masterpieces by Beethoven and Mozart? Why always pick on Berlioz? There are critics, it seems, so obsessed with his musical misdemeanours that even when driven to applause they automatically apologise for it.

And yet what a joy the whole thing, or nearly the whole thing, is!

[1] I think this is a fairly accurate figure. The average for seats taken up and paid for on *all* nights, including the 'event' ones, is sixty-eight per cent.

The music associated with Romeo's solitariness at the Capulets'; the oboe tune in the same movement; the funeral procession; the Invocation—these are some of the things that linger, long after the instruments have been put away, about the heart and mind. As to the love-music, it is a revelation (a word ruined by misuse, but here properly applicable), and it gains enormously by being heard in its setting, instead of, as usually, 'cold'. David Cairns, so sensitive a critic of Berlioz as of much else, has recently said of it "sensuality is transfigured". That is not, in my view, quite exact: rather the compound of *eros* and *agape* characteristic of young lovers is here of such passionate intensity that not only the self and the other, but the phenomenal world too, are experienced immediately as one, without particulars or differentiation: an infinity of love and an infinity of beauty, love's synonym. There is nothing like this in the whole range of love-music. *Fidelio* is not about *eros* at all, but about married *agape*. The duet in the first act of *Butterfly*, if greatly sung, stirs the pulses delightfully but with an impact exclusively physical. The ethereal loveliness of the *Otello* duet, one of the most moving ever written, remains throughout, from its magical opening to 'Venere splende', on a purely human, one might almost say a purely natural level. In *Tristan* the beauty and pain of a life-denying sensuality is apotheosized. Perhaps the nearest parallel to Berlioz is Monteverdi: I am thinking of the closing duet in *L'Incoronazione di Poppea*, when two sensualists, cruel and you would have said worthless though they have shown themselves, sing 'Pur ti miro' to music of heart-easing purity. But you listen with happiness rather than in the ecstasy that engulfs you at *Romeo and Juliet*.

I couldn't sleep till daybreak after that music, so drunk was I with its glory. It is the sort of music to make a cripple start up and fly to heaven.

§ 5

It was as a boy at the proms that I had my first experience of Berlioz, with the usual excerpts from the *Damnation*. I remember vividly how transported I was by the Dance of the Sylphs; and I should be inclined to say that even now I love it as much as anything in Berlioz, were it not that 'Voici des roses', the Invocation that immediately precedes it, moves me even more. There are moods in which I would sooner hear 'Voici des roses' than anything. There is an ache in it, for an earlier,

a kind of pre-moral beauty, peculiar to Berlioz: time after time, whether he is being tender, as in *L'Enfance du Christ*, or exalted and pitiful, as in *Les Troyens*, he expresses, like no other musician, the pang of loveliness.

I have been quoting myself in those last two sentences:[1] and I wonder now, as I look at 'like no other musician' ten years later, whether I still feel the same. I think I do. It is one of the weaknesses of my character to be always searching for comparisons, not only in music but in almost everything else: but search though I may, I can think of no parallel to that Berlioz 'pang of loveliness'. Or not in music. There is a parallel however in painting: and I have often tried in one or other of my anthologies to find some way of printing 'Voici des roses' side by side with the Botticelli Venus. Now I can do so, and this gives me great happiness. But I must not give the impression that 'Voici des roses' is of such pre-eminence in that miraculous score that nothing else is worth citing. So let me mention in passing just one other of the innumerable felicities that overflow in those pages: 'D'amour l'ardente flamme', and not only the melody itself, but the way it returns after some strident passages with an effect of the most moving pathos.

I have heard the *Damnation* more often than I could easily reckon, in many countries but chiefly in Paris, and in Paris not only in concert-halls but on the stage, Charles Panzera being particularly outstanding as a concert Mephistopheles. But my most poignant memory is of a Saturday or Sunday at Brimpton in the summer of 1936. Ernst Toller, who had written the 'Schwalbenbuch' in prison (he had fought very bravely for the oppressed in the early nineteen-twenties), was staying with us: he had just married a slim young girl who looked very gentle and happy. Well, we were sitting that blazing forenoon on our lawn overlooking the Berkshire Downs when someone suggested champagne; and as we sat sipping it Toller asked us whether we would like to see the girl dance. So we brought out the gramophone—we still had one then—and put on the Dance of the Sylphs: and the girl took off her sandals and danced, and that was that. Shortly afterwards they sailed for America, where he committed suicide. He was terrified by the Nazis (spiritually, not physically), felt sure they would win, and couldn't face it. I never knew a man who loved his fellow-creatures more. "The words 'I am proud to be a German', or 'I am proud to be a Jew'," he wrote in his autobiography, "sounded ineffably stupid to me. As well say 'I am proud to have brown

[1] *More for Timothy.*

eyes'. Must I then join the ranks of the bigoted and glorify my Jewish blood now, not my German? Pride and love are not the same thing, and if I were asked where I belonged I should answer that a Jewish mother had borne me, that Germany had nourished me, Europe had formed me, my home is the earth, and the world my fatherland."

§ 6

Another aspect of Berlioz' genius is his power of evoking a scene or emotion with a vividness and intensity that only the greatest of composers (or of poets or artists, for that matter) share with him. I remember listening to a broadcast of the *Symphonie Fantastique* on a hot summer evening in about 1952. The last two movements—the walk to the gallows, the Dies Irae, the tolling bell, the execution—suddenly affected me horribly. Always, before, I had enjoyed them as music, and was to do so again; but now I heard nothing—could only see and feel: see and feel a man walking, walking—a man who lived and breathed—in an obscene ceremonial procession that had been rehearsed as a play and would end with his being deliberately killed. Ah Christ!, I thought, this was a murderer, yes: but he was also the Christ who is all men, stumbling on the road to Calvary. A week before, heaven had been in that same little room as the last movement of Beethoven's Choral Symphony came through from Bayreuth: now, instead of beautiful life there was naked sado-masochism. . . . It is only by accident that the greatest of musical names has crept in, but let it stand.

It is a relief to turn from horror and shame to the gentlest and tenderest of all Berlioz' works, and the gentlest and tenderest, to put it loosely, in an objective as well as a subjective sort of way: I mean, no one could listen to *L'Enfance du Christ* without becoming, if only for a passing hour, gentler and tenderer himself. Two performances stand out in my memory. One of them was at the old Queen's Hall (I do not know why I keep on calling it the old Queen's Hall, as if there were a new one, but that is how I always think of it), and Beecham, who shared with Hamilton Harty at that time a supremacy in the interpretation of Berlioz, was I am pretty sure the conductor. We sat with the poet W. J. Turner, and I mention this because I want to celebrate him as one of the great Berlioz pioneers. The other outstanding performance was at the Bath Festival two or three years ago. Colin Davis conducted in the Abbey; Peter Pears, as the narrator, sang

BERLIOZ CONDUCTING · BY DORÉ (1850)

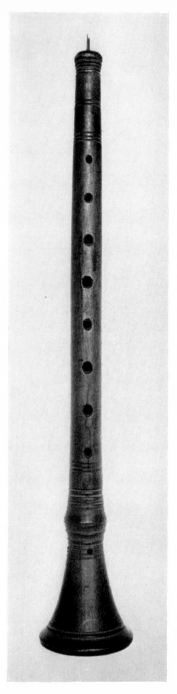

THE PIFFERA

THE ABRUZZI BAGPIPE

with a tranquil adoration, wholly devoid of sanctimoniousness, that
quite won me over (he has not always been to my taste); and April
Cantelo, as Mary, was peculiarly fresh and appealing. I can only
describe the performance as a holy one, and the Abbey as sanctified by
it. Happily memorable, too, was another performance conducted
by Colin Davis: this time in the midst of broken-down armchairs at
the Hermitage music-camp.

I cannot resist appending two little pieces of music here, because I
love them so: the figure that represents, I imagine, the baby's innocence
(there is something of very similar tone, if not of shape, in *Idomeneo*):

and the tune that Jacques Barzun justly describes as "the high point
of the emotional and musical sublime":

It is time I brought these paragraphs on Berlioz to an end, but let
me linger a moment more to recall a Christmas eve we spent quite
recently in Rome. We were at midnight Mass in the Aracoeli—one of
those indecorous affairs, with people strolling in and out, that express
with such immediacy the essence of Catholicism as all mixed up, in
a taken-for-granted sort of way, with daily life—when my ear was
suddenly caught by familiar tones in the distance: familiar but

unfamiliar too, for I was certain that this was nothing I knew. So we went out to investigate, and there at the porch were a couple of musicians with odd instruments that looked like bagpipes and oboes. I asked a bystander who they might be, and he told me that they were up from the Abruzzi, as was their custom at this time of year. Then it flashed on me that there was a resemblance between these rhythms and those of *Harold in Italy*, and that the scene of *Harold in Italy* was the Abruzzi; so when we got home I looked up Berlioz' 'Life'[1] and this is what I found:

"In the miserable oblivion and dishonour into which music has sunk in Rome I found but one small sign of honest life. It was among the pifferari, players of a little popular instrument, a surviving relic of antiquity. They were strolling musicians who, at Christmastide, came down from the mountains in groups of four or five armed with bagpipes and piffere, a kind of oboe, to play before the image of the Virgin.

"I used to spend hours in watching them, there was something so quaintly mysterious in their wild aspect as they stood—head slightly turned over one shoulder, their bright dark eyes fixed devoutly on the holy figure, almost as still as the image itself.

"At a distance the effect is indescribable and few escape its spell. When I heard it in its native haunts, among the volcanic rocks and dark pine forest of the Abruzzi, I could almost believe myself transported back through the ages to the days of Evander the Arcadian."

[1] Dent, Everyman's Library. Translation by Katherine F. Boult.

CHAPTER II

Before getting down to my plan of dealing rather more fully with my operatic initiation than was possible in that brief interview with Peter Heyworth, I must do a little tidying-up of what I said about production, for otherwise I risk being misunderstood.

I am not against the fresh production, and in particular the re-mounting, of familiar operas, as must be obvious. On the contrary, I am strongly in favour of it: strongly rather than passionately, for passion seems hardly demanded by such a comparative banality as the look of the stage when the sound of it is what really matters, though if the look of it blatantly outrages the composer passion rightly comes in. Many of the Covent Garden productions are wretchedly run down and some of them disturb the eye, and as a result distract the ear, by the evidence of their antiquity: even the Visconti *Don Carlo* is not what it was, and when I saw *Rosenkavalier* a couple of years ago there was a shabbiness on the stage that clashed as surely with all that elegance in the orchestra as Madame Crespin's singing did, delightful though some of it was, with the Marschallin as Strauss had conceived her and with the old Vienna that was her home. We made similar complaints in my boyhood, and such a state of affairs has probably always been the rule in most of the opera-houses of the world. What is rather at issue is the *emphasis* on production characteristic of recent years, when it has not been uncommon for the notices to deal almost exclusively with this aspect of the performance, an odd inch or so being kept at the end for voices and orchestra and the rest.

I have already conceded the propriety of a concentration on décor when the music is worthless, like Mascagni's, and would concede and indeed welcome it when the music is not absolutely worthless but comparatively so, as in the case of *Manon*, which was put on the other night at Covent Garden 'for' Signorina Scotto. Something very odd has recently been happening about Massenet: quite a cult of him has been developing among serious critics, one of whom recently des-cribed him as a better composer than Stravinsky. Certainly he is agreeable enough, or rather *Manon* is, in the attractive mustiness of the Opéra-comique at a Christmas matinée, when all the children and even the babies are brought out to hear it: I have enjoyed it on two or three such occasions myself, indifferent for the time being to the villainy of the orchestra or the peculiar scratchiness characteristic of minor Parisian sopranos. But away from that atmosphere its saccharine palls very quickly indeed; and the other night when the signature tune came gluily over for the thirtieth time—*tum* tum, *tum* te-tum, diddle-de tum te tum—I found myself thinking how much happier I should be if I had some Zeffirelli to look at. And *Manon* lends itself particularly well to such treatment: an inn, a Paris interior, pretty little harlots. But what they had actually done was to get out from the depository an assortment of old bits and pieces that reminded me, before I dozed off, of the heavily framed oils by Victorian masters that decorate the corridors of solid British hotels at the seaside or in the smarter provinces.

Why, if Massenet is to be revived, must it always be *Manon*? Possibly because there are quite a number of sopranos today with the prettiness of look, charm of manner and vocal equipment that the not very exacting name-part demands. But it is a pity, because there *is* a little Massenet opera that anyone who has ever seen it would eagerly wish to see again: *Le Jongleur de Notre-Dame*. It is so lovable that you think of it as fragrant rather than sugary, and so attractive in its picture of religious simplicity that you would hate to call it sentimental: and it is over before it can begin to pall. Zeffirelli could let himself go on it, and the Covent Garden people should give him the chance.

§ 2

To ascend in the musical scale, but not to the stratosphere, I would not only pass the recent production, a pretty elaborate one, of Rossini's *Count Ory* at Sadler's Wells, but would beg everyone to go and see it next time they put it on. The score is sprightly and full of small graces, but with little of real musical interest in it and nothing at all of sheer musical delight. This is just the kind of piece that cries out for the production it gets: full of prettiness and irony and colour, with bogus horses and similar leg-pulls galore. What might have been a rather boring evening if the music had been mainly relied on became a delightful entertainment. I had a similar experience in the early thirties with an even better Rossini production, one by the Fiat company of Milan. These people had an Opera Society that used to spend a whole year in the preparation of a single work. They would go out for the best artists and producer they could find; bring together a special orchestra of picked players; experiment with scenery and costumes until the result was exactly what they wanted; and then rehearse and rehearse to the point of perfection. We saw their *Barber* at the Champs-Elysées one evening. Toti dal Monte and Titta Ruffo were in the cast, and the décor, within an enclave boxed out of the stage, was ravishing.

There is a mystery about Rossini. I once wrote that just as Verdi is the most loving of composers, so Rossini is the most heartless: adding however that you could always enjoy him for something net and brandy-like in his sparkling Mediterraneanism. I based this judgment on such operas of his as I had then heard, namely *L'Italiana in Algeri*, *Cenerentola*, *William Tell*[1] and of course the *Barber*. This last is in its way one of the most attractive operas ever written, with its all but unique combination of wit, high spirits and gusty humour; but there is not a moment of genuine tenderness in it from first bar to last. And then I heard *La Pietra del Paragone* at the St. Pancras Town Hall. Rossini wrote this in 1812, when he was twenty, and it is full of tenderness: a tenderness he never recovered, unless it is to be found in *Otello* or some of his sacred music, which I have never heard. What happened then to spoil this brilliant man at so early an age? Is the explanation to be found in a letter he wrote to Pacini in 1866?[2] "This art [of music]," it runs, "which is based solely on sentiment and ideas, cannot escape the influence of the times we live in, and the sentiment and ideas of the present day are wholly concerned with steam, rapine and barricades. Remember my philosophical determination to give up my Italian career in 1822, my French career in 1829. Such foresight is not granted to everyone; God granted it to me, and I have been grateful for it ever since." Or was it his presumed syphilis that turned a young man who could write the tender passages of *La Pietra* into a lazy cynic? Or is there a third explanation? The question is worth clearing up.

There are signs that an uncritical enthusiasm for Rossini is on its way, and a revival of *Semiramide*, perhaps 'for' Joan Sutherland (as recently at the Scala), is not unlikely. So let me quote what Berlioz wrote when about eighteen: exaggeratedly of course, but I see no harm in judicious exaggeration when its aim is to ensure that an opinion passionately held should attract serious attention: "Rossini's operas taken together can hardly bear comparison with one line of Gluck's recitative, three measures of melody by Mozart. . . ."

[1] But there is a moving soprano aria in this.
[2] Quoted by Toye, *Rossini*. Arthur Barker.

§ 3

And now I want to explain a little more fully why I found Wieland Wagner's production of *Fidelio* so ruinous. I have already mentioned, when talking with Peter Heyworth, the stylisation of the prisoners' chorus, but there was at least one other example, almost as blatant, of the same misconception. There are three supreme moments within the supremacy of *Fidelio* as a whole. The first is that final expression of the idea (or central truth about human existence) that man is here as fellow-worker with God: the moment when Leonora presents her pistol precisely as the trumpet rings out, and the trumpet rings out precisely as Leonora presents her pistol. The second is Leonora's spoken 'Nichts, nichts, mein Florestan' after Florestan's 'Was hast du denn für mich getan?' (Lotte Lehmann used to move me more by the way she spoke those four words than by all her magnificent singing). The third of these moments is near the end: the Minister enters, and sings, to one of the simplest as well as one of the loveliest melodies Beethoven ever wrote, 'Es sucht der Bruder seine Brüder, und kann er helfen hilft er gern'. A second truth about human existence, almost as central as the first, has been revealed: 'a brother has need of his brothers, and when a brother can help he gladly does so'. It might be called, in the current jargon, an existential truth: does so, not should do so.

The essence of that third moment is twofold: first, the Minister 'comes', as the trumpet-call has promised: and secondly he comes as a brother to brothers.

Now in the Wieland Wagner production the Minister didn't 'come'; he was already there when the curtain went up, sitting or standing, dominatingly remote, above a crowd that seemed frozen, as in a cinema 'still'. And he looked as little like a brother among brothers as could be imagined: he looked like Sarastro, with the Urim and Thummim on his breast.

But the worst has still to be told: the spoken passages were entirely or almost entirely eliminated. I complained about this to one of the officials, and he replied in effect: "Oh, everyone knows what the work's all about, so the talk isn't necessary; and anyhow it's boring, and breaks up the music." What was it then, a concert or a dramatic performance? That Beethoven should have made of the *Singspiel* a vehicle for his sublimities does not affect in the least its essential character as a *Singspiel*: rather, the *Singspiel* has alone been found capable of expressing those sublimities. Beethoven knew what he was about when he used spoken dialogue (just as he knew what he was about when he broke into words at the end of his last symphony), and above all in the case of 'Was hast du . . .' and 'Nichts, nichts'; yet you often hear a performance of *Fidelio* in which that passage but no other of the spoken ones is cut, and the reason given is this: "You cannot let the music down at such a moment."

What is wanted for *Fidelio* is the simplest possible setting, with nothing outré, nothing specially emphasised, nothing the 'common man' would not immediately understand. Beethoven must be allowed to make his own unsurpassable impact. Like Shakespeare, he was a common man himself, with a common man's sensitivity, understanding and creativeness magnified a thousandfold. He was anything but a 'highbrow'; and I can imagine him shaking his fist at Wieland Wagner's doubtless reverential pretentiousness.

Peter Heyworth, it may be remembered, defended that prisoners' chorus as follows: "But surely men can be oppressed to a point where they *do* lose identity? That happened in the concentration camps, and the whole point of Wieland Wagner's production was that he made us experience *Fidelio* in the light of recent history." "Made us experience"! Is there a living soul, capable of understanding the work at all, who does not at once, and most painfully, make the connection? That is why to hear *Fidelio*, always an overwhelming experience, is now more overwhelming than ever. The Germans understand all this as well as anyone. When I returned to Germany in 1947, after doing relief work there the previous year, I was told on my arrival that they wanted me to hear a little music. I was taken to a broken-down hall with a few scattered people in it, and as I took my seat a couple of dozen men in ordinary working clothes filed on to the platform and proceeded to sing the prisoners' chorus. I was never told anything about them except that they had "got it up specially for me", but I suppose they and the orchestra were amateurs, though they might have been the Philharmonia chorus rehearsed by Pitz and conducted by Klemperer to judge by the effect they made on me.

I mentioned to Peter Heyworth a performance of *Fidelio* at the music-camp near Hermitage, and described it as one of the most moving I have ever heard—and I heard the one in Paris given by the Vienna Opera during its visit there in 1928, with Lotte Lehmann, Elisabeth Schumann, Richard Tauber and Richard Mayr, Schalk conducting. The comparison may sound extravagant, so let me explain.

§ 4

The music-camp has been going since 1926, when it was started by an amateur, Bernard Robinson, and a group of his friends. People have been going down there all these years for two purposes; to get the place in order and to make music. The music is mostly for themselves, but on one or two week-ends during the summer friends come in, a couple of dozen perhaps, to sit around and listen. We often went over when we were living at Brimpton: hearing for instance the *Quattro Sacri Pezzi* of Verdi and the performance of *L'Enfance du Christ* already mentioned, both conducted by Colin Davis. The players are mostly amateurs: when they are professionals they occasionally play an instrument other than their own (my daughter Livia, when a professional horn-player, used to play the viola). They sleep in tents, and spend ten days of their summer holiday there. Every sort of calling is represented: my friend David Higham, for instance, the literary agent, often sings in the choir, and another friend, John David Solomon, a schoolmaster, plays among other things the bass-trombone.

Fidelio is the only opera they have ever attempted, and the whole thing was on an amateur basis. They put up a stage in the old barn themselves, dug an orchestra-pit, made and painted the scenery, and provided singers and orchestra. And the result is as I have described. I can never listen to *Fidelio* without occasional tears: the tears, on that evening, were almost continuous. And the reason was this: we were there in the very room with them, were part and parcel of them, were experiencing in the closest possible way what they were experiencing; we were all 'common men', sharing elementary emotions— Beethoven and the publisher and the schoolmaster and the literary agent. For once, everything I have said about singing went by the board: who cared if one of the women couldn't manage this or one of the men foozled that? You did not even notice.

There is nearly always something specially delightful about amateur music-making. Provided it is reasonably competent, an amateur quartet in a friend's drawing-room can satisfy one more than the Amadeus in a concert-hall. But the comparison must not be carried too far. Folk-songs carolled by amateurs can be highly distressing: and so, for that matter, can folk-songs carolled by anyone.

§ 5

There was recently another production of *Fidelio* in which the rule of simplicity, of avoiding anything in the least emphatic, of refusing to underline the composer's intention, was broken with shocking effect. The Frankfurt performance at Sadler's Wells, on the whole decently mounted and more than decently sung, was going well enough, if not superlatively, until the dungeon scene. And then, as the curtains parted, we saw Florestan—crucified: he was standing erect, in that moment of deathly weakness (the vision of Leonora had not yet come to excite him), with his manacled arms stretched full out to make, with his upright body, the figure of a cross. As if Beethoven had not depicted Florestan's outraged humanity with sufficient vividness! As if we had to have it rammed brutally home, instead of its being allowed to steal on us, through Beethoven's magic, with an almost intolerable sense of pity: pity for a race of human beings who, in the unregeneracy of this earthly existence ('welch ein Dunkel hier!'), are always sending one another to Calvary.

But it must be said again that the simplicity I have been pleading for must be a 'common man's' simplicity, not the stylised simplicity of a clever modern producer. (There are operas, on the other hand, that positively demand a stylised simplicity: Stravinsky's *Oedipus Rex* is one of them.) So far as an opera like *Fidelio* is concerned, in one respect only is a sort of stylised simplicity allowable and even imperative. This is when all action comes to end, and the peculiar genius of opera ceases to have anything in common with that of an ordinary spoken play: everything is held up while the characters, in an ensemble, musically illumine the dramatic situation. When that happens, the singers must formally take up their positions, and remain not only motionless but gestureless while they sing what the composer has told them to. Examples are the canon quartet in *Fidelio*, the trio in *Rosenkavalier* and the quintet in *Die Meistersinger*.

§ 6

Lighting is all-important, as much in simple as in elaborate productions or even more so. There are few things so elemental, so direct yet so unforced in their emotional and spiritual appeal, as light and the absence of it: like the blaze of an August noon or the darkness of a moonless night. To go far afield from Beethoven, there was an example of this at the Edinburgh Festival five or six years ago. Callas was singing Sonnambula; and towards the end, as the happy excitement of 'Ah! non giunge' mounted higher and higher, the light mounted with it, not only on the stage but also, after the old Italian manner, in the auditorium too, until, as the curtain began to fall, the whole place was ablaze. There can have been few who did not experience, with a rush of emotion, a glory enhancing the glory even of singing like that.

‹

Courtesy Harold Rosenthal

THE WATER-ENTRANCE TO THE FENICE

THE LAST ACT OF *TRAVIATA* AT THE FENICE IN 1854, THE YEAR AFTER
ITS PRODUCTION THERE

CHAPTER III

I CAN NOW GO BACK to my boyhood. One of the main aspects of the operatic side of it, now that I come to review it long years after, appears as a fluctuating struggle for the possession of my musical self by Wagner and Verdi. But there are other things I want to record before going into that.

I am nostalgic by nature, as perhaps an unusually high proportion of Jews are: but am a messianist too by the same token, with a passion however not so much for a restoration of all things, which the nostalgia might suggest, but for something new and better. The messianism is nowadays far stronger than the nostalgia, but in my earliest boyhood it was the other way about. I longed above all things for two incompatibles: to be living in the operatic past of my father's conversation and to be living in a remote geological epoch, but in one of a somewhat more recent remoteness, with fantastic life—dinosaurs and giant conifers and the rest—proliferating on the steamy surface of a supertropical earth.

The geological nostalgia was to vanish by the time I was about eight or ten, though a passionate but soberer interest in geology lingered on into my later schooldays; and even now when I happen to see a probably fossiliferous cliff or similar formation I vaguely wish I had a geological hammer by me to 'tap the strata' with. The operatic nostalgia was to last longer, and is indeed still with me in a curiously attenuated form: in that of longing, for a passing moment or two, to indulge in the external trappings of the old kind of opera-going. When I first went to the Fenice, most elegant of opera-houses and specially dear for its association with Verdi—not only was *Traviata* first performed there, as everyone knows, but so were *Ernani* and *Rigoletto* and *Simone Boccanegra*—I not only insisted, as was natural, on arriving by gondola at the water-entrance instead of going by foot from the Piazza in the commoner fashion, but I thought, with a momentary pang, what a pity it was that I couldn't be wearing a white tie and a cloak with scarlet linings, and be carrying a gibus and a gold-headed ebony cane. When I had an office in Paris and was going a lot to the Opéra, in spite of such appalling performances that I always swore I would never go again but always did, I used to look with a

pang like my Venetian one at the old roués in *tenue de soirée* who
traditionally sat in the first three or four rows of the stalls the more
easily to ogle the ballerinas: and I once actually sat in the middle of
the front row myself—not for a like purpose, but at the first performance there of *Parsifal*, conducted with the aid of a metronome. I
always have the instinct to dress for Covent Garden, or at any rate for
'big' nights there, but never do: at this moment I feel sure that I shall
dress for the Callas *Tosca* next month, but am almost equally sure that
nothing will come of it. Another example of this eccentricity is the
regret I used to feel that I had never gone to the opera in St. Petersburg
in the old Tzarist days. I still occasionally feel it; and this is the more
odd in that I abominate the Russian *ancien régime* and anything remotely
connected with it.

All this is no doubt part and parcel of my pleasure in outmoded
elegances, which is forever fighting with, but never wholly losing to,
a persistent radicalism. Many years ago John Strachey, after a discussion
we had been having about one of the finer points of Marxism, showed
me a card he had just discovered for one of his mother's parties at about
the turn of the century, with the word 'trousers' in the bottom left-
hand corner: and he told me, when I looked blank, that it meant
'informal'—white tie and tails, but not knee-breeches. I was delighted,
and recalled my pleasure in something that had happened to me during
the summer of 1914. I was walking in Piccadilly Circus smoking my
pipe, when I ran into old Mr. Rooper (pronounced Roper), the father
of my Oxford friend Ralph. He was a charmingly antique gentleman,
with the best foreign blood in him—Ralph's second name was Bonfoy;
and after greeting me as if I were the King of England, or even the
King of France, he took me gently by the arm and said "My dear boy,
please forgive me for mentioning it, but a gentleman doesn't smoke
a pipe in the street." He then gave me a cigar, knowing I was fond of
them.

§ 2

There is a flavour to opera-going, as described to me by my father
before ever I knew it myself, that is recaptured as nowhere else in a
beloved book of my childhood, George du Maurier's 'Peter Ibbetson':
"My sweetest recollections of this period of my life are of the music
I heard, and the places where I heard it; it was enchantment! With
what vividness I can recall it all! The eager anticipation for days; the

careful selection, beforehand, from such an *embarras de richesses* as was duly advertised; then the long waiting in the street, at the doors reserved for those whose portion is to be the gallery. The hard-won seat aloft is reached at last, after a selfish but good-humoured struggle up the long stone staircase (one is sorry for the weak, but a famished ear has no conscience). The gay and splendid house is crammed; the huge chandelier is a golden blaze [alas, it has gone now, the one I knew in the old days at Covent Garden]; the delight of expectation is in the air, and also the scent of gas, and peppermint, and orange-peel [I remember no peppermint or orange-peel: what I remember is 'Squash, lemon! Squash!', the malarticulated cry of our lemon-squash man as the applause faded away after curtain-fall. We thought him the best critic of the lot, and always asked his opinion of any performance we might have missed: his reply was almost invariably the same—'I never heard a worse . . .'].

"The orchestra fills, one by one; instruments tune up—a familiar cacophony, sweet with seductive promise. The conductor takes his seat—applause—a hush—then taps—the baton waves once, twice, thrice—the eternal fountain of magic is let loose, and at the very first jet

> 'The cares that infest the day
> Shall fold their tents, like the Arabs,
> And as silently steal away.'

"Then lo! the curtain rises, and straightway we are in Seville— Seville, after Pentonville [Maida Vale]! Count Almaviva, lordly, gallant, and gay beneath his disguise, twangs his guitar, and what sounds issue from it!. . . .

" 'Ecco ridente in cielo . . .', so sings he, the most beautiful male voice of his time, under Rosina's balcony; and soon Rosina's voice, the most beautiful female voice of hers, is heard behind her curtains—so girlish, so innocent, so young and light-hearted, that the eyes fill with involuntary tears, and the heart has room for nothing else but sunny hope and love and joy! And yet it is all mere sound—impossible, unnatural, unreal nonsense!"

My father might have been talking to me, or I (*mutatis mutandis*, as indicated in square brackets) to Livia. But there is one thing I should have added, if I had been George du Maurier: the feel of my bottom on the cold stone steps as I read the libretto during the interval, in preparation for the act to come. I recall particularly a performance of *Siegfried*. Occasionally, towards the end of my schooldays, I was accompanied at Covent Garden by Cecil Botting, the Greek master of the Eighth. This blond, roundish man—his moustache had little waxed tips to them—was a great Wagnerian, but rather inexperienced, and I got a good deal of pleasure from helping him with his leitmotifs. He was always torn during the intervals between a desire to absorb my exposition and a sense of duty that kept nagging at him to mug up next day's Homer. He usually chose the latter, but on the occasion in question I insisted on his sitting down with me and studying the libretto. I shall take this opportunity of dragging in a little tribute to him. On top of his school work, he slaved away with an army of private pupils whom he coached for university scholarships and so on, as many of his relations were needy and he felt bound to support them; and he died in his fifties, worn out by overwork. But his sense of enjoyment was keen, and he loved good living; and once a year he gave all his pupils who were leaving, private or otherwise, a wonderful many-coursed dinner with all the appropriate wines. I smoked a very strong cigar at the one I went to, and was sick. I didn't quite realise his quality at the time, but I look back on him now as pretty nearly my ideal of a man.

What Peter Ibbetson is describing in the passage quoted above is a scene from his 'natural' life, before he murdered his uncle. But after sentence of death and its commutation a new sort of life begins for him: a 'non-natural' one, but far more real than the other. Every night for twenty-five years he and Mimsey Seraskier, the Duchess of Towers, who have loved one another as little children, 'dream true' together, she in the world and he in his cell, by a method her father had taught her: every night they live in her present and past and in the past of their ancestors, and then, as they go farther and farther back with Elysian happiness, in the prehistoric and primeval. For George du Maurier must have shared that other nostalgia of my boyhood, the one for remote geological epochs:

"Dear Giulia Grisi shall sing the Willow Song for us again and again, and you shall hear the applause. Ah, what applause! . . .

"Then a cigarette and a cup of coffee, and a glass of curaçao; and after, to reach our private box, we had but to cross the room and lift a curtain. And there before us was the opera-house brilliantly lighted, and the instruments tuning up, and the splendid company pouring in: crowned heads, famous beauties, world-renowned statesmen, Garibaldi, Cavour, Bismarck, now so famous, and who not? Mary would point them out to me.

"Now it was St. Petersburg, now Berlin, now Vienna, Paris, Naples, Milan, London—every great city in turn. But our box was always the

MARIO AND GRISI SINGING 'PARIGI O CARA' · BY GEORGE DU MAURIER

COVENT GARDEN IN 1858

same, always the best in the house, and I the one person privileged to smoke my cigar in the face of all that royalty, fashion and splendour.

"Then, after the overture, up went the curtain. . . . I think I may say that of music we have had our glut. For all through her busy working life Mary found time to hear whatever good music was going on in London, that she might bring it back to me at night; and we would rehear it together, again and again, and *da capo*.

TO THE OPERA BOX

"It is a rare privilege for two private individuals, and one of them a convict, to assist at a performance honoured by the patronage and presence of crowned heads, and yet be able to encore any particular piece that pleases them. How often have we done that!

"Oh Joachim! O Clara Schumann! O Piatti!—all of whom I know so well, but have never heard with the fleshly ear! O others, whom it would be invidious to mention without mentioning all—a glorious list! How we have made you, all unconscious, repeat the same movement over and over again, without ever from you a sign of impatience or fatigue! O Patti, Angelina! O Santley and Sims Reeves! O De Soria, nightingale of the drawing-room, I wonder you have a note left! . . .

"To think that we have seen—actually seen—*de nos propres yeux vu*—Napoleon Bonaparte himself, the arch-arbiter of the world, on the very pinnacle of his pride and power; in his little cocked hat and grey double-breasted overcoat, astride his white charger with all his staff around him, just as he has been so often painted! To think that we have even beheld him before he was First Consul—slim and pale, his lank hair dangling down his neck and cheeks, if possible more impressive still! And Mirabeau and Robespierre, and Danton and Marat and Charlotte Corday! we have seen them too; and Marie Antoinette and the fishwives, and 'the beautiful head of Lamballe' (on its pike!) . . . and watched the tumbrils go by to the *Place du Carrousel*, and gazed at the guillotine by moonlight—silent and terror-struck, our very hearts in our mouths. . . .

"Then we were present (several times!) at the taking of the Bastille; and going further back we have haunted Versailles in the days of its splendour and drunk our fill of all the glories of the court of Louis XIV; and have applauded Molière in one of his own plays, and have gazed at and listened to (and almost forgiven) Racine and Corneille, and Boileau, and Fénelon, and the good Lafontaine—those five ruthless persecutors of our own innocent French childhood!

"And, still ascending the stream of time, we have hobnobbed with Montaigne and Rabelais, and been personally bored with Malherbe, and sat at Ronsard's feet, and ridden by Froissart's side, and slummed with François Villon—in what enchanted slums! . . . And Bertha, with the big feet; Joan of Arc, the good Lorrainer (what would she think of her native province now?); and the very learned Héloise, for love of whom one Peter Esbaillart, or Abélard (a more luckless Peter than even I!), suffered such cruel indignities at monkish hands. . . .

"As we reached farther and farther back through the stream of time, the task became easier in a way; for with every successive generation the number of our progenitors increased in geometrical progression, until a limit of numbers was reached—namely, the sum of the inhabitants of the terrestial globe. In the seventh century there was not a person living in France (not to mention Europe) who was not in the line of our direct ancestry, excepting, of course, those who had died without issue and were mere collaterals.

"We have even just been able to see, as in a glass darkly, the faint shadows of the Mammoth and the cave bear, and of the man who hunted and killed and ate then, that he might live and prevail.

"The Mammoth!"

§ 3

We were living in Elgin Avenue, off Maida Vale, at the time, and, unbelievably, part of it was still semi-rural. From a point a few houses further down than ours up to a point not far short of the Paddington and Maida Vale High School, which I went to till I was about ten, there was a gap in what would nowadays be called the built-up area, given over to ups-and-downs, fields with clover in them and market-gardens. I loved the smell of the clover but disliked picking it, getting down on hands and knees to avoid doing so, just as today I love any kind of fragrance but hate cutting flowers for the house or letting others cut them. The market-gardens pleased me even more, particularly in autumn, when enormous multicoloured dahlias sparkled with the morning dew; and September and early October have remained my favourite months, though I like all times and seasons and have liked, till quite recently, all weathers. As for the ups-and-downs, these were small hillocks and valleys on either side of the road where pavements ought to have been: I spent a lot of time running up and down them, and they played an important part in my young geological life. Little piles of flints lay alongside them for building purposes, and I would go searching among these on my way to and from the Maida Vale High School for fossil sponges, which happened to be particularly abundant in the part of the Thames Valley the flints came from. Once I found something far more special than a sponge, namely the cast of a shell, particularly fine; and I hurried home to identify it, if possible, in my two-volume Geikie, a text-book of geology that I greatly treasured and was always poring over.

There is a tie-up in my mind between Geikie and what was at that time one of my minor operatic pleasures. We had an old high box-room in the attic of our Elgin Avenue house, full of packing-cases and black-domed trunks and discarded umbrellas and the like; and one day, to my immeasurable delight, I discovered there a few old Telegraphs that had been taken up perhaps for some job of packing and thrown carelessly in a corner. Thrown away, such treasures, in which performances of opera might be announced! It became a favourite occupation, in summer when the sun was high, to sit reading in the full glare on our narrow balcony—and the chances are that it would be Geikie if it wasn't Algernon Blackwood or Sherlock Holmes—and then to break off and go searching for still more copies of the Telegraph in the dimness and dust above. For those were spacious days for all who were not poor, and opera announcements were as different as you could imagine from their present successors. The chances were that after drawing a few blanks I would come upon some issue with a summer date, summer having meant, from time immemorial, the operatic 'grand season'; and there, by the left-hand margin of the middle left-hand page, not all wretchedly crowded up as today into a mean half-inch but overflowing for a generous foot, would be a dozen announcements of forthcoming performances, each with a good solid inch to itself and each giving fully, down to the Steuermann in *Tristan* or the Messaggero in *Aida*, the names of the performers. The date might be nineteen-hundred, or eighteen-ninety, or even one of the late eighteen-eighties: five years back, ten years back, twenty years back: and I became as familiar with the minor names—I have the shape of them still in my mind, though not the exact spelling—as with the Pattis or de Reszkes or Nordicas that came popping out from the page every now and again to give me a sudden stab of delight. The curious thing is that, although I was only just beginning to go to the opera, I knew exactly which role each one of these performers had been playing—or was playing for me at the moment, for that is how I thought of it. This odd expertise was a product of unconscious detection—comparison, elimination, etcetera—combined with a masterly knowledge of operatic literature: libretti, I mean; for there were lots of them about, and there was nothing I liked better than reading them in bed at night, looking out on the way for particularly famous arias, and comparing the English with the Italian or German opposite so that, when I came to hear the work myself, I might be able to follow it perfectly. For there was no opera in English at the Covent Garden of my day until Beecham came along, or only as an occasional eccentricity: we worked hard for our enjoyment, mastering in advance the original text. I have never cared for opera in English: as often as not the musical line is ruined, to say nothing of such a locution as 'Good-bye, now' (which sounds more like an Irish-American concierge seeing you off than Violetta saying 'Addio' to old Germont), or of such another as 'To treat a woman so!' (a far graver offence, in its ruin of a highly dramatic situation, than the one old Germont is attacking his son for). In general, what was jargon in the original can rarely be dejargonized by English-ing it, and the odd libretto of literary merit commonly sheds in translation a good deal of such merit as it originally had. Besides, the person who cannot be bothered to do his homework is also, as often as not, the person who wants to know what it is all about and no more, if as much: at a performance by the Welsh National Opera Company of *Nabucco* at Bournemouth a few years ago, someone in the row behind us was explaining the plot to the man on his left under the apparent impression that 'Nabucker' was the hero, or perhaps villain, of a 'musical' set in contemporary Palestine. The expositor, so far as I could gather—and I listened with malicious care—had not even bothered to read the meagre description in the threepenny programme; he seemed to be relying on local gossip. Still, opera in English is better than no opera at all.

The domestic stock of operatic text-books was supplemented later on by a wonderful gift to me from my great-aunt Rosetta. Already an old lady at that time, she had been a great opera-goer in her day, and had accumulated, partly, I imagine, by inheritance, a magnificent store of the small, closely-printed booklets in yellow and orange and blue, published by firms in the Haymarket and Wardour Street and St. Paul's Churchyard, that had been the ordinary libretti of a generation or so before mine. She gave the lot to me, and I have them still. All the famous old classics, as my father used to call them, were there, the Sonnambulas and Dinorahs and Otellos (Rossini's), the Africaines, the Prophètes and the Etoiles du Nords: things already obsolete in my day, when the vogue for Wagner was already at its height, and a taste even for Bellini was considered rather grotesque, for all that Wagner himself (but they probably did not know this) had thought well of him. Occasionally—the libretto, in such cases, had clearly been bought at the actual performance—a small slip of paper, lightly fixed to the title-page, would set out the names of the cast: printed anyhow, as though of no great importance: but—the Ravoglis in *Orfeo*, Tamberlik in the *Prophète*, Albani in *Puritani* and *Hamlet*, Nicolini in *Robert the Devil* ("Carriages may be ordered for 11.50"), Patti, Scalchi and Maurel in *Semiramide* (1878), Patti and Faure in *L'Etoile du Nord* (1873), Ella Russell, Nordica, Lassalle, Scalchi and Edouard de Reszke in *Ugonotti*: and—Mario! "Ah, did you once see Shelley plain?"

§ 4

The little stone balcony in Elgin Avenue is associated for me with a nostalgia other and deeper than the two I have already described, unless indeed all nostalgia is one. I was standing on it one August, a boy of six or seven, and suddenly felt myself caught up I knew not whither as hussars came riding down from a neighbouring barracks, and the paving stones echoed to their horses' hooves, and the street was afire with the afternoon sun, and everything was silent.

By the same token, when, later on, I started waiting outside Covent Garden for the gallery to open, it was something sacramental in Floral Street itself that was the greatest felicity of all. In that narrow, rather sordid street, with opera house on one side and high blackened buildings (for they seemed immensely high) on the other, there would come, in the early evenings of that June or July weather, patches of sunlight from a sun itself unseen. And then, for all the bustle and noise in the world's greatest city, and for all, or perhaps because of, the distant traffic—distant, though in fact only just beyond our deep and narrow chasm—there would happen, in the interior castle of one's spirit, a lull, a suspension, a silence and a peace in which joy and sadness, both incomparably intense and yet of an utter tranquillity, were one. The late sun in cities has always had this effect on me. I suppose something of the kind was meant by Omar Khayyám, when he talked of 'the brave music of a *distant* drum'; and many people experience it, I think, when faintly, in a sunlit street, they catch the tones of a penny whistle or barrel organ, or the singing of a human voice. There are days in Aix-en-Provence, its blazing streets empty as the sun goes down and then footsteps ringing out—foorsteps, they

might be, of the mailed soldiery in some long dead Caesar's legions—
when the sadness would be unbearable were it not the purest happiness
as well.

I shall not attempt to explain the experience of which I have been
speaking, and which, I am certain, a great many people share: I shall
only say of it, as of many other experiences which are bound up with
sights and above all with sounds (and this is where music comes in),
that any explanation in purely physical or 'materialistic' terms is
ludicrously beside the mark. So I shall content myself with repeating
the word 'sacramental', adding only that, if any experience of great
beauty brings such sadness with it, this is because, for the most part
unconsciously, we feel ourselves exiles still from our proper home. All
physical things are sacraments, and the world is so beautiful because it
is a sacrament of the Supreme Beauty. To quote what Oscar Wilde
himself quotes from Théophile Gautier, 'I am one of those *pour qui le
monde visible existe*': exists absolutely, but at the same time exists as
an intimation. If I could write my own epitaph it would be something
like this: "Always, even in the midst of the greatest evil and horror,
he loved the world".

§ 5

Bound up, I believe, with the sacramentalism of the world and
human existence was another experience in Floral Street and on buses
to the Queen's and Albert Halls and the White City and anywhere
else I might be going to hear music. It was an experience happy
beyond expression for one who was still very young and only beginning to grow familiar with the masterpieces: the experience of awaiting
recognition. To have heard a piece of music once or twice, to hear it
veiled in your consciousness and struggling to reveal itself, and to
know that very soon, at a moment that must inevitably come, you
will see it face to face—that is a felicity such as few other experiences
can equal, and of the same nature, maybe, as the quiet of expectation
with which a saint awaits the beatific vision. Or one could put it in
another way: one could speak of a sculptor seeing something in a
block of stone and struggling to reveal it. The two ways of putting it
are really identical, for in a unitary—the final—experience subject and
object are one.

The pleasure of recognition (which is not the same as the pleasure
of *awaiting* recognition) is of course the commonest of musical
pleasures, and commonest of all in the case of music heard but once, or

rarely, before. But it can be present in a rather different sense, and be almost intolerably poignant, at a first hearing, and it can be present at a hundredth hearing, when you think you remember everything, but are suddenly aware of detail after detail that has been lying at the back of your mind. Klemperer is the great contemporary master of such revelation.

I have heard several explanations of this pleasure. One is a narrowly physical one, something to do with nervous reactions and the satisfaction that accompanies them. Another involves jargon about the womb. But I believe for my own part, being of a metaphysical and religious turn of mind, that it is a question of ἀνάμνησις: I believe that when we greet a melody or any other piece of *materia musica* with a shock of delighted recognition, even occasionally on a first hearing and always with greater and greater delight as we grow more and more familiar with it, we are, in a Platonic sense, 'remembering'. I shall call in Plato and some others to help me out. But to quote the passages that follow is not to suggest that we have heard the actual melody 'There', or, to speak more truly, are forever hearing it deep within us: it is to suggest rather that this melody is one of the innumerable expressions of, and recalls, the reality we have known 'There' or are forever knowing:

"Thus far I have been speaking of the fourth and last kind of madness, which is imputed to him who, when he sees the beauty of earth, is transported with the recollection of the true beauty; he would like to fly away, but he cannot; he is like a bird fluttering and looking upward and careless of the world below; and he is therefore thought to be mad. And I have shown this of all inspirations to be the noblest and highest and the offspring of the highest to him who has or shares in it, and that he who loves the beautiful is called a lover because he partakes of it. For, as has been already said, every soul of man has in the way of nature beheld true being; this was the condition of her passing into the form of man. But all souls do not easily recall the things of the other world. . . . Few only retain an adequate remembrance of them; and they, when they behold here any image of that other world, are rapt in amazement; but they are ignorant of what this rapture means, because they do not clearly perceive. . . .

"But of beauty, I repeat again that we saw her there shining in company with the celestial forms; and coming to earth we find her here too, shining in clearness through the clearest aperture of sense. . . ."[1]

[1] Jowett's tr., courtesy of the Trustees, Jowett Copyright Fund.

"There are Souls who are reminded by earthly beauty of the Beauty Yonder, and these love the earthly as an image; those that have not attained to this memory do not understand what is happening within them, and take the image for the reality."[1]

"But somewhere in my soul, I know
I've met the thing before;
It just reminded me—'twas all—
And came my way no more."[2]

"We, who are parts of Adam, heard with him
The song of angels and of seraphim.
Our memory, though dull and sad, retains
Some echo still of those unearthly strains."[3]

"Calm grows the air around,
Arrayed in beauty and unwonted light,
Salinas, at the sound
Of music exquisite
That thy skilled hand doth cunningly indite.

"And at that sound divine
My soul, that in forgetfulness hath lain,
With a new light doth shine
And unto memory plain
Of its first splendid origin attain . . .

"Up through the fields of air
It wings, till in the highest sphere it dwells,
And a new music there
It hears, music that wells
Undying and all other kinds excels."[4]

"The reactions music evokes are not feelings, but they are the images, memories of feelings [of feelings, as Plotinus might have said but Hindemith does not say, 'yonder']."[5]

[1] Plotinus, translated by Stephen Mackenna. By permission of Faber and Faber.
[2] Emily Dickinson.
[3] Rumi, from *Rumi: Poet and Mystic*, translated by Reynold A. Nicholson. By permission of Allen and Unwin.
[4] Luis de Leon, *The Lyrics of Luis de Leon*, translated by Aubrey Bell. By permission of Burns and Oates.
[5] Paul Hindemith.

CHAPTER IV

I SUPPOSE IT WAS a pretty odd affair, given my age, that operatic life of mine before the 1914-1918 war; and it says a good deal for my parents that they allowed it, though I do not know what else they could have done short of turning me out of the house or having me certified as a lunatic: as they would have been justified in doing (subjectively), for there were clearly times when they thought I was mad. (I am speaking, it will be understood, of almost another century. After all I was in my teens, my middle and late teens for most of the time: and nowadays there would be nothing particularly astonishing about that sort of night-life, except for its *venue*.)

Night after night I wouldn't get home till about one in the morning; for it would have been unthinkable to leave the Covent Garden gallery until, for all our shouting and clapping, we couldn't get another recall, and then there was the walk to the corner of Wellington Street and the long bus-ride back to Elgin Avenue. A cold supper was always ready for me in the parlour downstairs; and this comes back to me as consisting almost entirely of beetroot-salad, doubtless by some oddity of misremembering, for there was always enough food on the table to satisfy my invariably ravenous hunger. (I would have had nothing to eat since lunch, except on 'Ring' nights with their dinner interval, as a sandwich at the bar would have cut into my savings and so have jeopardised my attendance on some future occasion; and a present happiness, however final in its own right, was always experienced as involving a coming one—no sooner had Destinn finished 'O patria mia' than I would think, with the spiritual greed, the greed for joy, that has always been one of my weaknesses, "Next Thursday I shall be hearing it again". Even lunch, for the same reason, might have been nothing but a banana and a bar of chocolate.)

My mother never protested against these cold suppers, and would often indeed arrange them on a couple of plates in pretty-looking patterns as one might arrange flowers: nor in general did she ever show herself unsympathetic with my musical proclivities, though she was not very musical herself, in spite of her studying the piano with Maggie Oakey and having once had a five-minute lesson from that lady's famous husband, the buffoon-pianist Vladimir Pachmann. She, my mother, once said to me, when I happened to mention that I was going to *Don Giovanni*, "You'll find it very *heavy*" with great emphasis on the adjective and a sort of contemptuous sniff. But I owe her, musically, a great deal: for maladroitly though she played whatever it might be, and as often as not it was a Victorian show-piece (with a carillon of furiously pealing octaves) called something like "Midnight Wedding", she also played Chopin, and I have loved him, particularly in a living-room, one's own or someone else's, ever since. (I have always thought it slightly improper to play Chopin in a concert-hall, though this is not of course borne out by his own practice. The only pianist I should nowadays make an exception of is Richter: to judge by his Schubert—I have never heard his Chopin—Richter would play him with such intimacy that the concert-hall would quickly be forgotten.)

My feeling for Chopin was reinforced by a whole series of happy experiences. My Uncle Assur, the favourite uncle of my boyhood (he was a bad painter, sang ballads in a gentle tenor, particularly loathed *Götterdämmerung*, which he called 'Gotterdamnthething', and was the kindest man on earth), was in love with a lady called Elsie Grant, who taught the piano and played it with a touch as charming as her looks. Assur had a big studio in the garden of No. 1 Elm Tree Road, where he lived with his mother, my grandmother, of whom I was also exceedingly fond; and he would often give little concerts in it, at which Elsie Grant was always the star performer. The whole complex—Elsie Grant, Uncle Assur, old Mrs. Michaelson, leafy St. John's Wood, the studio (with the collection of cracked but beautiful Dresden and Chelsea that Elsie Grant used to keep there) and above all the grand piano, for ours was only an upright—fascinated me irre-sistibly; and I used to adore being taken there when I was still a very small child, not perhaps more than four or five. One day, remembering my mother's Chopin, I asked Elsie Grant to play some for me and she played a couple of waltzes, I thought most beautifully; and that con-firmed me in a love of him that has always had something peculiarly gentle and peculiarly personal about it. Assur's studio came smilingly into my mind on two later occasions: when I first saw *Les Sylphides* in 1912, for those two waltzes were in it; and when I first heard Bellini, for it is his Chopinesque character that makes him as attractive to me as Donizetti is boring (with the exception of *Don Pasquale* if heard rarely enough). Not that I like everything of Bellini's either: *I Puritani*, apart from a few ingratiating melodies, is as musically tedious as it is dramatically absurd.

§ 2

But if my mother was not unsympathetic, my father became so. He worked hard over that first *Traviata* he took me to, marking some principal arias in the libretto (which I have before me—I notice a little tick nine lines down from 'E strano' to show where the recitative ends and the melody begins) and making me con it: and he kept whispering to me at the performance, sometimes unnecessarily (as 'ballet') and sometimes helpfully (as 'cabaletta', when Melba broke into 'Sempre líberaah'). But presently, as my enthusiasm grew, I began to bore him with my raptures and minutiae, for in spite of his origins he was essentially an English moderate—a Telegraph man, though 'a staunch conservative', rather than a Morning Post man: a bit indeed like the recent Archbishop of Canterbury, Lord Fisher of Lambeth, as I was to discover later on. He had a habit of talking about me in my presence as 'he'; he used to mutter things to my mother like "Destinn, Destinn, Destinn! What *chuzpah*![1] Has he never heard of Adelina Patti? The boy's *m'shuggah*."[2] The Gollanczes in general, to be sure, thought little of post-Patti singers. My Aunt Lena, for instance, accidentally attended the hitherto unknown Tetrazzini's debut, and remarked a day or two later, in a tone of sly venom, "My opinion, Madame Tetrazzini's going off". But I had an uncle, Morris Gollancz, who went to the other extreme. Said to be an even greater Hebrew scholar than my Uncle Hermann—subsequently Revered Rabbi Professor Doctor Sir Hermann Gollancz—he held down, with the utmost difficulty I was told, a job as watchmaker's assistant at a pound a week, and though the most Jewishly orthodox of them all was the only perfect Christian I have ever known. The smallest criticism of anyone would invariably draw from him a shy and lisping "Muthn't thay, muthn't thay" (his mouth had been distorted by typhus). I once took him to an *Aida*, for he adored music and was even poorer than I was. I could see that the tenor, who was atrocious, distressed him: but when, as we left, I remarked that this was no Caruso, he muttered "Muthn't thay, muthn't thay".

I was clashing with my father at this time, even I am afraid sneering at him, about a lot of other things too, of greater ultimate importance than the respective merits of Patti and Destinn: about his moderate Toryism, his moderate antifeminism, his absurd and not at all moderate patriotism. ("Thank God I've never left these shores" he protested, in a

[1] Impudence.   [2] Crazy.

voice that seemed to stand at attention, on the outbreak of war: but he stopped short, for all that, of substituting an 'e' for the 'z' in our name, as another branch of the family did, though in fact it isn't German at all, but derived from a diminutive Polish village. "Don't they know," he exclaimed to my mother, when two of the mutators were having tea with us one *Shabbas*, "that the name's unique?" As indeed it is.)

I must have been insufferable in my youthful arrogance and insistent proclamations of radicalisms, and have never ceased to regret it: I find myself bitterly regretting it at this moment as I sit here in Eaton Place, which he would have so ardently approved of as signifying that I had 'got on'. It was only as he lay dying that the barrier between us came down, for I asked myself if somehow, without saying anything—he was shy, and would have been embarrassed by a confession—I could get through to him at the very last moment and make him understand how sorry I was. And so remembering the love of music that he had inherited from his own father and passed on, for my happiness, to me, I bought a huge pile of gramophone records: forgotten old things that he had heard in his boyhood, such as the shadow-song from *Dinorah* and 'O Paradiso' from *L'Africaine* and the drinking-song from *Lucrezia Borgia*. Hour after hour, until he wanted to sleep, I played them to him. It was the tiniest of reparations, but the good old man, for good old man he was, and fundamentally humble and forgiving, paid it back a hundredfold: a day or two before his death he suddenly muttered something to himself that it would be inappropriate for me to put down here, though I did so, for there it was appropriate, in 'My Dear Timothy'. . . . And so the wheel had come full circle.

CHAPTER V

I HAVE SAID THAT one of the main aspects of my operatic life before the 1914-1918 war strikes me now, thinking back, as a fluctuating struggle for the possession of my musical self by Wagner and Verdi: a struggle that went on for many years longer, and was determined only in the nineteen-thirties, and then, decisively but with lingering regrets that persist even now, in Verdi's favour. And the struggle in those earlier days, before 1915, was above all between *Aida* on the one hand and *Tristan* on the other.

§ 1

The climate of that time must be remembered, as well as my musical heritage: the latter favoured Verdi, the former Wagner. The Verdi renaissance was as yet not even on its way: Verdi was still widely dismissed as a barrel-organ composer, and I remember the amused but affectionate contempt with which two ladies, 'regulars' in the gallery (to identify them with my contemporaries, one of them always wore a deep red rose, and they were considerable bridge-players), used to talk about *Aida* or *Traviata* during the intervals; agreeable stuff, they used to say, and superbly sung, but not of course the real thing, not *serious* like Wagner and especially *The Ring*. Verdi was a man of tunes, some of them pretty or even rather beautiful or with a gay lilt to them, but cheap or banal on the whole; given to orchestration thin and noisy by turns; in a word, pretty crude, though attractive enough as a vehicle for great singing: while Wagner was the greatest composer since Beethoven, and perhaps surpassed him. *Aida*, my rose-lady might add, was of course a considerable advance on *Traviata*, the rather vulgar *Rigoletto* and the impossible *Trovatore*: for at the beginning of my time *Otello* and *Falstaff* were rarely mentioned, and anything earlier than *Rigoletto* never, except perhaps by some eccentric who had heard *Ernani* in Italy. *Tannhäuser*, *Lohengrin* and the *Dutchman* were spoken of, on the other hand, almost as reverentially as *Tristan*, *Meistersinger* and *The Ring*. I am referring to majority opinion, for Verdi had his keen partisans and there were Wagnerians who allowed criticism of the Master: and exclusively of gallery opinion at that, for I could have no knowledge of what was being said amid the splendour below or in the cosmos outside. But my description is probably a fair one of the musical climate in general, at any rate in England: things may have been different in France, where Debussy was influential, and even in Germany, where the Verdi revival, I fancy, was already under way

Opinions of the music as such, of Verdi's and Wagner's respectively, were closely involved with theoretical considerations: enthusiasts for 'music-drama' tended to regard Verdi's as more or less negligible, while careless lovers of 'mere' opera criticised Wagner's as boring and heavy, with the orchestra intolerably drowning the singers. For the concept of music-drama dominated everything. Music-drama, in the opinion of Wagnerians, was one thing and opera another; and Wagner, by creating the first, had not only left no future for the second but had invalidated most of its surviving specimens. With perhaps some exceptions (a few murmured Mozart and a few others Gluck, but then Gluck, after all, was John the Baptist to Wagner's Jesus) you could no longer, you know, take the old things seriously.

It must be explained that the Wagnerian writings, now exclusively food for musicologists and historians of music, were still being devoured by quite a number of serious music-lovers. I had myself, not exactly devoured them, but tasted of them quite extensively, several months before that first visit of mine to Covent Garden: I I would rush off to the Hammersmith Public Library during the lunch intervals at St. Paul's with my banana and bar of chocolate, and settle down to an hour's absorbed reading. And I would always emerge starry-eyed. What a marvellous conception! This union of the arts in a perfection of interdependence, each of them reinforcing the others and nothing lost, everything gained—could a more splendid consummation be imagined? At first I kept it all to myself, fearing I should be accused of disloyalty to my father's operatic past, and even uneasy on my own account, for might I not be jeopardising my enjoyment of the Italian opera I was so eagerly looking forward to? But after becoming a regular opera-goer I could restrain myself no longer, and would often expatiate on the topic at Sabbath lunch, for which my father, of course, was always at home. If there was one thing that bored him more than 'Destinn, Destinn, Destinn', it was The Art Work of the Future. "Leitmotiven!" he used to call across me to my mother. "Nothing but a lot of repetition!" He had once tried The Ring himself —'with cuts'.

§ 2

I was in this situation when I heard my first *Aida* and was immediately bowled over, as much by the music as by the singing, and as much by the drama as by both. Wasn't *this*, then, a perfect union of the arts, or at any rate of two of them, drama and music?—for I could give little attention to the setting, which however, now I come to think of it, wasn't particularly makeshift, as I told Peter Heyworth, but to the best of my recollection perfectly adequate, with the Nile scene looking quite beautiful to my no doubt unsophisticated eyes. But ah, hadn't Verdi been influenced by Wagner when he wrote *Aida*? No, I answered myself, it couldn't be that, for I had felt the same, if less intensely, about *Traviata*, and there could be no question of Wagnerian influence in that case. Still, the Wagnerian conception *was* a splendid one. So the conflict began.

I could not keep away from *Aida*: I certainly heard it more often than any other opera up to 1914 except *Tristan*. Destinn was always the Aida—anyone else would have been unthinkable; Kirkby Lunn was usually the Amneris; and for Radamès we had (apart from Caruso) Martinelli and two 'big' tenors from Paris and Brussels, Dalmorès and Franz, who, though not ideal for the music, didn't let it down either. Dinh Gilly was the best of the Amonasros: his voice, which had a ring of passion in it rather like Destinn's, was of a beautiful amplitude throughout the whole of its compass, the top notes being particularly powerful and sure; he sang with a real sense of drama, even on occasion ferociously; and his presence was magnificent, boxer's nose and all. But Scotti was very fine too, and so was Baklanoff, whom I heard only once. Sometimes, for additional richness, Marcoux would sing Ramfis, and Huberdeau Il Rè.

What moved me most, as that music unfolded itself in a gradually fuller revelation night after night and became more and more familiar, was the simple beauty of melodic line in the music of Aida herself. It eased the heart: one smiled with it, even when it was sad or despairing. But the beauty of the composer's intention was bound up with, was at the mercy of, a comparable beauty in its realisation: there could be no question, as in the case of that amateur *Fidelio*, of merely adequate voices and a merely adequate use of them not mattering. You might almost say that, in a Verdi aria, beauty in the line and beauty in the rendering of it are indivisibly one: a poorly or even no more than adequately sung *Aida* is not *Aida* at all, and anything less than a superbly sung one loses half its glory. That is why I have kept away from any performance of *Aida* for so many years now: Amneris can still be finely sung, and probably Amonasro too, but there is no tenor I know of who could begin to sing Radamès as Verdi intended, nor any soprano for Aida herself. Callas has nowadays in the main the wrong sort of vocal technique; and as for Vishnevskaya, the recent Covent Garden Aida, I do not believe, to judge by what my friends tell me, that, fine in many ways though she is, I should find her in this role to my taste. (But I had forgotten Leontyne Price, whose Aida I missed: she must be a magnificent one.)

§ 3

If *Aida* moved me, *Tristan* also moved me, yes of course, but above all intoxicated me in a way *Aida* could never do in those earlier days and has never done since. Intoxicated: that is the irreplaceable word, trite though it must sound. For three or four years, until the curtain came down on all such possibilities in the summer of 1914, *Tristan* was half my life: I lived in the anticipation of it, in the experiencing of it, in the remembering of it. Apart from the difference between being moved and being intoxicated, it was not a matter (then), as in the case of *Aida*, of the finest singing being integrally important and indeed crucial: when you are being swept by a tornado only the tornado is present to your consciousness, and there can be no question of 'distinguo'. Later, in the twenties and thirties, when I was to hear the great Isoldes, I was to learn what a tremendous difference great singing could make in this case too: but it was never to have for me that quality of the *sine qua non*, nor can ever have in the nature of the case, which it has always had, and must always have in the nature of the case, for the rendering of Verdi.

As a matter of a fact I remember nothing, with two exceptions, about those *Tristan* performances before the first world war, nor do any of them stand out in my mind above the rest. The exceptions are van Rooy's glorious Kurwenal and Hans Bechstein's very moving Hirt. But I find on reference to my defective and mutilated stock of programmes that I heard, among others, von Bahr-Mildenburg, Edyth Walker, Felia Litvinne and Saltzmann-Stevens as Isolde; Kirkby Lunn as Brangäne; Peter Cornelius as Tristan; Weidemann and Clarence Whitehill, additionally to van Rooy, as Kurwenal; Robert Radford as King Marke: with, as conductors, Hans Richter, Bruno Walter,

Franz Schalk, Thomas Beecham and (in an off-season) Hamilton Harty.

"Short of fainting," wrote Berlioz to his sister when still a very young man, "I could not feel a stronger impression than that of seeing Gluck's masterpiece, *Iphigeneia*. . . . It's about the limit of what one can stand.'[1] That was exactly my reaction to *Tristan*. If heart-easing serenity might have described my emotion at *Aida*, ecstasy or rapture was the word now: and it was in the second act, from the distant tremolo and shimmer of the horns at the beginning to 'heiss erglühter Brust, höchste Liebes-Lust' towards the end, that it was at its most continuous. Then there was the young sailor's almost intolerable longing as the prelude ended and the curtain went up: the 'Tristan! Isolde!' when, after those bewildered moments, the potion could no longer be denied and the lovers stood at gaze; Brangäne's voice on the watch-tower: and, perhaps most moving of all, the joyous tune on the shepherd's pipe, comparable only, as a divine moment in opera, with the trumpet call in *Fidelio*. Even the Liebestod rarely moved me as much. Between performances phrases were always ringing in my head as I did my Latin prose or skimmed my Homer: 'Welches Land? Kornwalls grünen Strand' and 'Tod geweihtes Haupt! Tod geweihtes He-erz!' and 'Was hälst du von dem Knechte?' and 'Kurwenal! Hör'! Ein zweites Schiff'. I was obsessed.

§ 4

Meanwhile I was exploring other works by Verdi and Wagner. I approached my first *Rigoletto* with a good deal of uneasiness, for in spite of my joy in *Traviata* I was a bit intimidated by the narrower Wagnerians, who thought it vulgar: and indeed (perhaps for that reason) this is an opera that failed to engage me wholeheartedly till the middle twenties. The performance was a fine one and Tetrazzini, who sang Gilda to McCormack's Duke and Sammarco's Rigoletto, was soon revealing what florid singing could be like. She was the most brilliant and lively of the coloratura sopranos I've heard, and I was to hear her in *Traviata*, *Ugonotti*, *The Barber* and *Lakmé* (put on for her —the bell song) as well as in *Rigoletto*. But there have been others I've liked better. I came to prefer, in the twenties or thirties, Maria Ivogün, a favourite with Bruno Walter: when I heard her as Zerbinetta at Charlottenburg I suddenly found myself thinking of the birds in the Pastoral Symphony, there was such a cascading freshness

[1] Quoted by Barzun.

about her technically miraculous coloratura. Galli-Curci, who arrived between the two, sang spectacularly but often off the note: all in all she was rather a myth. Beautiful also in the earlier Rigolettos was Lydia Lipkowska, one of a pair of Russian singers whose vocalisation resembled the dancing of the more *petite* of the ballerinas who were conquering London just then. The other was Maria Kousnietzoff. I fell in love with them both.

The memory of Sammarco, my first Rigoletto, has been dimmed for me by that of the more recent Joseph Schwarz, whose magnificence in the part can be put side by side, as one thinks back, even with Caruso's as the Duke. The combination of pathos and furious venom, which is the secret of the role, was rendered by that powerful voice with superlative mastery: you would have thought the 'cortigiani' unsurpassable but for the 'vendetta' that followed it. As for Caruso himself, no other of his roles could rival that of the Duke for the variety of vocal expression it allowed him: from the brio and peculiar, almost cutting incisiveness of 'Questa o quella' to the tender legato of his avowal to Gilda. And the high notes!

§ 5

For the rest, and apart of course from *Otello* and *Falstaff*, I heard nothing by Verdi from the gallery of Covent Garden except a single performance of the *Ballo*: this was in 1911, but I had gone out a year earlier for some scratch performances of it at the Coronet Theatre in Notting Hill Gate, the same theatre where my wife and I, in the first years of our marriage, were to see a film once a fortnight. I never heard *Trovatore* as a boy: I doubt whether the Covent Garden people ever put it on in those days, and I shouldn't have wanted to hear it anyhow. For it was thought of as the barrel-organ opera *par excellence*: even my father despised it (those glorious tunes!); and the Wagnerian side of me was too powerful to stomach the impropriety of listening to anything that clashed so shockingly, as I assumed, with Wagnerian principles. My whole position indeed was highly complicated, even seemingly, but only seemingly I think, paradoxical. I was still nostalgic for the old Italian opera, but shrank at the same time from anything too, from the Wagnerian point of view, outrageous, unless I had reason to believe that the music as such was worth hearing: and if the music wasn't, then even the best singing, Destinn's possibly excepted, could be no adequate compensation. Fine music finely sung

was among the highest of musical experiences, and Wagner be dam-
ned: but bad music even greatly sung has never been to my taste.
Tetrazzini may have been singing Lucia after I had begun going to
Covent Garden, for she had made her British debut in it with the San
Carlo people at an off-season only a few years earlier, and I well
remember the public excitement she caused, for the newspapers used
to 'feature' prima donnas at that epoch as nowadays they 'feature' the
Beatles: but if I could have heard her in it and didn't, then the reason I
kept away was that I assumed, perhaps by instinct, that the music was
tedious, as I was to find it—insufferably tedious—when I first came to
hear it with Joan Sutherland a very few years ago. I did not feel this
about Bellini, as I have mentioned, and indeed was always hoping that
at any rate *Norma* would be put on: and again my instinct was to prove
sound when Ponselle sang in it so finely a few years after the first
world war. I cannot imagine why, in spite of my love, amounting to
adoration, for *Traviata* and *Aida*, I took it for granted that *Trovatore*
was musically intolerable: it may have been because I had heard the
anvil chorus so often thundered out on my mother's piano—but then
this had also been the case with the soldiers' chorus from *Faust*, and I
had drawn no such erroneous conclusions. Or it may have been that
Trovatore was the very symbol of antiwagnerian *Italienismus*, and so I
avoided it as much for Verdi's sake as for Wagner's.

There could be no question in that climate of *La Forza* or *Macbeth*, of *Luisa Miller* or *Simone Boccanegra* or even *Don Carlo*, not to
mention *Nabucco* and *I Lombardi*: hardly anyone in England had so
much as heard of them, except a few who had been influenced by
Dent. It was while I was at Oxford that this sensitive musician and
musicologist was preparing the way for an operatic renaissance of
Mozart, who had meant to Covent Garden audiences only *Figaro*
and the *Don*, and had meant them infrequently: his 'The Operas of
Mozart', still far the best book on the subject, appeared in 1912, and
I bought it within a week of publication. It can be imagined with what
pleasure I read the first sentence, in which he quoted with approval the
remark of 'an eminent living composer' to the effect that 'there were
only three really great writers of operas—Mozart, Wagner and Verdi'.

§ 6

My own enthusiasm for Verdi has waxed and waxed, and I have
never lost an opportunity of hearing his rarer works, so that now
there are only six wholly unknown to me, namely *Oberto*, *Il Finto*

Stanislao, Giovanna d'Arco, Alzira, Il Corsaro and *Aroldo*.[1] This very year we filled a gap by attending a dress rehearsal of *Jérusalem*, the Paris version of *I Lombardi*, at the Fenice: it is a poorish work (though redeemed by a chorus closely resembling 'Va, pensiero'), but what a thrill it was to sit in that *bonbonnière* of a place with only about a hundred others on a blazing Venetian forenoon!

At the same time, I feel that the Verdi renaissance is getting a bit out of hand. One should hear every one of his operas at least once, but why rave about them all as if they were masterpieces? The other night *Attila*, a work full of boring and sometimes laughable crudities (literally laughable: the audience laughed), was revived at Sadler's Wells: and people were rushing about in the intervals asking wasn't it all really marvellous? Still, this must be said: even in the worst vulgarities of some of his earlier works the same truth can be heard struggling for expression as was to reveal itself, pure gold, in the surpassing grace and delicacy of the old man's *Falstaff*. So perhaps an indiscriminate veneration for every bar he wrote is no great matter. But what I fear is that the contagion may spread—there are signs of this already—and come to involve Italian opera in general, so that we may be faced with revivals of *Lucrezia Borgia* and the like. This would be a pity, so long as most of Gluck, as well as many minor works of great interest, remains virtually or entirely unknown. There is far more to be said for reviving some Meyerbeer, such as *L'Africaine* and *Le Prophète*. After all there is at least one piece of nearly great music in *Ugonotti*, the love-duet 'Tu m'ami', whether it was actually written by Meyerbeer himself or by the first fiddle, as rumour has it: so who can say what treasures may not be hidden in some of those other scores my father used to rave about?

§ 7

I shall say nothing about *Falstaff* and *Otello*, the works themselves, except that both are supreme masterpieces: and little about the way I have heard them performed. I talked to Peter Heyworth of Zenatello's Moor and would only add now that I have never heard his equal, though Slezak ran him close: which is not to suggest that either could be compared to Tamagno, who is said, for what that is worth, to have made the chandelier rattle in the roof of the Lyceum Theatre. I would even go so far as to say that opera-goers too young to have

[1] But I have heard *Aroldo* in the meantime.

heard Zenatello's piercingly clean but ample and rounded 'Esultate', with the grace-note, its glory, sung to thrilling perfection, can have little idea of what that music can mean. Nor were his partners less admirable. Scotti's Iago was vocally and dramatically the subtlest I have heard and seen, and Desdemona was Melba's best part. Given the immaculate purity of her vocalisation, her psychological deficiencies, in the musical sense, were almost a positive advantage (I am thinking particularly of the willow-song and the Ave Maria): better to let the music speak for itself, as if through a piece of human near-mechanism, than run the risk of interfering with its own immaculacy.

I was not to hear *Falstaff* until 1914, and then for two performances only: the house for both, in that great Wagner season (*Parsifal*, *Lohengrin* and *Die Meistersinger*, as well as *The Ring*), was half empty. Scotti was in the name-part, with Claudia Muzio as an adorable Alice and Kirkby Lunn as Dame Quickly. Scotti's voice was perfectly suited to the music, particularly to the lightness and rapidity of 'Quand' ero paggio': as it was, by the same token, to the Don's 'Finch' han dal vino'.

CHAPTER VI

I MUST RETURN NOW to Wagner, and this really means trying to describe how I felt about *The Ring*; for to confess the truth (and if I say confess this is because the climate is now as heavily Wagnerian again as it was in my boyhood) nothing of Wagner's has ever meant much to me except *Tristan* and *The Ring*—and of course *Die Meistersinger*, which no one but an insensitive boor can have failed to adore at some period or other of his musical life, and which I have always adored and, with a few harmless reservations, adore still.

But my attitude has been a good deal more negative than 'never meant much to me' suggests. I took an immediate dislike to *Tannhäuser*, which I heard only once from the gallery—in the middle of my *Tristan* period—and have rarely heard since: a scandalously narrow basis, no doubt, on which to judge, but then I go to what pleases or interests me, and have no duty in the matter except to myself—and often lose a lot, surely, by refusing in such cases to explore further. I had already heard the overture several times at the proms, and had been impressed by the dramatic gravity of the pilgrims' chorus and stirred by the Tannhäuser tune and 'the pulse of life' (as the programme note called it), though not to excess: so I had looked forward to hearing the work alive and whole. But the evening was a failure. In the opera itself (and, I was to feel later, in the overture too, though when Klemperer conducted it the other night with the Philharmonia he almost persuaded me to the contrary) there seemed neither depth to the gravity nor inwardness to the excitement: under the noise there was an absence of genuine life that made the whole thing seem contrived. The orgy, in particular (little though I knew about orgies), sounded hollow and bogus: what a contrast to the love music in *Tristan*, which was even more than a unique expression of passion, it was passion, the Idea of passion, itself (though I knew little about passion either, but was already starting on Plato). Or, to put it in another way, the whole thing, under its externalities, was, spiritually rather than musically, foursquare. Again, 'O Star of Eve'—Clarence Whitehill sang it in English, for this was one of Beecham's English seasons, and the familiar language somehow made it sound worse— affected me most disagreeably, like many of Wagner's earlier tunes, because of something Germanised-Italian about them: neither one thing nor the other, as Churchill remarked in a different connection. The aria was of course terribly hackneyed, but this was not the reason for my malaise: for so is Verdi's Brindisi, and I could hear it a thousand times with delight.

I liked *Lohengrin* a good deal better. In this case also I was familiar with the prelude (I had heard it often at the proms) and my heart would flutter a little as the divided fiddles began their high symphony; and I enjoyed it at the actual performance, with some other bits and pieces like the bridal procession (not chorus) and the prelude to Act III. But a lot of it affected me as either barren or sentimental and 'mein lieber Schwan' made me squirm. I felt no differently last year when the Hamburg troup—the same that gave us *Lulu*—performed the work at Sadler's Wells.

On the whole it was the *Fliegende Holländer* (with Destinn or Signe von Rappe as Senta) that I liked best in early Wagner. There is a glory of the sea in it that compensates for a lot that is tedious.

§ 2

And now *Parsifal*, which I first heard the year of its première in England. There had been great excitement as 1914 approached, that being the year in which the ban on performances anywhere but at Bayreuth—a ban that had been universally respected except in the United States—was to be lifted; and I mention as a curiosity a programme I have dug out, dated 1913, of "Tableaux from Wagner's Court Festival Drama *Parsifal*, specially designed and staged by Byam Shaw, A.R.W.S., the Augmented Orchestra conducted by Sir Henry J. Wood, by permission of the Queen's Hall Orchestra Limited." There are eight Tableaux with numerous subdivisions, beginning with 'The Killing of the Swan' and ending with 'Redeeming Love'; and at the bottom there is a note: "The statement that these Tableaux were given by permission of Madame Wagner was incorrect, and was made under a misapprehension. The permission was given by Messrs. Schott & Co., the publishers and owners of the copyright." I cannot say where the performance was, for the programme had been closely trimmed, as usual, before being pasted into my exercise-book, with the *venue* eliminated: but I imagine at some such place as the Palladium or Coliseum, to judge by the typography.

Parsifal is a work that causes me acute discomfort. It would be foolish to deny that it overflows with musical beauty of a high order,

if not to my mind of the highest; though there are themes in it, like
the main Parsifal one so often repeated, that have always struck me as
at once blatant and banal, and moreover as quite arbitrary: a dozen
other patterns of sound would have been, in point of characterisation,
no less appropriate. The whole system of leitmotifs, so far at least as
the representation of persons rather than objects is concerned, tends to
such arbitrariness, if only because they must necessarily be so brief: a
few notes can perhaps characterise a sword or a spear, but not a man or
a woman. Wagner's system can be beautifully subtle in its ability to
recall a character at a given moment, and in the way it allows him to
combine two or more motifs with great musical-dramatic effect (I shall
deal more fully with all this later on): but in respect of the sheer
portrayal of character it acts as a positive hindrance. The great masters
of characterisation in opera are Mozart and Verdi, not Wagner. Still,
there are degrees of appropriateness: the motif of the young Siegfried is
suggestive in its necessarily limited way, that of Parsifal quite irrelevant.

But what I dislike most in *Parsifal* is the richly cloying quality
of music intended to express a religious atmosphere and religious
emotions. It has been called sensual or sexual, but I should not describe
it quite like that myself: I should describe it rather as the expression,
by a man of high sensuality but little feeling for religion, of a religious
atmosphere and religious emotions as he thinks they ought to be
expressed. It is this spuriousness in the music that, for all its melodic
and harmonic beauty, and its complete sincerity on the conscious level,
makes me feel so queasy. I ought to add that by 'a feeling for religion'
I imply no dogmatic beliefs, but openness to the spiritual and holy.

The music in *Parsifal* that comes closest to expressing true religious
emotion is that associated with the peace of a Good Friday morning,
and this I have always loved: for Wagner was particularly sensitive to
the phenomena of nature, and nature, both in its gentler and in its
sublimer aspects, can give intimations of the spiritual even to those with
comparatively little feeling for it. But other music in this genre
surpasses his, by reason of its greater purity: Beethoven's for instance
in the Pastoral Symphony, and Gluck's in *Orfeo*.

§ 3

I come to *The Ring*, on which, together with *Tristan*, the passionate but selective Wagnerism of my boyhood and very young manhood
was based. I heard my first cycle in 1910, and, apart altogether from

that, this was in itself a very special occasion, for Hans Richter, who had conducted the original Bayreuth performance in 1876, was at the rostrum. What a pang of history, of the past that had now become my present, hushed me as the lights went out, and staring down from B.49 at the dim orchestra far below, through field-glasses that had been my father's and were now mine, I caught a glimpse of that legendary figure! I remember him as huge and bearded, rather like Brahms: but I saw indistinctly, and the years may have fashioned my impression.

From 1910 till the war broke out in 1914 I tried never to miss a cycle: I saw at least one every year, and usually two. Richter was succeeded, in that order, by Franz Schalk and Nikisch, who conducted for two seasons running, 1913 and 1914: I preferred him, in a very uninstructed way, even to Richter, but then I was already under his spell as Elena Gerhardt's accompanist at her *Lieder* recitals. I have the casts, and many of the names are historic ones of the second rank: but I shall mention three only (all of the first rank) because I remember nothing at all about the rest, in point either of what they looked like or of how they sang. The exceptions are van Rooy as the usual Wotan; Hans Bechstein as Mime; and Paul Bender as the Wotan of 1914. (van Rooy and Hans Bechstein, it may be recalled, are the ones I remember so vividly from *Tristan*.) There are two possible explanations for my forgetfulness of the rest. One is that I had no ears for anything but the orchestral splendour, though this would not explain my memory of Bechstein and van Rooy. It seems more probable that the singers, with the exceptions noted, simply failed to impress me, perhaps by comparison with the standards currently prevailing in Italian opera. However that may be, I am certain that these performances were vocally inferior, even far inferior, on the whole to the ones we heard at Covent Garden between the wars.

Long before my first cycle I had been working hard at the literature by way of preparing myself for the revelation to come. While I was getting up the Artwork of the Future at the Hammersmith Public Library, I was buying any booklet I could lay my hands on that expounded *The Ring* and particularly its *Leitmotiven*. There was one by Frieda Winkworth, another by Cleaver and Clump or Crump, and Gustav Kobbé's 'How to Understand Wagner's Ring'. (Kobbé is now famous for 'The Complete Opera Book', re-edited a few years ago by Lord Harewood.) Kobbé's was the best of all, for it not only printed no less than seventy-four motifs in good clear script, but gave a number of important combinations as well. I have been looking through it, and find a lot of things like 'Alberich departs, still in the form of a vaporous column' and 'a motive divinely and heroically beautiful, it often assumes a tender mood, like the chivalric gentleness which every true gentleman feels towards a woman". It would be easy enough for me to jeer, now that I am over seventy and have heard *The Ring*, I suppose, a couple of dozen times or more: but then I was a generous thirteen or fourteen, and being fresh to it all would have been in no mood to criticise a little rhodomontade, harmless in any case, even if it had occurred to me as such. What I wanted was solid information about the motifs, Kobbé gave it to me, and I still think of him with affection.

Soon I was learning the 'poem' almost by heart, against Frederick Jameson's version in English: and now I hardly needed Kobbé to feed my happy expectation (though 'happy' gives little idea of my impatient eagerness), for there it all was, set out and communicated direct to me by Wagner himself. The grandeur of its conception; the immensity of its scale; its combination of almost geological remoteness with passionate living creatures; the physical heights and depths in it, its rocks and rivers and open air; the giants and dwarfs, the *Wurm*, mysteries like the Tarnhelm, Wotan's kiss and Brünnhilde's age-long slumber; and, then, for overwhelming climax, the doom of old shibboleths and the world's salvation, which fitted in perfectly with my young radicalism—what a joy to be living, as I should shortly be living, in a world like that, a world even more wonderful than this one, and this one was wonderful enough!

When the moment came at last I could hardly believe it was there, and I listened in rapture to that genius of an opening: the E flat on the double basses, the seminal, utterly simple progression (or so it sounded) of the rising horns, and then the parting of the curtains and the disclosure of the Rhine.

I have been reading through the libretti and eking them out at a few points with the piano scores I used to con in those days (sitting on the second or third stair below the clattering bar during the minor waits, or at a table in a restaurant, Simpson's or Romano's, during the dinner interval, which always seemed far too long to me) in an effort to sharpen my memory of the things that entranced or impressed me most during my first couple of cycles: and I shall mention a few of them here, because it is a pleasure to recall my happiness at *The Ring* until criticism became insistent, but with another motive too, namely to balance things up. There is much in *The Ring* I now detest, and comparatively little that gives me joy, as I shall presently make clear; but I hope I shall never be so foolish as to deny that only a towering genius could have conceived it and brought it to birth.

What enthralled me most, then, in *Rheingold* was the fresh-ness of its open-air atmosphere, together with a couple of motifs usually described as those of Freia and Eternal Youth, but bringing to my heart as I listened the sense of newly mown grass at the Paddington and Maida Vale recreation ground, and of clover in my fields by the ups-and-downs, and of glistening dew on those great purple dahlias in the market-gardens beyond Elgin Avenue.

Then there was the Tarnhelm motif, with its marvellous suggestion of empty air—a feat as difficult in music as in painting—and of the mystery of non-being: and the Valhalla one, so tranquilly proud in its grandeur. And of course I was highly amused by the descent into Nibelheim, and was forever tapping out the Nibelung motif, that first spring, with the handle of a fork or the flat of a spoon on the dining-room table: my father would shake his head and mutter *m'shuggah*. And finally, and perhaps best of all as so typically Wagner-ian, the moment when, as everyone gazes at Valhalla and Wotan pauses before greeting it, the motif of the Sword rings out piercingly, to show that he has found a way to salvation. I had been looking out for it, but it thrilled me all the more when it came.

The next night—a day or two usually elapsed between *Walküre* and *Siegfried* and between *Siegfried* and *Götterdämmerung*, but *Walküre* always followed directly after *Rheingold*—I had to wait for my first peak till Sieglinde offers Siegmund the mead to a melody that reveals its full beauty, and particularly that of the *gruppetto* it ends with, only when sung by an artist of absolutely top rank, if possible of the Viennese school: the legato, the breath-control and the beauty of the voice itself must all be perfect (Lotte Lehmann, later on, was specially entrancing in this role). I sang inwardly with all the love-music, and at the second cycle waited breathlessly for the door to fly open against those sweeping arpeggios, and for 'Winterstürme' to begin. (I was later to see a 'modern' production in which the door didn't fly open because it wasn't there: another example of a perverse outrage to the composer's intention.) Earlier had come the play, so intellectually beautiful, with the Sword motif; first when it sounds, ending *pianissimo*, as Sieglinde gazes at the tree-trunk, and later when it returns, to the rise and fall of the orchestra, as a gleam flashes out from the embers and the hilt fitfully appears.

The second and third acts of *Walküre* captured me first at the point at which Brünnhilde warns Siegmund of his coming death, to music as broad and grave as some of Handel's; then by her announcement of Siegfried's birth, with his triumphantly positive motif, now heard for the first time, leaping up and dominating everything—an example (the attacking sword at the end of *Rheingold* is another) of that prophetic use of leitmotifs which binds the whole drama together and gives the listener a sense of being privy to cosmic mysteries. But it was the closing scene, from the Farewell to the slumber and fire music, that turned happiness into ecstasy.

What moved me most in the first act of *Siegfried*, after the sound of April mornings in the boy's melody as he beats at the weapon tinkered by Mime, was the tune, full of a young man's longing for a

beauty once known but now lost, that accompanies his musing about fledglings in spring; and the moment when Siegfried recalls seeing his image in the crystal brook and his motif comes shimmering from the orchestra, with a poetry at the opposite extreme to the literalness of so many of these identifications. Then, after the *Waldweben*, I was at once seized by the introduction to Act III, which struck me as far and away the most splendid orchestral passage, so far, in the whole cycle; and I was not to alter my opinion even when *Götterdämmerung* had come to an end. The sweep, the glow, the passion and the constantly intervening incisiveness carried me away. But the best of course was yet to come. First the scaling of the peak and the cutting away of Brünnhilde's corselet and greaves. (This is the happiest example of imitative music I know. There are two sorts of such music. The better reveals the essence of the thing imitated: the worse, of which Vivaldi's *The Four Seasons* is typical, merely mirrors it, more or less palely, as a phenomenon.) And then—Brünnhilde's greeting to the sun, her 'O Siegfried! Siegfried!', and 'Ewig war ich, ewig bin ich....'

Götterdämmerung failed to impress me quite as much, but of course I loved the duet between Siegfried and Brünnhilde and Siegfried's journey to the Rhine, and most of all perhaps the funeral march. Here the array of motifs is wholly in place, bringing to our ears, as nothing else could, Siegfried's entire life as we ourselves have been living it. Even the orchestral climax moved me less.

§ 4

Apart from the musical-dramatic interest of the work, though all mixed up with it, was something that savoured more of the detective stories I was already enjoying than of anything more exalted: I mean the game of spotting the motifs. I call it a game and so fundamentally it was, though a success in any respect on any occasion promised an enhancement of musical-dramatic pleasure in that particular respect on all future occasions: for once you had noticed that motif A was combined with motif B at section C near the beginning of D, deaf ears would never again deprive you of an intended nuance. Anyhow, we would whisper to ourselves 'motif W, very soft' or 'motif Z there, as well as X and Y': and sometimes we would whisper the precious information to a neighbour, intimately and even conspiratorially. I was sitting at a cycle in the late twenties next to a great lady, who instructed her lord in this matter every time a familiar motif came through sufficiently loud for her to spot it: bad enough, I thought (for my defection had already begun), to suffer these unnecessary identifications by the Master himself, but to have them rammed home by an outsider. . . .

(To break in on myself with a trivial episode relevant to the Wagner-Verdi business, a couple of hours ago I switched on the wireless, for The House of the Arrow, one of my favourite antiques, was due at 8.30 on Saturday Night Theatre. But I was a few minutes early, and suddenly found myself in the middle of a glorious Mediterranean duet—Vic Oliver's Variety Playhouse was nearing its end—that made me leap from my chair and gesticulate with ludicrous abandon. The music was as familiar to me as God Save the Queen, but for the moment I couldn't place it: middle Verdi of course, but which? Then it came to me: barrel-organ Trovatore.)

§ 5

And still another thing The Ring gave me: a sense of occasion that made it stand out as unique, very much as Wagnerians regard a visit to Bayreuth as a pilgrimage. There was to begin with a peculiar solemnity about the whole enterprise: over a stretch of days one would be living—continuously, for the gaps between *Walküre* and *Siegfried* and between *Siegfried* and *Götterdämmerung* hardly counted as time—a kind of existence far removed from the ordinary one. (There were people who went to the opera on irrelevant nights during a cycle: I despised them.) Then there was the sense of adulthood at last achieved, for I was just seventeen when I went to the Richter performances (seventeen then was much younger than seventeen now) and the flavour lingered on into the later cycles. Finally there was the beautiful hour for starting—five for *Walküre* and *Siegfried*, even half an hour earlier for *Götterdämmerung*—and above all the dinner interval. To walk down Wellington Street and debouch into the Strand, with its horse-buses and hansom cabs; to walk back again as the light was dying—this somehow made both worlds more wonderful, and each simultaneously more wonderful than the other. There was an occasion, not during a *Ring* cycle, when I was specially moved, in a way bound up, maybe, with intimations of far-off things, by the shock of contrast between a world in which people talk and a world in which people sing. This was on the last night of the 1909 season. I had heard *Louise* only once and was anxious to hear it again, and it had been billed for that evening. But I was still under parental discipline, it is forbidden to ride on Saturday until Sabbath has 'gone out', and Sabbath 'goes out' very late indeed in high summer. So I decided to walk. But I underestimated the time it would take me to get from Elgin Avenue to Bow Street, and arrived very late. There could be no question of B49, so I made for the gallery slips; and as I tiptoed through the little door out of the darkness I was suddenly seeing the lanterns ablaze on Montmartre and hearing the sadly gay music of the milling crowd. . . . You sometimes get an emotion like that if you are shut out from a concert and hear, as you wait in the corridor, the playing within; or if you walk into the hall past a room you cannot see in which the orchestra is tuning up, as often happens to me when I take the artists' lift on South Bank. . . . But what I felt at the *Louise* performance may also have been due, in a minor degree, to the fact that Paris, as yet unvisited, was pulling at me.

§ 6

After that first couple of cycles the passages I have mentioned moved or impressed me more and more as they grew increasingly familiar, and many others revealed themselves: not to mention the grand design, the orchestral colour, the vast surge and sweep of the work as a whole. Doubts, it is true, were beginning to creep in, but I hastily brushed them aside; and it would be fair to say that when the war intervened in 1914, to be followed by a pretty complete gap in my musical life for a decade or more, I was still a dedicated *Ring* man.

RICCARDO WAGNER LOOKING PENSIVE

GIUSEPPE VERDI LOOKING WRY

CHAPTER VII

AND NOW I SHALL try, in the present chapter, to give an idea of what the Wagner and Verdi performances were like from the mid-twenties, when I resumed opera-going, to the mid-thirties, when I abandoned it again for a period; and then, in the following chapter, to deal with the whole Wagner-Verdi conflict in me as it began before 1915 and was finally decided during the later period. I shall say nothing however about the *Meistersinger* till I come to the chapter on Salzburg.

I

WAGNER

For many years after 1926 the Wagner performances were of extraordinary splendour, so that my incipient doubts of 1914 had a great deal to fight against. Even the initial year, 1926 itself, came close to justifying that description, for after a *Sigfrido* in Florence (with Commendatore Amadeo Bassi as the hero and portraits of Riccardo Wagner and Guiseppe Verdi in the programme, the former looking pensive and the latter wry), we found awaiting us, on our return to London, a *Ring* under Bruno Walter with Olczewska as Fricka, Erda and Waltraute; Melchior as Siegmund; Lotte Lehmann as Sieglinde; Melchior as the young Siegfried; and Frida Leider as the *Götterdämmerung* Brünnhilde. For these were the Vienna days, dominated at first by Bruno Walter and later by Beecham: the Vienna days, because Lotte Lehmann and Elisabeth Schumann made the atmosphere. And if I have been a little cautious in the way I have described the 1926 cycles, this is because a certain lack of concentration —of concentrated greatness in any single performance—must be debited to it. I cannot find, for instance, that Frida Leider was part-nered by a comparable Siegfried in *Götterdämmerung*, or Lotte Lehmann by a comparable Brünnhilde in *Walküre*.

For the full splendour, however, we had to wait only one more year. The 1927 *Walküre*, again under Walter, ranks with the Destinn–Tetrazzini–Zenatello *Ugonotti* and the Destinn–Caruso–Dinh Gilly

Aida as one of the three or four supreme performances of my time. Here is the cast: Melchior (Siegmund), Friedrich Schorr (Wotan), Frida Leider (Brünnhilde), Lotte Lehmann (Sieglinde) and Sigrid Onegin (Fricka). I doubt whether there had been anything like it before, even in the best Bayreuth days, when Materna, Alvary, Rosa Sucher, Schumann-Heink and Lilli Lehmann were at the height of their powers: and am sure there has been nothing like it since.

So it went on, year after year, with ups and downs, or rather a few downs, but usually on at least a comparable level. Alexander Kipnis was outstanding as Hunding in 1929, and, the same season I think, Rudolf Bockelmann replaced Friedrich Schorr as Wotan and the Wanderer. Several years later Elisabeth Rethberg was almost rivalling Lotte Lehmann's Sieglinde. Then in 1936 Kirsten Flagstad sang her first Brünnhilde, and at once leapt into the sort of fame reserved for a Melba but never a Destinn, a Paderewski but never a Schnabel, a Kreisler but never a Ysaÿe. These popular acclaims, rarely based on comparative merit and by no means always on personality considerations, are wretchedly inexplicable.

The other Wagner performances matched those of *The Ring*. By 1927 Leider was singing Isolde, and Flagstad succeeded her in 1936. Robert Heger conducted a *Parsifal* in 1927 with Melchior, Mayr and, quite casually, Elisabeth Schumann as one of the Flower Maidens. Schorr sang the Dutchman in 1930, and the following year Lotte Lehmann sang Elsa, with Olczewska as Ortrud.

To say a word or two about only the most brilliant of the stars in so exceptionally brilliant a cluster, Frida Leider was far and away the finest Brünnhilde or Isolde I had heard up to then, and of the few others I have heard since only Birgit Nilsson is comparable. There was such a sweeping passion in her voice, such a generosity of power and so incisive an attack, that you wondered whether tenderness could also be there until the tenderness came. Her biting ferocity in the first act of *Tristan* was matched, and perhaps even surpassed, by the quiet beauty of her lyricism in the second and her grave exaltation in the third; and if you admired her piercing 'hojotoheijah' in the *Walküre*, sung for once without the slightest sense of strain, you admired the more, by contrast, the perfect control of her *piano* in 'Siegmund! Sieh auf mich! Ich bin's, der bald du folg'st'.

Flagstad, though exceptional, was not in the same class. Her singing was clean and pure, even, in its way, perfect: but she was cold, a little like Melba or Joan Sutherland. As for Melchior, his voice was genuinely heroic, and he could use it with ringing passion: but there was little of the sheer beauty in his singing that compels, not merely admiration, but gratitude. This was not so in the case of Schorr and Bockelmann, the Wotans and Kurwenals of the period; there was a rounded amplitude in their voices, and a steadiness on top, that made them comparable to, if not quite on a level with, van Rooy. If there was anything to choose between their Wotans, Schorr was the more godlike, Bockelmann the more human and gracious; I preferred both to Hans Hotter, who came later, and was not always quite as steady as he might have been, at any rate on the occasions I heard him.

I shall write about Lotte Lehmann and Elisabeth Schumann in another connection, but Maria Olczewska belongs properly here. This was a contralto I have never heard surpassed, though Simionato may equal her and Stignani may have done so in her prime. Her versatility was quite out of the way—her Orlofsky was as good as her Azucena, her Fricka as her Amneris; and her voice, capable alike of playfulness and gravity, was devoid of the 'plumminess' that has been criticised in, for instance, Kirkby Lunn, whom I had particularly admired as a boy in *Samson and Delilah*. (This 'lollipop' had appealed to me in youth almost as much as it apparently appealed to Sir Thomas Beecham in old age, and I suspect would modestly appeal to me still if finely sung. Sugar no doubt, but the best sugar; at the one extreme of French opera, as *Carmen* is at the other. For a year at least it gave me an intense pleasure of the easier sort as I was getting to know the tunes: 'Mon cœur s'ouvre à ta voix' and 'Printemps qui commence', 'Amour! viens aider ma faiblesse' and the love-duet, and most of all the pretty chorus for female voices, 'Voici le printemps', with its insidious orchestral accompaniment. There is a certain affinity between this last and 'Voici des roses': the Berlioz being alpha plus and the Saint-Saëns beta minus.)

As for Bruno Walter, the dominant conductor of that Wagnerian decade, it is difficult for me to speak of him objectively: for I have always loved him above all other conductors, though Klemperer far surpasses him in Beethoven, and I have preferred Toscanini, Furtwängler, Pierre Monteux and Thomas Beecham in the music of various other composers. But there was something specially gracious, almost charismatic, about his interpretation of Wagner when the music allowed of it (though he never sentimentalised Wagner—beyond Wagner's intention—as, it must be confessed, he could sentimentalise Mozart); and he had a gift of communication, of sympathy with his audience, that almost made one feel one was conducting oneself. His sensitive nostrils were as indicative of the musician as of the man. His moulding of phrases was superb. He was a supreme master, nearly as great a one as Klemperer, of orchestral unfolding.

II

VERDI

But if 1926–1936 was, from an interpretative point of view, the Wagner decade *par excellence*, a galaxy of Verdi performances shone, as a whole, only less brightly than the pre-war ones, for all the lack of a Destinn or Caruso; and there were individual performances that even surpassed some of those in the earlier series.

Just as the 1926 Wagner was ushered in for us by *Sigfrido* in Florence, so the 1926 Verdi had a prelude, of a very different kind, at the Scala. On the evening of April 11th we found ourselves in Milan, intending to spend the night there on our way south, and hurried to the Cavour (which has now disappeared). We chose this hotel for two reasons: first, because it was a stone's-throw from the Scala, and secondly because I remembered, or thought I did, that Verdi himself had always put up there, and that, when the old man had been carried in triumph from opera-house to hotel after the first night of *Otello*, it was from its balcony that Tamagno sang the 'Esultate' to the crowds milling below. It seems I was wrong, for Toye states flatly that Verdi always stayed at the Albergo di Milano, and Toye is rarely inaccurate: nevertheless I shall continue to cherish the apparently mythical association. Anyhow, the first thing we did on arrival was to ask the concierge whether we could have a couple of tickets for the Scala that evening, neither knowing nor caring what was on. The concierge immediately exploded into a mixture of fury and derision, shouting over to his mate—in semi-English, to make certain we should understand, much as my father had been in the habit of calling me a *m'shuggana* to my mother and my face—'he wanta two ticket for La Scala! For *stasera! Due biglietti!*' Then the two of them went off into paroxysms of laughter, and we crept away to the dining-room: but we had hardly given our order when he came rushing in (the place was a very informal one) and shouted '*Miracolo! Due biglietti*—returnèd! And *niente supplemento—prezzo originale!*' But the antipasti were just arriving, and we looked enquiringly at one another; whereupon he clutched me by the arm, and shouted in a fury of impatience '*Avanti!* Noa eata! *Cinque minuti!*' So we rushed off, and were mercifully allowed in just as the curtain was going up, with no time for a programme. (It happens that my seat was almost exactly B49—at the extreme end of the central block: but on the fourth row instead of the second, and in the stalls instead of the gallery.) And there was the *Traviata* ballroom before us, very gay and richly appointed, with one of the most insidious of operatic waltzes teasing our ears. I was at first a little disturbed by the antics of the man in front of me, who was waving his hands to the music (doubtless with a seraphic look on his face), as I have often been tempted to do myself at the sound of familiar melodies: but directly the 'Libiamo' started my attention was held. This was no ordinary Violetta! When the curtain came down I bought a programme, and the lady turned out to be Claudia Muzio. I learned later that she was returning to the Scala that evening after an absence of a decade or so in America. She may even have been singing Violetta there for the first time. Anyhow, it was an occasion indeed, and I wondered afterwards whether they had been drinking real champagne: I thought I detected bubbles through my field-glasses. Toscanini was the conductor.

Back in London after our fortnight in Italy, we were to hear, that first year of our operatic renewal, three performances of *Otello*, still with Zenatello but now with Lotte Lehmann as Desdemona (exquisite in the fragrance and courtesy of her singing throughout, but particularly in the first duet and in the willow-song and Ave Maria), and, at two of them, Mariano Stabile as Iago. We were indeed constantly hearing *Otello* throughout this period, with for instance Zanelli, Melchior and Martinelli as *protagoniste*. Martinelli came near to equalling Zenatello: Melchior was often thrilling, but what the role really calls for is an Italian *tenore robusto* or *robustissimo*, not a *Heldentenor* from the North. Of more recent Otellos Vinay has probably been the best: but there has never been, on the nights I have heard him, either the tenderness or the passion I have always been waiting for. On only one occasion, however, have I failed to enjoy a performance of this opera: that was a couple of years or so ago at Covent Garden, when del Monaco was singing. This is a tenor not at all to my taste, whether as Otello or as Aeneas, a part we heard him create at the Scala première of *Les Troyens*: but my taste may be defective, for I understand he is highly thought of not only in New York but at the Scala itself. My friend Bob Giroux of New York, who has a collection of pre-dog records second only to Desmond Shaw-Taylor's, once gave me a lesson in *Otello* singing: he first put on a more or less contemporary record of del

Monaco in the closing scene of the opera, and then an ancient one, with piano accompaniment, of Tamagno in the same heart-breaking music. Anyhow, two incredible feats were accomplished by del Monaco at Covent Garden that evening: I found myself on the verge of disliking the work itself, and left before the last act. What I longed for at that moment was a little Schubert chamber-music, or Yehudi Menuhin in the Chaconne.

But I must mention another Otello we often heard during our thronging decade of operatic splendour: Arthur Cox at Sadler's Wells. This was a peculiarly English Otello, English in an almost Shakespearian sense (as Frank Mullings was), with a voice, properly plain and gruff, that sounded enormous in a small theatre; and English, for once, seemed the right language. About this time there was a veritable Verdi festival at the Wells, with Joan Cross adding Violetta and Leonora (in the *Forza*) to her Desdemona. A singer again of somehow specifically English charm, frail to look at, dedicated to her art, and ranking very high indeed if not quite at the top, she was one of our favourites.

The Wells itself, which we were beginning to frequent just then, was a development out of the original Old Vic, which I had often visited as a boy: down amid the fly-blown shops and dingy sexualities of the Waterloo Bridge Road, it suggested dirty railway compartments, and tenth-rate pubs in ill-lit streets, and underground lavatories. But it delighted me, or at any rate the side of me that didn't hanker for opera-cloaks and St. Petersburg, by its genuine proletarian quality— you could get in for tuppence, I think: even the stage-box cost only a shilling or so, and I sometimes sat in it with a party of friends to get a closer view of old Charles Corri, who conducted his squeaky orchestra of about thirty, and the stage as well, with an extraordinary presence of mind that could cover up a thousand mishaps. It was at the Old Vic that I first heard *Don Giovanni*. The Leporello eat spaghetti (as part of his performance) while the stalls sucked oranges. I enjoyed it far more than many stuffed-shirt performances, but almost equally ill sung, that I have heard at Covent Garden more recently. Charles Corri was still conducting at that 1933 *Otello*, but the gallery had gone up three hundred per cent, namely to sixpence.

Before leaving the topic of Sadler's Wells I must pay a tribute to one of the most lovable of its stars, I mean Arnold Matters. With a voice of perhaps less than top quality, he not only excelled as an actor but revealed, in every role he undertook, a character so naturally gracious that he did more than delight his hearers, he moved them. A noble Boccanegra, he surpassed himself as Figaro. His parenthetical

Royal Opera Covent Garden

Proprietors . The Grand Opera Syndicate, Ltd.

General Manager . Mr. NEIL FORSYTH
Musical Director . Mr. PERCY PITT

[1914]
THIS EVENING'S PERFORMANCE

LAST NIGHT OF THE SEASON

Tuesday, July 28th, at 8

VERDI'S OPERA

AÏDA

(In Italian)

Il Re	MURRAY DAVEY
Amneris	LOUISE KIRKBY LUNN
Aida	EMMY DESTINN
Radames	PAUL FRANZ
Ramfis	GUSTAVE HUBERDEAU
Amonasro	DINH GILLY
La Sacerdotessa	AMY EVANS
Un Messaggiero	DANTE ZUCCHI
Premiere Danseuse	FELYNE VERBIST
Conductor	ETTORE PANIZZA

Stage Manager · *M. FERNAND ALMANZ*

For future Announcements see inside

SIGNORINA DESTINN

[Dover Street Studios

'Susanna!' on discovering, in the last act, that it was she and not the Countess endeared him to everyone.

§ 2

We heard *Aida* in the twenties and thirties as often as we heard *Otello*. The last of the old performances had been on July 28th, 1914, which ended the season. Destinn was, almost symbolically, in the name part. We would not let her go: twenty-two times—I counted them—she returned to acknowledge our shouts. Then I took up my stand in Floral Street, and, coming out with Dinh Gilly, she gave me a rose. War was declared five days later.

And now, from 1926 onwards, there were two particularly beautiful Aidas, both outstandingly gifted with the kind of legato the music specially demands: Dusolina Giannini and Elisabeth Rethberg. The latter, in particular, interpreted to perfection the Verdian tranquillity: the sense of what the Greeks called γαλήνη in some of his quieter music. She was indeed near to equalling Destinn in all but vibrancy and passion. We also heard Scacciata at the Scala, Gina Cigna at Palermo and Anne Roselle in Vienna.

All these references to Italy, Sicily, Vienna, Paris, etcetera must be giving a totally false impression of our life at this time, for they suggest that we were always wandering about the Continent in an atmosphere of leisured ease. This was far from being the case: our holidays rarely exceeded a fortnight, though we occasionally ran over to Paris for a short week-end in addition or even to Venice for a long one (at Easter), and this was before travelling by air had come in. But we never missed an opportunity of hearing any music available, unpromising though it might be. We once found ourselves in Siena for the night, a rather dingy Siena in those days, lacking even a decent hotel. A lot of bills were about, announcing, with the irresistible caption *novità*, an opera by some unknown composer, probably Sienese, and nothing could have kept us away from it. Something tattered about the house was more than balanced by our intimacy with the performers, for the orchestra was on a level with the audience, there was no barrier between them, and we were given such excellent seats, right in the middle of the front row, that we might have been members of the orchestra ourselves. We understood not a word, and were displeased by the singing; so when our attention was caught by the flautist we felt that it would not be too heinous to concentrate on him. He was teaching his craft to a little boy at his elbow, and would nudge the tiro to come in when occasion demanded: interrupting for this purpose his major concern, which was the incessant plastering of his hair with spittle and its subsequent combing with the aid of a diminutive mirror. I was reminded of a libel I had heard on an orchestra that detested its chief: when a woman player was waiting for her entry she used to knit.

I have also been asked how so much music could have been combined with the conduct of a busy publishing business, as well as with the para-political activity that was already taking much of my time even before I became engulfed by it. The answer is germane to the subject of this memoir. When as a young boy I had got home from Covent Garden and eaten my supper and done an hour's homework, it might be two in the morning or later; but I had to be up betimes none the less, for I was a keen classic, thought little of the Virgil or Homer routine, and wanted to range further afield and get on to Longinus or the Greek lyrics or whatever it might be. So I would knock six times hard on my forehead, repeating as I did so 'six o'clock'; and six o'clock it would be, almost to the second, when I found myself staring about me. At first I had to dash cold water on my face to keep my eyes open, but to be awake, fresh and alive, at six or earlier soon became second nature. This established a habit that has never left me: three and a half hours' sleep, with at least a half-hour's rest after lunch, has always been enough for my needs, and I have suffered nothing from this useful regime except an occasional bout of insomnia. Anyhow I make up by dropping off in taxis and sleeping half round the clock on holidays, and taking a couple of seconals on a Friday night every three months or so and dozing happily almost the entire week-end in consequence.

§ 3

It was in 1929 that we heard, at the Paris Opéra, our first *Traviata* since the Melba and Tetrazzini ones and the others of that remote epoch: a charming *Traviata*—charming, for that house, by exception —with Fanny Heldy as Violetta. It made quite a stir: it is the one referred to by Toye in his 'Verdi' when, writing of "the Verdi Renaissance in Germany which has been so remarkable a feature of musical history during the last few years", he adds: "Nor, in fact, has this revival of interest in Verdi's work been confined to Germany, though found there in its most striking form. For instance, to take but the most recent examples . . . *Traviata* was, I am informed, the outstanding success of the Paris Opéra last winter. . . ." It was I who had done the informing.

Then, a year later, came the best of all Violettas, that of Rosa Ponselle. I hate snobbish talk about wine, with its knowing, *faux-naïf* terminology, and I may be talking ignorant nonsense: but as I think of Ponselle and try to convey her quality a comparison comes into my head. There are clarets that are too full for me, and others that have grown thin, and a little musty, with age; but I was given the other night a wine that tasted beautifully equable yet was quite devoid of an exaggerated *velouté*. That was what Ponselle sounded like. And yet Violetta was not her best role. The previous year she had sung Norma, and the fioriture in 'Casta Diva', which she played with like a Callas in her prime, and the legato in 'Mira, o Norma' were as if Bellini had written them for her. She was partnered in *Traviata* by Gigli, a tenor I never greatly admired, despite a beautiful voice and an often pleasurable technique: he was typically 'Italian', sobbing and almost crooning in a way Caruso never did.

§ 4

Stabile was the usual Falstaff at Covent Garden, and Joan Cross a lovable Nanetta at the Wells: but the most enjoyable performance of Verdi's masterpiece I have ever heard was at Charlottenburg in 1927 under Bruno Walter, a performance at the opposite pole to the Zeffirelli one I criticised in my interview with Peter Heyworth. I have just asked my wife her impression of it, and she has replied "breathlessly beautiful", which is my impression too. Everything was befittingly intimate, whatever the size of the house may have been; the sets, particularly that for Windsor Park, were just right in their simplicity; and the stage traffic, again particularly in the closing scene, was perfectly managed. But we nearly missed that experience. This was our last day in Berlin, and the train left the Friedrichstrasse Bahnhof at midnight: but *Falstaff* ended at midnight too, and to have cut the last act would have been unthinkable. So we consulted the concierge at the Adlon, a fat man who wore his cap to one side and was reputed the most knowledgeable of his tribe in all Europe, and he arranged that our luggage should be put into our *wagon* at the Friedrichstrasse Bahnhof, and that we should pick up the train at the Zoo station (nearer the Charlottenburg opera-house), where it arrived at about a quarter past twelve and made a wait of five or ten minutes. He would fix up a car to meet us after the performance, arranging a curious method of identification: I was to wave a yellow duster (a presage of things to come) which he gave me for the purpose. I am usually in a panic when things like that are under way, fearing every imaginable mishap; but on this occasion the last act so entranced me that I did not worry at all. We caught our train in the nick of time, and our luggage was safely there: and so was a cold supper of chicken and asparagus salad, which the concierge happened to know I specially liked.

CHAPTER VIII

My doubts about *The Ring* up to the summer of 1914 were swallowed up in my rapture, and were not of such a nature as to modify it to any appreciable degree. (I had no doubts about *Tristan* till later.) Indeed I realise their existence more vividly now than I did at the time. But they were there, below the surface or just above it.

§ I

The first faint stirring of doubt was about the *length* of certain dramatically static passages, accompanied by the slightest misgiving about the whole Wagnerian theory and system of music-drama (as opposed to opera) itself. And I think I can place the passages in question. I have been looking through that old vade-mecum of mine, Kobbé's 'How to Understand Wagner's Ring', and I find a line in faded pencil, with three exclamation marks, against the following passages:

"The ensuing scene between Wotan and Fricka [in the second act of the *Walküre*] has been subjected to an immense amount of criticism and ridicule. Even Wagnerian commentators are somewhat timid in their references to it. The plain facts concerning this scene are these: it is somewhat long, and hence, from a *dramatic* point of view, perhaps too extended, as it delays the action. But if it may be *partially* condemned *dramatically*, it must be *entirely* and unreservedly praised *musically*. Indeed it is musically so fine that to an intelligent listener all sense of lengthiness disappears. . . . As she advances hastily towards Wotan her angry, passionate demeanour is reflected by the orchestra, and this effective expression of Fricka's ire is often heard in the course of the scene." (My italics for 'dramatically' and 'musically', which I had underlined in Kobbé; the rest are his.)

"It will be observed that a considerable portion of Wotan's narrative [later in the same act] covers some of the events which were enacted in *Rheingold*. Hence a portion of the narrative is unnecessary, and

D

therefore undoubtedly faulty from a purely dramatic standpoint. It may also be not unjustly questioned if in other portions the narrative does not go into details beyond the dramatic requirements. Both the scene between Wotan and Fricka and the narrative are too long to be given in their entirety in a performance which begins as late as eight p.m. When, however, Wagner's works are performed as they are at Bayreuth, where the performances begin at four in the afternoon and there are long intermissions during which the listeners can saunter about the grounds surrounding the theatre, not a note should be omitted. There cannot be under such conditions the faintest suggestion of fatigue from an undue mental strain, even on the part of those who have become so accustomed to the insipidness of the old-fashioned opera that they are appalled at the mere thought—provided they retain the power of thinking—of mental effort in connection with a musico-dramatic work. Whatever fault may be found with Wotan's narrative —or rather portions of it—from a purely *dramatic* point of view, it is *musically* most expressive from its first accents, uttered in a choked, suppressed voice, to its eloquent climax. The motives heard will be recognised, except one, which is new." (The italics are mine.)

I can reconstruct quite faithfully what preceded these markings of mine and what followed them. I wonder for a passing moment at one of my earlier cycles whether the Fricka-Wotan duologue isn't a trifle long, but I hurriedly brush aside the idea, for I am committed to Wagner and am a person of strong artistic loyalties: it is a matter, I tell myself, of my not having done enough homework—if I could follow every word I should feel differently. But I am also (a) a person of at any rate average intellectual integrity, and (b) a worrier in matters of art (for years, to give an example, I felt a quite neurotic anxiety as to whether I might not be all wrong about 'modern' pictures, and only a few months ago bought a couple of them, in the hope that, as a result of daily intercourse, I should grow to like them better). So when, at my next cycle, I again find that Fricka-Wotan duologue a trifle long, or even a trifle longer, I again brush aside such a heresy for the time being, but directly I get home go straight for Kobbé, in the certainty that his wisdom and knowledge will reassure me, and demonstrate that this anyhow infinitesimal fly in the ointment does not really exist. And what do I find? "But if it may be partially condemned dramatically, it must be entirely and unreservedly praised musically". And then, as I read on with growing uneasiness, I find the following about another passage: "Undoubtedly faulty from a purely dramatic standpoint, but

musically most expressive . . . not a note should be omitted." I
explode with fury: "Grotesque! And the man calls himself a Wagnerian! Doesn't he know that the very essence of music-drama is the
perfect fusion of music and drama? Doesn't he realise that this is how it
differs from 'old-fashioned opera', in which, as he is always telling us,
the drama is sacrificed to the music. Isn't that what his whole book is
about? He must be *m'shuggah!*" So the immediate effect of this
encounter with Kobbé is a furious reaction against my own semi-
hesitation, which has anyhow been shamefaced, about the duologue in
question; and I begin to wonder, in the stress of my self-accusation,
whether I found it long for a horribly disquieting reason that Kobbé
himself suggests. "Indeed it is musically so fine that to an intelligent
listener all sense of lengthiness disappears." Then perhaps I am not an
intelligent listener? A painful verdict, for it must mean that I am incapable of appreciating the highest things in music, but only the
obviously delightful ones. Or maybe I was "fatigued from an undue
mental strain". Then perhaps I ought to go to Bayreuth and saunter
about the grounds during the long intermissions? But my father, even
if he could afford it, and he cannot, would think this *hyperm'shuggah*:
and anyhow there is nothing really in it, for the first act of *Walküre*,
which comes immediately prior to the more important of the offending
passages, is plain enough sailing, and you can saunter about the streets
of London as happily as about the grounds of Bayreuth during the
long dinner-interval if you do not want, or cannot afford, a big
meal.

But the episode was comparatively trivial, and so were similar ones
that probably followed it between 1911, when I suspect it occurred,
and the outbreak of war; for of my 'staunch' Wagnerism, in any but a
grotesquely exclusive sense, during this period there can be no question. The decade 1926–1936 was increasingly a different matter, in
respect, I mean for the moment, of the purely theoretical question—
music-drama versus opera—rather than of strictly musical or moral
considerations; and I shall cut out any dallying with intermediate
stages and come immediately to what I now feel.

Wagner's basic idea was of course the one put forward by the
Camerata Fiorentina round Giovanni de' Bardi at the end of the six-
teenth century. Their concern was "the revival of classic Greek music—
an obvious endeavour when seen as a parallel to the Renaissance revival
of Greek sculpture and architecture. On the assumption (which was
correct) that Greek tragedies were originally sung rather than merely
spoken, the Florentines reached the conclusion (which was faulty) that

music should always be subservient to words rather than remain autonomous."[1]

Giovanni elaborated as follows: "In composing, you will make it your chief aim to arrange the verse well and to declaim the words as intelligently as you can, not letting yourself be led astray by the counterpoint like a bad swimmer who lets himself be carried out of his course by the current and comes to shore beyond the mark that he has set, for you will consider it self-evident that, just as the soul is nobler than the body, so the words are nobler than the counterpoint. Would it not seem ridiculous if, walking in the public square, you saw a servant followed by his master and commanding him, or a boy who wanted to instruct his father or his tutor?"

And again, in the words of Vincenzo Galilei (the astronomer's father), who was a member of the group:

"If the object of the modern practical musicians is, as they say, to delight the sense of hearing with the variety of the consonances, and if this property of tickling (for it cannot with truth be called a delight in any other sense) resides in a simple piece of hollow wood over which are stretched four, six, or more strings of the gut of a dumb beast or of some other material, disposed according to the nature of the harmonic numbers, or in a given number of natural reeds or of artificial ones made of wood, metal, or some other material, divided by proportioned and suitable measures, with a little air blowing inside them while they are touched or struck by the clumsy and untutored hand of some base idiot or other, then let this object of delighting with the variety of their harmonies be abandoned to these instruments, for being without sense, movement, intellect, speech, discourse, reason, or soul, they are capable of nothing else. But let men, who have been endowed by nature with all these noble and excellent parts, endeavour to use them not merely to delight, but, as imitators of the good ancients, to improve at the same time, for they have the capacity to do this and in doing otherwise they are acting contrary to nature, which is the handmaiden of God. . . . The noblest, most important, and principal part of music are the concepts of the soul expressed by means of words, and not the sounding together of several voices as the modern practitioners say and believe."

The result of all this was *Dafne*, the first opera, probably produced during the carnival of 1597.

Now what Wagner imagined was that it was his mission to fulfil

[1] Levarie, *Musical Italy Revisited*, The Macmillan Company, N.Y. The quotations that follow are from the same source.

the Florentine initiative, on a far more elaborate level and with arts other than music and drama brought in. But it was a mission that in the nature of the case he, being Wagner, could never fulfil.

For whatever one may think at the last about the quality of Wagner's music, that he was a musical genius—even, as a Rabbi said of his master (not about music but about sanctity) in the way he put his shoes on—cannot for a moment be denied: while as a dramatist he functioned, if now and again with considerable and once or twice with supreme mastery, as often as not hardly at all. The inevitable happened: music ran away with him. As to his quality as a dramatic poet you have only to read any dozen pages of *The Ring* and somewhere or other you are likely to find your answer. Or, for the matter of that, almost the whole of the second act of *Tristan*.

In a nutshell: what you primarily listen to in Wagner—in nearly all operas indeed, but above all in Wagner—is not the words but the music, while what Giovanni de' Bardi intended was the opposite.

Not that Giovanni got it right either. Whether or not, and I should of course deny it, "the words are nobler than the counterpoint" in God's hearing, for an ordinary music-lover the music must in any case tend to swamp the words, simply because he *is* above all a music-lover: while the impact of the words, in the totality of their effect, their effect as dramatic literature, over the opera as a whole, can never be enhanced, must always be diminished, by being set to music—provided they are of the self-sufficient greatness that alone can result in great drama. (I discussed something of this before in relation to concert-music, when writing about the Britten War Requiem.) Which is not of course to deny that, however much the words may suffer, the new thing, words plus music, is far intenser in its impact on a music lover than the old thing, words alone.[1]

The truth is that what should measure the excellence of an opera is neither music nor words, but drama: and to serve the drama there has usually had to be, in practice, a certain compromise between words and music. The ideally great opera (impossible, for the reason given, of achievement) would be a great drama (*a*) with great words enhanced by great music and (*b*) with great music enhanced by great words: and it must be said in Wagner's favour that if there is to be a compromise —if words on the whole are to be sacrificed to music or music to

---

[1] I have had to be summary and dogmatic about a question—the relation of music to words—that has been minutely discussed from the earliest days of opera down to Strauss' *Capriccio*.

words—the former is preferable, though this procedure, in his case, was the opposite of what he consciously intended. The distinction between opera and music-drama is in fact a myth: an opera is a music-drama to the degree of its approach to the operatic ideal, and a music-drama fails to be a music-drama to the degree of its departure from it. From this point of view, there are not a few music-dramas, usually called operas, that must rank, *as* music-dramas, higher than *The Ring*: for instance *Fidelio*, *Orfeo* (Gluck's), *Orfeo* (Monteverdi's), *Figaro*, *Don Carlo*, *Otello*, *Falstaff*, *Elektra*, *Wozzeck* and Debussy's *Pelléas*—with the last, again *as* music-drama, the greatest of all.

§ 2

The mention of Debussy comes in well here, for I want to write a paragraph or two next on the leitmotif system, especially as it functions in *The Ring*. Debussy's famous remark about the characters presenting their visiting-cards every time they appear was already current in the Covent Garden gallery before I heard my first cycle: the platoon of anti-Wagnerians used to tease the battalion of Wagnerians with it. I was furious (my partisanship) but determined (my intellectual integrity) to listen as carefully as possible, with a view to discovering whether there was anything in it. Nothing, I decided at my first cycle or two: on the contrary, as they became increasingly familiar (and they were already pretty familiar by the time my earliest *Götterdämmerung* had ended), most of the motifs, or at any rate many of them, thrilled me more and more. I have already mentioned the game of 'spotting the motifs', and this went on for years. But here again, and again as a matter of little importance, to be hastily brushed aside, an occasional question began insinuating itself. Must we really have Wotan's spear motif, so often in its plain and original form as it seemed to me, eternally crashing in? That is the only case I can remember, though I daresay there were one or two others. But as with music-drama versus opera so now with *Leitmotiven* the process accelerated after 1926, and ten years later I had come to my present position, which is this:

The leitmotif system, as developed in *The Ring*, can be of the greatest dramatic force and poetic subtlety, but it can also be a terrible bore. A great deal of course depends on the musical interest of the motifs themself: but, apart altogether from that, it can serve, as perhaps nothing else can, a number of dramatic and psychological purposes that have delighted me as much as they must have delighted everyone else familiar with the tetralogy.

(1) It can make one privy to what is going on in the mind of a character, and that is to add a new dimension to drama. I have already given two instances—the announcement of the Sword motif at the end of *Rheingold*, and its reappearence in *Walküre* when Sieglinde tries to make Siegmund look at the tree-trunk.

(2) It can convey to the listener, by way of an organic enrichment of the orchestral web, something he could learn otherwise only from an extraneous *compère*. When for instance Siegmund is telling Hunding of his father, and of how, after one of the forest combats, no trace of him could be found, the Valhalla motif, sounding as a background in all its grandeur, makes the listener understand, what is known to neither Siegmund nor Hunding, that the father is Wotan. The tragic irony in such passages, which 'lets one in' on the cosmic pattern, can rarely have been surpassed in the history of drama.

(3) Its power to produce a climax can be extraordinary. To continue with the sword motif, its great leap as Siegmund wrests from the tree-trunk the weapon his father has left for him is one of the most thrilling moments in the whole tetralogy.

(4) Equally remarkable can be its power to recall earlier happenings. A particularly beautiful example is the echo of Siegmund's and Sieglinde's love-music as Wotan pleads with Fricka to forego her threatened vengeance.

(6) Finally (though the topic is endless) the possibilities inherent in a combination of motifs require no illustration. Anyone familiar with *The Ring* will recall a hundred examples.

But a qualification or two must already come in. Some of the simplest effects will mean nothing to anyone listening to his first cycle: what significance, for instance, can that initial announcement of the Sword motif have for him except that of a fine cutting phrase? And if it be objected that he ought to have done his homework, so he ought: but can the self-sufficient validity of a work of art be defended by such a plea? You are not compelled to 'get up' a Shakespearian tragedy in the certain knowledge that unless you do so you cannot possibly avoid missing some of the finest things in it.

Then the combination of motifs. This is in theory a wonderfully suggestive technique, particularly for anyone reading a score by the fireside. But in practice, and in the theatre, the matter is different. The simpler and more immediately striking combinations are easy enough to follow, but many of the subtler and more complicated ones will almost certainly be missed, unless the score is known almost by heart; and if you are repeatedly oblivious to references crucial for Wagner's purpose, the leifmotif system is *pro tanto* a failure.

The main point, however, is this: the constant repetition of motifs, whether beautiful in themselves or boringly commonplace (the Giants, Hunding, the Walküre etcetera), and particularly when they are brought in as mere 'visiting cards', ends by producing such tedium, in respect of motifs as such, that even when they are used for purposes of outstanding significance their effect may be diminished. My mother, who followed all current developments, including, I remember, Freud, wrote a play at the height of the *Leitmotiven* boom, to be accompanied by music: the latter consisting solely of a dozen motifs, to be severally played by an orchestra of a hundred every time the appropriate character entered or spoke. She used to give readings of this drama, which turned on mesmerism or reincarnation, I forget which, for the benefit of Belgian refugees: and every time she had occasion to say, for instance, 'Lady Betty', she would mutter with a sniff in a *sotto voce* aside 'Lady Betty motif'. I was furious, for I thought she was parodying the master: but I was to think later that, though her genius hardly equalled Wagner's, her method, in one particular, was not such a parody of his after all.

Wagner's invention of the leitmotif system was a brilliant one, but he let it run away with him; and I often found myself wishing, during my last cycles, that he had used it with more discretion, for then one would have had the wonders, when they came, without the irritation that so often intervened. There are at least two examples in Verdi of how moving an occasional use of motifs, or musical reminiscence, can be. The first is the passage, already mentioned, at the end of *Otello*, when the Moor, in his death agony, sings the words of the duet from Act I to the same music, now unutterably heart-breaking: 'Un bacio . . . un bacio ancora . . . un altro bacio'. The other is when, in the last act of *Traviata*, the dying woman reads Alfredo's letter, speaking not singing it, to the accompaniment of their old avowal.

§ 3

As to the music itself, I remember only one positive criticism I made of it in my gallery days, but I remember that very vividly indeed. It was of the tune, usually known as Redemption by Love, to which

Sieglinde sings her joyful reply when Brünnhilde has told her that she is to be the mother of Siegfried, greatest of heroes:

It is a tune of the highest significance, though it will be heard only once again during the course of the tetralogy, for at the end of *Götterdämmerung*, when Valhalla is blazing, it will soar above the orchestral tumult and dominate everything. It is fair to say, then, that Wagner intends it to indicate or symbolise or sum up the whole meaning of *The Ring*. And what is it? A trivial and banal little tune, as incommensurate as could well be imagined with the grandeur and solemnity of the idea it is meant to embody: and made all the worse by the pomp of its orchestral panoply at the surging climax.

For the rest, a glance at the list I have already given of the things I specially liked in my boyhood will suggest a list of the things I probably didn't, and certainly didn't in the twenties and thirties. I think particularly of the forging songs (all but unbearable in their shallow heartiness) and the Valkyries' Ride, which are typical, under the surface of their imitative brilliance, of something I find dislikeable, and even detestable, in a certain amount of Wagner's music: something hard, square, or literal, though these adjectives give as little idea of what I am trying to express as banal does. There is no inside to such music: no heart, no spirit. *Tannhäuser* in particular is full of it.

There is comparatively little music in *The Ring*, however, that I should complain of on this score: on the contrary I should at once agree that most of it is of all but the highest beauty. The trouble rather is, as I came to feel a long time ago, that it is *too* beautiful, which is to say that its beauty is not the highest of all: or call its beauty an impure beauty. *The Ring* ended by satiating me, not in this passage or in that, but as a whole. The greatest music never does this, however familiar it may have grown: I have heard the Pastoral and Choral Symphonies far more often than I have heard *The Ring*, but the one never fails to refresh me, or the other to reveal heaven. I can perhaps clarify what I mean by confessing that I always longed for a Schubert trio or Mozart quartet after the curtain had fallen on the richness of *Götterdämmerung*.

Richness, ripeness—that has a good deal to do with it. Coleridge coined a neologism to describe a certain literary style: he speaks of its 'too-muchness'. (Similarly Taine speaks of the 'violent saucery' of

Victor Hugo.) There is a too-muchness about the music of *The Ring*: about its beauty, its power, its pathos, its epicism. What I like best of Wagner's, apart from and on a level with *Die Meistersinger*, is the Siegfried Idyll, if played under happy conditions. I was sitting on a blazing forenoon last summer in my cottage near Hambleden, and noticed, on looking into the Radio Times, that the Siegfried Idyll was being played almost at once; so I switched the machine on. The cottage is a tiny one with plenty of windows, so that if you sit in the living-room you are practically in the garden; and it was in this freshness that the music came through to me, played by the few instruments that Wagner wrote it for. The effect was magical, and for a moment my love-hate towards Wagner turned to love.

But there is not only a too-muchness about the music of *The Ring*, there is a too-muchness about *The Ring* more generally. It is too vast in conception, too grand in design, too large in its attitudes, too epic in its emotions: the heights it climbs to are too high, the depths it descends to too deep. There is an air of *hybris* about it: its vastness is not a vastness *ad majorem dei gloriam* as the Choral Symphony's is, but a vastness for its own sake. By 1936 the feeling of satiety that was becoming dominant for me in respect of the music, despite a few lovelinesses I could still enjoy without reservation and my pleasure in such magnificent singing, was spreading to the work in itself. I began wondering whether I should ever want to see it again, for the reasons already given and for a more important one still to be explained; and I do not think I have in fact ever seen it since in its entirety, though I have gone to a number of individual performances of this opera or that, either because I suddenly felt a desire to hear a particular piece of music again—and phrases of lyrical magic come stealing into my mind as I sit here—or because I wanted to sample some singer, like Hotter or Nilsson, who had newly arrived. But the spell, I imagine, has been broken for ever.

This attitude of mine to too-muchness may be idiosyncratic, a reaction against my own considerable flamboyance. All that fantasy about opera-cloaks is combined in me with a special liking, though the word is inadequate, for things of quiet and peace. A sort of worshipful hush in the presence of tranquillity, already strong in me on the Elgin Avenue balcony more than sixty years ago, has grown with the years, and this may partly explain why a passionate enthusiasm for Wagner has become a reluctant distaste for him. By the same token, I now prefer chamber-music to opera: I have always loved both, but the order of my loving has changed. For all that, I hear more opera than chamber-music: I am no traitor to my first passion.

§ 4

I think that before going on to my last point about *The Ring* I had better get *Tristan* out of the way. When I stopped going to *Tristan*, only one of the things I was feeling about *The Ring* applied to it, and that in a somewhat lesser degree. I was not troubled about any music-drama question in the case of *Tristan*, for I had never thought of it as a music-drama at all but always as a symphony with voices: though considered as music-drama it would rank very high if cut a bit in Act II (King Marke) and Act III (Tristan). Similarly, the question of motifs did not arise: though every now and again I was delighted by a particular reference, the motifs in general affected me as so much symphonic material. Finally, there is not a note in *Tristan* that can be thought of as banal, tedious, or 'square': all is either beautiful in itself or beautifully appropriate to its place in the symphonic scheme.

If in the end then I could no longer feel about *Tristan* as I had felt in my schooldays and when at Oxford, this was for the same reason as in the other case: it was *too* beautiful. I arose from it, not refreshed, not exhilarated, not purged by emotion, not with spirit enhanced, but satiated: with some rapt memories of the past few hours, but satiated none the less. I should have felt the same, I think, about the legendary carpet of Khursraw, made for the vast audience-hall of the palace at Ctesiphon: "an eternal garden," someone has called it, "forever at the perfection of its vernal loveliness." I say this with great sadness, not at all as I have said it about *The Ring*, for *Tristan* is a wonderful work, and for many years was close on being central—I might perhaps go even further than that—to my musical life: I well remember our romantic line of talk in the Covent Garden gallery, and how we used to proclaim that, if it ever came to committing suicide, the way to do it would be to fling oneself from gallery to stalls during a performance of *Tristan*. So I feel that a chapter in my musical life, and a supremely happy one, has been finally closed. Or perhaps not finally. I had not been to *Tristan* for many years when in 1962 I found myself repenting. I had broken my thigh two years earlier, and was at last mobile enough to go abroad for a long holiday. The night before we were to leave, Birgit Nilsson was singing Isolde at Covent Garden, and I suddenly wanted to go. The experience was a very moving one, apart altogether from Birgit Nilsson's superb performance. I cannot pretend that I felt what I had felt in the old days, but neither did I feel what I had been feeling more recently. So perhaps next time I hear *Tristan*—and I am suddenly persuaded that I shall hear it again and perhaps often—I shall recapture the ancient emotion, and the boy and the old man will have joined hands.

§ 5

I have left to the end the greatest of all my objections to *The Ring*, because in one sense, but in one sense only, it is extra-musical: I am referring to its morality. This aspect of it caused me little trouble in my gallery days: I probably thought "a bit of a bounder, Siegfried, but still . . .". Nor did it worry me much for a few years after 1926. But when, in the early thirties, Hitler was emerging more and more menacingly it began worrying me a very great deal.

I know that what I am going to say is 'old hat', but I must say it none the less. Richard Wagner, on one side of his nature, was a man we should nowadays describe, in a rough and ready sort of way, as of fascist mentality (which did not come in with Hitler, or with Mussolini either), coloured by something essentially, if not exclusively, Teutonic; and it is above all in *The Ring* that this side of his nature emerges. By a fascist mentality I mean a preference for war as against peace, for violence as against gentleness, for retaliation as against forgiveness: a glorification of strength and a contempt for weakness: an exaltation of health and a disdain for suffering: an aggrandizement of women, but only as handmaidens of men. And by Teutonism (not for a moment to be thought of as the mark of all or even of most Germans) I mean a predilection for vastness as against proportion, for cloudiness as against precision, for an inflated romanticism and a vague nobility, as well as a devotion, more rabid than among people in general (except perhaps Jews), to the old race and stock. Or say if you will that *The Ring* is the work of a pagan, in the unloveliest sense of the word. Or finally call it antichristian (and that an antichristian should have written *Parsifal* is another reason for my dislike of that counterfeit work).

I am anxious to make myself clear. If I find *The Ring* distasteful in the present context, this is not because Wagner had an element of fascism in him: if Hitler himself, improbably, had written a piece of interesting music devoid of evil (for 'pure' music can have evil in it, witness *Turandot*), I should have gone to hear it without prejudice, and gone again and again so long as my interest in it lasted. Nothing could be more detestable than to boycott the work of a man you think evil, provided that what you think evil in him does not come out in his music.

No: I dislike *The Ring*, not because Wagner was (I repeat, on one side of him) a fascist, but because the work is packed with fascism. Some of my friends, when I tell them this, seem greatly surprised: surely, they say, what matters is the music? That is a low view of opera: the music may indeed outshine everything else in all but the finest of operas, yet opera remains opera and something more than a concert in all but the worst of them. The greatest music ever written for an opera is Beethoven's for *Fidelio*: and *Fidelio* is the opera in which, to a degree greater than in any other, 'plot' and stage wring the heart. Beethoven was on my side in this matter—everyone knows what he said about *Don Giovanni;*[1] and what is good enough for Rothschild, as my father used to say, is good enough for me. That Beethoven may have been mistaken in believing *Don Giovanni* immoral (after all, the Don goes to Hell) is as little relevant as that I may be mistaken in believing *The Ring* immoral. What comforts me is that the two of us, giant and dwarf, both include in our estimate of an artistic creation a judgment of its morality.

When I call *The Ring* immoral I mean that it glorifies evil: and I just do not want to watch evil being glorified four nights more or less running, and on three of them at inordinate length. And not, above all, that particular evil. How could I sit there and watch it with the gas ovens, the mass executions, the men and women digging their own vast communal grave burnt into my consciousness? For make no mistake: the spirit of *The Ring*, for all its pseudo-nobility, *is* the spirit of fascism. I am not going to spell it out: I am not going to argue with people who cannot see, for instance but only for instance, that Siegfried with his pride, his strength, his arrogance, his ruthlessness first to Mime and then to Wotan, is the young hero of a fascist's dream. And Wagner uses every resource of his musical genius to make us admire him: just as he does the same to make us jeer at Mime. How typical of a fascist to make the most contemptible of his characters an ugly little misshapen dwarf! You can almost see a doctor coming to take him off for medical experiments.

And now, having said all that, need I insist that, as I have tried to indicate already, I am not equating Wagner, from a moral point of view, with Hitler or his like? What I have said is that Wagner had a fascist side to him, and that this comes out in the general spirit of *The Ring*:

[1] "Il prétendait que Mozart ne devait pas prostituer son talent sur un sujet si scandaleux"—*Mémoires sur la Restauration*, by Mme d'Abrantès.

I have not denied, nor would dream of denying, that he had another side to him too. He was capable of great tenderness, even in *The Ring* itself: he could write 'so küsst er die Gottheit von dir'. Nor have I suggested (I shall suggest the opposite) that what I find in *The Ring* I find in everything else that he wrote: I am merely concerned to explain why, for so many years now, *The Ring*, apart from all musical questions, has not been to my liking.

§ 6

I would wish to say a word in conclusion about the relation of music-loving to personal life. (Music-*loving*: that music-*making* is intimately bound up with the music-maker's inner life, which may be quite other than its outward manifestation might suggest, must be obvious—and this makes nonsense of the stuff about Beethoven, Beethoven the man, perpetrated by those Viennese psychoanalysts.[1]) People have often told me that they see no connection between a love of music on the one hand and the inner life of the man who loves it on the other: for me, on the other hand, the relationship between the two has always been close, sometimes terribly close. An instance may explain what I mean. There was a short period during my schooldays when I believed myself to have committed a fleshly sin that outlawed me from everything beautiful and good. (My error was twofold: it wasn't a sin, and I was yet to realise that 'we must be in charity with ourselves as well as with our neighbour'.) The sense of corruption became overwhelming. The smell of the grass was still there, but was now all the more alien for its sweetness; the sun still shone, but not for me. And most agonising of all was my relation to music, the quintessence of beauty and goodness. The shame I should feel in its presence was something I should be unable to bear: so I kept away.

II

As for Verdi:
If I say little about him in the present connection, by way of rounding off this chapter of comparison between my feelings for him and for Wagner as these have developed, that is because almost everything that

---

[1] 'Beethoven and His Nephew', by Editha Sterba and Richerd Stern. Dennis Dobson, 1957.

needs to be said has already been said by the way. Save perhaps one thing only, though this has probably also been said: since that first *Traviata* my love for him, as I have got to know him better and better, has constantly increased, and where it could not increase it has remained undiminished. The music that I first loved him for, the *Traviata* 'Libiamo', still stirs my pulses whenever I hear it, even if merely whistled or hummed; and this is not a matter of boyhood association but of something in its character and pattern, something in its musical ethos, unimportant though the piece is, that speaks directly to me with irresistible effect.

For what I love above all in Verdi's music is the sun in it, its clean beauty, its soaring or leaping phrases, its glorious cantilena. I love it with an immediate, personal love, in the way one loves a human being. And I also love, by a kind of transference that takes no account either of virtues or demerits, Verdi the man, as I love no other composer, not even the greatest, Beethoven.

One of the reasons for this is his sheer humanity. Few have had as keen an awareness of evil as Verdi: but there is a sadness about the music associated with the most evil of his characters—you hear it above all in *Otello* and *Macbeth*—to be found in no other composer, though Britten gets close to it in some of the Claggart music in *Billy Budd*. D'Annunzio wrote the final epitaph for Verdi in his memorial ode: 'Pianse è amo per tutti', 'He wept and loved for all'.

What a joy it is, in spite of everything I have said about the danger of overdoing the Verdi cult, to reflect that there are works by Verdi still to explore, to grow familiar with in the unfolding kind of way that is one of the chief pleasures of musical experience! I had always dismissed *I Due Forscari* as more or less worthless, I do not know on what authority, until an evening, some twenty years ago, when I happened to tune in to it on the wireless. At first I went on tinkering away at some sentences I had been writing before dinner, when suddenly—there it came, the great melody, sweet and easy and rounded and strong ('out of the strong came forth sweetness'); and then another and another and another, pouring out, flowing on, with an inevitable prodigality like nature's in spring. So what could one do but just sit there and listen, and beam happily, and bless the old man? He is all heart, and will forever have mine.

So the conflict between Wagner and Verdi that began in me more than half a century ago has ended decisively in Verdi's favour. But remembering all that Wagner has meant to me over

by far the greater span of my musical life, I am reluctant to leave
it at that: so let me add that if anyone were to ask me which of
all operas, performed as finely as possible, I should like to rush
out and see at this moment, I might answer, after some hesitation,
Die Meistersinger.

CHAPTER IX

APART FROM VERDI and Wagner, the three great experiences of my operatic boyhood were *Orfeo*, *Pelléas* and *Elektra*. That neither *Fidelio* nor anything by Mozart should come into the list must seem extraordinary, but I think I know part at least of the answer and shall try to explain it later on.

I

ORFEO

I had known about *Orfeo* as long as I had known about anything musical at all: for my father was always talking about the Ravogli sisters, and among the libretti bequeathed to me by my great-aunt Rosetta is one of *Orfeo* with the Ravoglis in the cast. (Let me celebrate her by printing her full name—Rosetta Friedlander: "one of the Swedish Friedlanders" according to my mother, for another of our family legends was that a maternal ancestor had been dentist at the Court of Gustavus Adolphus, and we even had a dark, heavily crackled painting of him—of the dentist, not of Gustavus—in our parlour at Elgin Avenue, somewhat resembling those ancestral portraits you see in New York.) There is no date on that precious libretto, but it was probably about 1890, for according to Bernard Shaw Giulia sang Orfeo in the November of that year to Sofia's Euridice. His enthusiasm for her—"I confess myself infatuated"—must have been the only one he shared with my father, who regarded my Shavianism as among my major *m'shugaases*, and would often remark to my mother "The Ibsen, the Shaw, the Maeterlinck! Has he never heard of Lessing?"—'Nathan der Weise' being one of his own great addictions. The whole of Shaw's notice[1] is worth reading: no better critique of *Orfeo* has ever been written.

Fired by the parental talk, I began looking out for *Orfeo* in odd places, for this was one of the operas which, like a lot of others, you couldn't hope to hear at Covent Garden. I got into the habit of

[1] *Music in London*, Constable.

scanning the programmes of the Carl Rosa and Moody-Manners people, and of scratch organisations like the one at Notting Hill Gate I have already referred to; and many attractive or less attractive experiences resulted. I journeyed out to Holloway, for instance, to see a performance of *Mignon* by the Carl Rosa people—an expensive adventure in respect of the bus fare rather than of the ticket, which cost I think tuppence: and it ought to have been worth the money, for the cast was an international one, consisting of, among others, Mr. Gordon Thomas 'the New Welsh Tenor', Mr. Leslie Austin 'from the Opera Houses of Munich, Eberfeld and Nuremburg', Miss Edna Hoff 'from the Stadt Theatre, St. Gallen', and, as *protagonista*, Miss Claude Albright 'from the Opera House, Bremen, etc.' The conductor was Walter van Noorden himself, owner of the enterprise, but might as well have been his partner at the rostrum, Eugène Goossens, most famous of musical fathers. However, I was rather disappointed. I had heard a lot of talk about how wonderful Patti had been in the polacca, and with my own ears had heard Tetrazzini sing it in Rosina's lesson-scene along with the Variazioni of Proch (a battle-horse for Rosinas second only to a vocal waltz by Tosti or Arditi, I forget which, or to 'Home Sweet Home', if it was a question of showing off sentiment or legato or both); and I had wondered whether the whole opera might not be on the same level. If I did not quite find it so, a good deal of it, and not only the gently fragrant 'Kennst du das Land?', was pleasing enough to my musical nostrils, and I was always on the look out for it later on: we were to hear it at the Scala and in Palermo and Rome.

But I owe Walter van Noorden a debt of gratitude for something more important than that. He introduced me, not I think at Holloway but at Brixton, to an opera I have cherished from that day to this, and not only for itself but for the musical gallicism it symbolises, namely *Carmen*: and, what is more, to the best Carmen I have ever heard though I have heard dozens, to wit the legendary Zélie de Lussan. This American lady, who had rivalled Minnie Hauk in the part, and was said to be surpassed only by Calvé, devoted a great deal of her time, just before her retirement, to the Carl Rosa Company, and that I should have heard her must rank as one of my greatest pieces of good fortune. Her fine mezzo had a keen cutting edge, without detriment to its seductiveness, as the role requires but rarely gets; and she acted as well as she sang, but was never guilty of forcing the pace, at any rate on the night I heard her, in either capacity. Good Carmens are exceedingly rare: even Destinn, I hate to confess, was said to be an almost ludicrous failure in the part, and so was Kirkby Lunn. The only Carmen I heard at that time who came near to rivalling Zélie de Lussan was Maria Gay.

Another opera I sought out in unusual places was *Hänsel and Gretel*, which I heard first at a students' performance at the Royal Academy of Music. The para-religious semi-sentimentality of its melisma gave me a good deal of gentle pleasure, in contradistinction to my sense of nausea at the religiosity of *Parsifal*; so I sought it out again, this time at the Coliseum, where Ruth Vincent, round about 1911, sang in the 'Angel Tableau' and Act III under the auspices of Thomas Beecham. (The affair must have pleased me, for I wrote in the programme 'Admirable performance. A most hopeful sign. We may yet have a national opera!'.) Music-halls in general were tending at this period to become halls of music or semi-music, with a strong accent on *verismo*. The same year, 1911, *Pagliacci* was put on at the Hippodrome, "personally produced and conducted by the composer, Signor Leoncavallo, with his own Italian Company"; and it was succeeded by *Cavalleria*, "personally Conducted, twice daily, by the Composer, Pietro Mascagni. Augmented Orchestra of 65 Picked Instrumentalists. Chorus of 50 Voices specially brought over from Italy by MASCAGNI. NOTE: Owing to the enormous strain upon the Principals, there will be three complete Casts, and they will be changed entirely at every performance". But 1911 was not to be the end of it. Next year the other twin was back: "R. Leoncavello will conduct for the first time tonight, and twice daily for a week, his entirely New and Original Opera in Two Scenes, *Zingari* (Gipsies), Specially written and composed for the London Hippodrome by LEONCAVALLO".

But it was not at Brixton or Holloway, at the Hippodrome or Coliseum, that I was to hear *Orfeo*, but somewhere nearer home: namely at the Savoy Theatre, opposite the Savoy Grill, which twenty years later I was to become so intimately associated with, or it with me: gastronomically, not financially (except, so far as I was concerned, in a negative sense). For it was announced in March 1910 that the following month, at 2.15 in the afternoon, there would be six performances of *Orfeo* at the Savoy Theatre under the patronage of Her Royal Highness Princess Louise, Duchess of Argyll: that the Euridice would be Viola Tree: and that the Orfeo, as well as the producer, would be Marie Brema.

Now Marie Brema was as legendary as Giulia Ravogli herself, and I was to discover a family link with her (though I did not know it at the time) when my Aunt Rosetta gave me her little store of libretti.

For stuffed into the Covent Garden one with the Ravoglis' names in it was a cutting from the programme of another performance: "To-night, Tuesday, December 8th, at 8, *Orfeo*, terminating with the celebrated air 'Che faro'. Orfeo, Mademoiselle Marie Brema. Con-ductor, Signor Bimboni. Followed at 9.45 by Mascagni's opera *Cavalleria Rusticana*. Lola, Mademoiselle Marie Brema. Conductor Signor Arditi". There is no date or place: but the date must be 1891 and the place the Shaftesbury Theatre, for it was then and there, during Lago's famous season, that Arditi conducted the British première of *Cavalleria*. The typography of the programme is so de-lightful in its debased Victorianism (every experienced opera-goer will know what I mean) that I have had an itch to reproduce it, but cannot find room.

Marie Brema was fifty-four when I heard her. She had been famous as a Bayreuth Ortrud, Fricka and Kundry, and had created a furore in Paris as Dalila and Amneris: her range being so great that in 1902 she sang the *Götterdämmerung* Brünnhilde under Hans Richter in Paris, having already sung the Angel in *Gerontius* at the Birmingham Festival of 1900.

§ 2

I went to at least three of those six April matinées, and then returned to the Savoy for another series in December. I remember little about the production, except that the sets, beautifully simple and satisfying, were in rich but low colours, rather autumnal, like a more subdued Matthew Smith. But no later performance has ever come near to effacing the memory of those early ones: and as for Marie Brema herself, neither Mary Jarred, who sang the role so finely at Sadler's Wells, nor Kathleen Ferrier, lovely as she was, could seem to me her equal. (And the same must apply to Sigrid Onegin and Kerstin Thorborg, for their superb—as I now remember them—performances in the Bruno Walter-Salzbug *Orfeos* have only this very moment come into my mind.)

But the work as a whole, performed as it was, made so over-whelming an impact—though overwhelming is too excitable a word for association with such serenity—that individual impressions, except of the music, were lost. Within a few minutes of the curtain going up (the prelude is nothing—Berlioz justly calls it 'une niaiserie incroy-able') the hush, 'the old awe' had 'stolen over me', and I was in the quiet of eternity.

To make any attempt to describe this familiar emotion (or state of being) in my own words would be foolish, so I shall quote again from that sonnet by Wordsworth:

"Thought was not: in enjoyment it expired . . .
Rapt into still communion that transcends
The imperfect offices of prayer and praise,
His mind was a thanksgiving to the power
That made him; it was blessedness and love."

And I shall add Spinoza:

"Blessedness is not the reward of virtue but virtue itself."

And Bernard Shaw, in the notice already referred to:

"In the Elysian fields . . . virtue and effort are transcended: there is no need to be good or to strive upward any more: one has arrived, and all those accursed hygienics of the soul are done with and forgotten."

Music may have perfect physical purity without any spiritual reference: 'Carmen' is an example. But in the music of the Elysian Fields perfect spiritual and perfect physical purity are combined—or rather are one and the same, indistinguishable—in a continuum of unbroken peace. Examples of such a union are common enough: I think at random of the first few bars of the choral melody in the Ninth Symphony when it first steals in on the 'celli; the flute tune Tamino plays as he goes through the ordeals of fire and water; innumerable instances in the late Beethoven quartets; and the slow phrase of 'heavenly length' in his fourth symphony. But for the sustaining of these celestial harmonies at such a length *Orfeo* is equalled, within the limits of my musical experience, by only three other works for the stage, which I shall come to presently. One might say of it as a whole what the Abbé Arnaud said of a single air in the same composer's *Iphigénie en Aulide*: "With that one might found a religion". Moreover it triumphantly proves, a century before Wagner set out to prove it, that music-drama surpasses every other form of drama in the strength of its appeal, its power to move and delight, and the glimpse it can give us of a reality latent in, but transcending, this earthly one; and finally by the large simplicity of its music it lies open to a great body of men and women who are transported by Handel's Largo but would be baffled by *Pelléas*. For the last reason it is perhaps more precious than any other of the great operas with which it ranks.

The music haunted me; and when I went to Oxford I bought a piano

score (which I have before me) and got a musical friend to play it to me
night after night. Soon I knew it almost by heart. The day after I
became engaged my bride and I went on the river at Cookham, and
I hummed one of the ballets:

She looked blank, so I tried another:

"You're terribly out of tune," she said. "No one could recognise it."
I felt extremely irritated, and may even have wondered for a moment
whether I had made a mistake, and I do not mean in the music. Then
she began laughing, and I got quite angry. (This was the first of my
irritations with her, and was to be, for any musical reason, my last:
the only one that persists being at dinner-parties, when, asked for her
opinion about something, she always says what she thinks. As her
opinions are as radical as mine, but we dine, like Disraeli, mostly with
Tories, this can be embarrassing.) People often laugh when I try to sing
or hum, so I avoid doing so whenever possible: but if I have been

rash enough to cite a musical phrase when involved in some argument, and am asked to identify it vocally, there is no way out. My friend that admirable critic Philip Hope-Wallace, sitting beside me at Betty Askwith's wedding, clearly found it all but impossible to behave decorously when I attempted the hymns.

§ 3

I have heard most of the other operas by Gluck that are ever heard at all, but often enough for real familiarity only *Alceste*, which was done pretty often in the middle twenties at the Paris Opéra, with Germaine Lubin and Georges Thill. (We missed the French performances at Covent Garden in 1937, which was just after my desertion of music for para-politics.) But with one exception—*Iphigeneia in Aulis*—I have not heard a Gluck opera for years, and how I hunger for him! Could not Sir David Webster and Lord Drogheda be persuaded to put on a series of revivals, or, if anything more lavish is impossible, then at least *Orfeo*? But not, above all, with a Zeffirelli décor, except perhaps for the scene in Hades.

§ 4

I must append a note about Monteverdi's *Orfeo*, which we heard at the Costanzi in 1934 under Tullio Serafin. Produced in 1607, only seven years after Peri's *Euridice*, the first surviving opera of the *Camerata* period, it gives a vivid idea of what those Florentine theorists were after, though it doubtless far surpasses the earlier example. But apart from its historical interest I have thought of it, ever since 1934, as the work I would sooner hear again than any other of the operas I have heard only once, so manifold is its loveliness: Orfeo's invocation to the woodland groves, with the quiet but growingly insistent enthusiasm of love in it; the setting of the messenger's 'La tua diletta sposa è morta' and his reply 'Ohimè', exact, the latter, for all its simplicity, as a musical expression of grief; Orfeo's song of gratitude to Hope, and her reply; the sinfonia that describes Charon's slumber; and above all Orfeo's appeal to Charon, 'Possente spirto, e formidabil nume'. The last, with the increasing urgency of its ever more elaborate coloratura, and the variety of aspiration in its exquisite accompaniment, is a miraculous expression of a singer devoting resource after resource of his musical art, and then another and another, to the desperate achievement of a supreme object. "I cannot force my way in", voice and orchestra are saying, "I cannot take the kingdom of heaven by violence: but listen to spirit and beauty, and relent." . . . I felt throughout, at that performance in Rome, the same hush, the same careless sense of being engulfed in an eternity of peace, as I had experienced at the other *Orfeo*. As to *L'Incoronazione*, I have already referred to the duet that ends it: but though that is the peak, the whole work abounds in quiet beauty and dramatic force.

II

PELLÉAS

There was an unusual event in Beecham's great winter season of 1910, the year that gave the public in general *Elektra* at Covent Garden and *Orfeo* at the Savoy, and gave me in particular my first *Ring*, the one under Richter: on March 9th I saw Debussy's cantata *L'Enfant Prodigue* done as an opera—a preparation for what was to follow. But I was pretty familiar already with a good deal of Debussy's music, particularly with *L'Après-midi*, which I had often heard at the proms and other Queen's Hall concerts, though its heyday for us, when Nijinsky danced it so unforgettably, was to be two years later: and with his piano music too, for Elsie Grant had often played it at my special request in the intimacy of Uncle Assur's studio. So I was well prepared for *Pelléas*.

Edvina was singing Mélisande the night I first heard it, and Vanni Marcoux Arkel. I have already said a word about Vanni Marcoux in my talk with Peter Heyworth. The combination of delicacy and a certain ruggedness in his beautiful bass, which was not however a particularly big one, perfectly fitted him for the part: and so did the smoothness of phrasing in which he excelled. Edvina was not so much to my taste. I had already heard this lady as Marguérite and Louise; and though there was an attractive freshness in her voice, and an unaffected honesty in her singing, she wavered too much for my pleasure, though she improved season by season. But it was not till December that year, after the grand season was over, that I was to hear as Mélisande a singer and actress of the kind that, once heard in a role, comes to mean it for ever after in the listener's consciousness,

Maggie Teyte: who I cannot help thinking, to judge from rumour, must have greatly surpassed her more famous predecessor, Mary Garden. Her adorable *mignonnesse*, a quality of mingled freshness and gravity in her smooth gentle singing—it was this that made her Cherubino so exquisite—and the childlike ingenuousness of her acting, if acting it must be called, moved me to an affection for her such as I have felt for few other singers.

§ 2

I was at the beginning of my thraldom to *Tristan* when I first heard *Pelléas*; and if I was moved almost equally by works so disparate, this was because my own nature is a mixed one. It was to the grandiose, extravagant, excitable, flamboyant, romantic, passionate side of me that *Tristan* overwhelmingly, intoxicatingly appealed: the side of me I was fond of calling 'vital' (I recently came across one of my letters to my mother from Oxford—she bequeathed them to me —and it starts with 'I'm feeling tremendously vital today'. What a disagreeable sort of person I must have been, and probably still am!). And it was the other side of me, the essential one, I like to think, the side of me that is peaceful and hushed, grateful and adoring, that made me sit there at *Pelléas* with an emotion of quiet bliss and of love for its innocence.

I was ready for *Pelléas* for another reason too: I loved Maeterlinck, not the later Maeterlinck, after he had gone to live in France, of *Monna Vanna*, *Mary Magdalen* and *The Blue Bird* (which I actively disliked when I came to read it), but the earlier Maeterlinck of *Ariane et Barbe Bleu*, *Aglavaine es Selysette*, *Alladine et Pallomides*, *Intérieur* and *La Morte de Tintagiles*, as well as of *Pelléas* itself. What appealed to me in him was something that cannot be called mysticism, for it was but a para-mysticism of the vague Celtic sort and not the true mysticism of Plotinus, Wordsworth and Blake, but the air of gentle mystery in those earlier works, the sense of shadowy presences, of an intangible reality, hovering just behind the curtain. (*Intériur* is almost symbolic of this feeling of his: and anyone who has glanced up at a lighted room from a dark garden, and has watched people walking and talking behind the window-panes, must have shared it with him.) Debussy, child of impressionism, was akin to Maeterlinck in his sensitive awareness of evanescent beauty, so that he was destined to be the composer of *Pelléas*.

§ 3

That I should have first heard *Orfeo*, *The Ring* and *Pelléas* within two months of one another, and in that order, has a certain intellectual beauty: for what the three masters were alike concerned with was the fulfilment of Giovanni de' Bardi's ideal of music-drama, Gluck by returning to but improving on Peri, Wagner by returning to but improving on Gluck, and Debussy, in conscious revolt against Wagner, by going right back to Peri, but with the resources that three centuries of musical development, including Wagner's contribution to it, had given him.

Now the actual music of *Pelléas* is literally incomparable: in its economy and discretion, its intimate delicacy, its reticent but eloquent clarity, the depth of emotion in its quietness, its blend of tenderness and restrained but almost intolerably intense passion, and a French precision and grace in it unalloyed by that thinness of musical content so often to be found in French music. Innumerable examples could be given: to cite a few only, the lovely preludes to the work itself, to Act I scene 3 and to Act II; the orchestral postlude to Mélisande's 'Oh! Pourquoi partez-vous?' at the end of Act I; the first love-scene, when Mélisande lets her hair fall; the orchestral climax after Golaud has come upon them, one of the very few big climaxes in the whole work; and the scene of Mélisande's death. And yet there is something to be even more grateful for than the music. I do not say that *Pelléas* is my favourite opera, for sheerly musical appeal remains paramount with me provided only that the dramatic effect is not too obviously outraged, and from this point of view I love *Orfeo* and *Figaro*, *Otello* and *Die Meistersinger* even more: but I do say that Debussy has, not indeed completely achieved the ideal music-drama, for that, as I have said, is impossible, but has come to the very verge of achieving it.

What I mean is this. To quote Debussy's own words: "I have been reproached because in my score the melodic phrase is always found in the orchestra, never in the voice. I wished—intended in fact—that the action should never be arrested; that it should be continuous, uninterrupted. I wanted to dispense with parasitic musical phrases. When listening to a [musical-dramatic] work, the spectator is wont to experience two kinds of emotion: the musical emotion on the one hand; and the emotion of the character on the other. Generally, these are felt successively. I have tried to blend these two emotions and make them simultaneous. Melody is, if I may say so, almost anti-lyric, and powerless to express the constant change of emotion or life. Melody is suitable only for the *chanson*, which confirms a fixed sentiment. I have never been willing that my music shall hinder . . . the changes of sentiment and passion felt by my characters. Its demands are ignored as soon as it is necessary that these should have perfect liberty in their gestures as in their cries, in their joys as in their sorrows."

That Debussy has carried out his intention with final exactitude is undeniable. But even so an all but perfect music-drama would not have resulted unless three other conditions had also been fulfilled. The first is that the words themselves must be worth hearing, must be suitable for declamation, and must be devoid of the banality or in-appropriateness that often renders opera in English so ludicrous. The second is that the words must come to the audience with the immediate clarity of those in an ordinary play, instead of, as happens so frequently in opera, being taken in, if at all, only at the cost of a distracting strain. And the third is that the setting of the words, whether beautiful in the ordinary sense or not, must have the appropriateness that amounts, in this connection, to musical beauty.

That the first condition has been fulfilled in *Pelléas* is obvious. As to the second, when I first heard *Pelléas* my French was even worse than it is now; I had read the libretto perhaps twice, certainly no more; but only a comparatively trifling number of the words escaped me. It is the third condition, however, that I have chiefly in mind.

The text of *Pelléas* is not great literature, and this is why the work as a whole cannot be described as achieving the ideal of music-drama. But it is language of a truly poetic simplicity: and Debussy has worked miracles with his setting of it—two miracles, to be exact. He has preserved the rhythms of natural speed with scrupulous fidelity; and he has at the same time endowed the words with such a poignancy of expression as could have been given them, if spoken, only by the greatest of actors. I think of the fear in Mélisande's 'Ne me touchez pas, ne me touchez pas!'; the agony in her 'Oh, oui, oui, oui' when Golaud has asked her whether anyone has done her harm; the hysteria in Pelléas's 'Il n'y a pas de temps à perdre' when he is telling Arkel of his friend's coming death; the sense of inevitable tragedy in Golaud's 'Mais dis-moi quelque chose; n'importe quoi, je ferai tout que tu voudras'; the gravity and pity in Pelleas's 'Ce sont trois vieux pauvres qui se sont endormis'; the simple beauty in Mélisande's 'Je vois une rose dans les ténèbres'; the passion in Pelléas's 'Toute ta chevelure, Mélisande, toute ta chevelure est tombée de la tour!'; the sadness, a little later, in his 'Toute la nuit, toute la nuit'; and, above all perhaps, Yniold's 'Il fait clair, petit père'—how the rhythm haunts me now as I sit here!—in that scene of Sophoclean irony when the light comes on in Mélisande's room. And yet there is a miracle, perhaps, even greater than these: I mean the wonderfully varied expressiveness Debussy gives to that simplest of words 'Oh'. In sum, I have no shadow of a doubt that Debussy is the greatest of all musical dramatists.

III

RICHARD STRAUSS

The première of *Elektra* was on February 19th of the same 1910. The work had been violently attacked on both moral and musical grounds: morally as brutal (and brutal it certainly is, but with an honest and primitive brutality, not with the brutality of *Siegfried*, all noble and boyish, or of *Turandot*, that brilliant essay in brooding sadism); and musically as discordant and cacophonous to an outrageous degree. It is difficult to realise, in the middle of the nineteen-sixties, that Strauss was at that time considered the arch-revolutionary. Schönberg, though already vilified in Europe, was hardly known here to the larger musical public, and in any case was only just developing the first of his distinctive styles.

The excitement I felt as the evening approached is as vivid to my memory as it is all but impossible to convey: just as you can rarely convey the smell of a place with a hundred associations that hangs about your nostrils long years after, as in the case of the Covent Garden gallery with me. There were several elements in this excitement, so mingled as to produce a sensation I had never experienced before and was never to experience again until the first night of *Boris*. First of all there was that sense of occasion I referred to when writing of Britten: one that I am feeling at this moment, three o'clock on the afternoon of January 21st 1964, as I sit writing in my office a stone's-throw from Covent Garden and think that in four hours' time I shall be walking round the corner to hear Callas in *Tosca*. But mixed up with it was something quite different. I was then in the first flush of a radicalism that verged on Jacobinism, and it was spreading out from the sphere of human relations (I detested my father's anti-feminism), of crime and punishment (I was determined to become Home Secretary and abolish the death penalty), and of social organisation (poverty must be abolished), to cover life as a whole. So I rejoiced at all this outcry about

Strauss' revolutionary cacophony: the more revolution the better—not but that, of course, the fine old tradition, the tradition behind *Traviata*, was not equally desirable. So I waited impatiently in the queue that night in a spirit of high adventure—with the feeling, a little vague but glorious, that somehow I was striking a blow. And then I was already enthusiastic about such music of Strauss as I had heard at the proms and elsewhere, and I had heard a good deal. I knew most of the tone-poems well, and had reservations about only 'Tod und Verklärung', which I thought rather splurgy: 'Don Juan' was the one I liked best, and I could not hear it often enough. Apart from the sensuous chromaticism that put a smile on your face and a sway into your body, its vitality, as I am sure I called it, was what carried me away: that great leaping tune you had to wait for, but found so exciting when it came! I used to hammer it out (a couple of fingers was all I could manage) on the piano, with a thump on the second note and an unconscionable pause thereafter. And then there were the *Lieder*, and especially *Morgen* (which I forgot to mention as among the very few gramophone records we had in those early days on Campden Hill Square). If these were what they were, what might not *Elektra* be!

I was not disappointed. The performance was magnificent. The Elektra was Edyth Walker; the Chrysothemis Frances Rose; the Orestes Weidemann; the Klytemnestra Anna von Bahr-Mildenburg; and the conductor Thomas Beecham. Mildenburg was overwhelming. A great dominating figure, with string after string of gaudy jewels swinging about her bosom (and reflected in the music), she sang this mezzo role to perfection, just as a day or so later she was to sing the soprano Isolde (under Bruno Walter, whom I was then to hear for the first time) with equal success. In March Weidemann was replaced by Paul Bender, one of the great baritones of my time, with a graciousness in his voice that Bockelmann was to remind me of. Strauss himself conducted some of the performances. I went four or five times within the month, and then returned for more performances in the autumn season of the same year. After that I was always on the look-out for a performance, but was rarely to find one, at any rate that I could go to, though I heard Mildenburg again in 1913. And I am always on the look-out for one still, and still with that sense of peculiarly-flavoured excitement I felt when awaiting the première. I think the best Elektra I have ever heard is Gerda Lammers, who took the place of Christel Goltz in an emergency a few years ago.

There is a point about the British première that I wish some archivist who may happen to read these pages would put me right on. I have it in

mind that the orchestra on that occasion was the orchestra Strauss
wrote for, one of about a hundred and twenty players, and that they
overflowed into the neighbouring boxes, now part of the stalls circle.
Is this so? Or is it the invention of a fading memory?

(We are just back from *Tosca*. It confirmed me in my view both
of Zeffirelli and of Callas. Maybe I can put in a note about it somewhere.)

One sat there, at that first *Elektra*, as a tensely committed participant in the onward flow of the tragedy. Here again was music-drama,
from the formal point of view, at very near its rare best: the drama, in
spite or rather because of the music, was central. If, again from the
formal point of view, it cannot equal *Pelléas*, that is because you cannot immediately and effortlessly take in every word, for the orchestral
surge often forbids it. But you can at any rate take in enough for an all
but perfect realisation of what is happening—provided you know
enough German—even without a previous knowledge of the text.

But, apart from that, surpassing beauties were already coming out at
me on that initial occasion, beauties that carried me away more and
more as they became increasingly familiar: and new ones were
constantly emerging. As I want, I dare say vainly, to keep this writing
down to manageable proportions I shall cite only three. The first is
when, in Elektra's great monologue that begins with 'Allein! Weh,
ganz allein', and immediately after the words 'zeig dich deinem Kind!',
'come to greet thy child', the nobly simple and beautifully extended
melody, played by that great body of strings in unison, rises rapt and
still from the orchestra, with a dramatic, a universalising effect no
ordinary play could ever achieve (I delight in printing it opposite).

At every subsequent performance I thought with special happiness,
just before the curtain rose, "I shall soon be hearing that heavenly tune":
how I wish I should soon be hearing it now!

Then within moments of Elektra's 'Agamemnon! Agamemnon!' at
the end of her monologue comes the Chrysothemis music: which, if
sung by a voice fresh and powerful enough (freshness and power are
both essential), can be immensely moving in the way it surges above
Elektra's darkness. And finally the Recognition. This is one of the half-
dozen or so greatest scenes in all opera.

That *Elektra* is an authentic masterpiece I could never doubt, nor
could I ever grow tired of it. I cannot say the same about any other of
Strauss' operas.

§ 2

When Beecham died he was on the whole shabbily treated by the press: you might have thought him in the main an eccentric given to quipping and posing, rather than, side by side with Henry Wood, one of the supreme musical benefactors of our time. If, into the bargain, he made some excellent jokes ("Ha! critic as well as performer!", of a Gräne who broke wind at a rehearsal of *Götterdämmerung*), so much the better. As an entrepreneur he was unrivalled; and though as a conductor he may not have ranked with the greatest of his contemporaries—Weingartner, Klemperer, Bruno Walter, Toscanini—from the lack, maybe, if for the most part a trifling one, of musical scrupulosity, to me at least he gave the keenest pleasure, more, the keenest delight, from his earlier days right down to the eve of his death. A coming Beecham concert was always something to look out for, especially if it promised, for instance, Berlioz, Mozart, the *Meistersinger* overture or God Save the King. The only thing I ever had against him was that he carried his love of 'lollipops', and particularly French ones, too far.

1910 was a prodigy of a year for him. He had already given a first winter season, the *Elektra* one, at Covent Garden: he was to give a second, the *Salome* one, when the Syndicate should quit Covent Garden at the end of the usual grand season: and now, with the grand season in full swing, he took His Majesty's (where he had already run an 'Afternoon Theatre' the previous year) for 'Opera in English'. It was there that he put on, and himself conducted, Richard Strauss' *Feuersnot* ('Beltane Fire', as the programme had it): not only *novità in Inghilterra*, I think, but never to be done again here. Robert Radford was in the cast, along with such admirably competent singers as Denis Byndon-Ayres and Caroline Hatchard, who, with Carrie Tubb and Maurice D'Oisley and a few others, will always have a place in my affections as typifying the Beecham entourage.

In justice to Beecham, I shall give a partial list of the operas he produced or revived in 1909 or 1910, apart from *Elektra*, *Salome* and *Feuersnot*: Ambroise Thomas's *Hamlet*, Sullivan's *Ivanhoe*, Massenet's *Werther*, *The Tales of Hoffmann*, *Fledermaus*, no less than five operas by Mozart, and two English works by contemporaries, namely Delius's *A Village Romeo and Juliet* (which I liked so much that I begged my way in to a couple of private performances at the R.C.M. in 1934) and Ethel Smyth's *The Wreckers* (which I also liked, though the extraneous consideration that I was an ardent suffragist and she was an ardent 'suffragette' may have influenced me). The man's enterprise, and the catholicity of his taste, were prodigious: for it must be remembered that he had founded the New Symphony Orchestra back in 1906, and that this very year, 1910, he was to found the Beecham Symphony Orchestra, led by Albert Sammons and with Lionel Tertis as first viola. And yet there are people who shrug their shoulders when you mention him.

§ 3

I first heard *Salome* on December 17th, and then again on the 20th, the 29th and the 31st, with Aïno Ackté in the name-part and the fine bass-baritone Clarence Whitehill as the Prophet. It was preceded on the last two occasions by *Heldenleben*: Beecham must have believed in good measure, just as the Paris Opéra, when we frequented it in the late twenties and early thirties, would have thought it cheating to put on *Bohème* without *Pagliacci* or *Rigoletto* without *Coppélia*. There is a lot to be said for this: there were years when nothing would have pleased me better than *Götterdämmerung*; a supper interval; and then the Gallic *Carmen*.

I have mentioned these December dates to show that I could not keep away, that first year, from *Salome*. I have never been able to do so since, have rarely missed an available performance, and have heard the majority of the outstanding Salomes of my time: Göte Ljungberg, Ljuba Welitsch, Inge Borkh, Christel Goltz, and the girl, I forget her name and have lost the programme, who sang so brilliantly with the Frankfurt people the other day at Sadler's Wells. The work fascinates me and I suspect will always fascinate me, and yet I dislike it. I find three kinds of music in Strauss, the good or even great, the bad or very bad, and a kind that draws but repels me at the same time, what fascinates being itself what repels: and in *Salome* I find little if any of the first, a certain amount of the second and a great deal of the third. Typical of the second category, the plain bad, is Jokanaan's music, and it struck me forcibly as such at the very first of my hearings: it has that 'square', surface quality I have criticised in the case of Wagner. There is a hack gravity or solemnity, a hack propheticism about it: this is how a man who is not a prophet, who cannot feel himself into the mind of a prophet, imagines, and expresses with painstaking contrivance, how a prophet might sing. Even worse, and this again I was sensitive to at a first hearing, is the Dance of the Veils: the more astonishingly, in that the sensual is very much Strauss' province. This is stuff, under the glitter, of the wretchedest banality.

Typical of the music that fascinates and repels me simultaneously is the shifting web of euphonic seductiveness built round the chromaticism of 'Ich will deinen Mund küssen, Jochanaan'. I do feel it mildly seductive (which is why it fascinates me) but rather nauseating too, as I have never found the lyrical passages in *Don Juan*: and in case anyone should argue that it is meant to be nauseating I do not mean nauseating in that sense, physically nauseating, but musically nauseating, nauseating for the cheap and easy way in which the idea of seductiveness is expressed. To point the contrast, take *Turandot*: a good deal of the music is nauseating, because so is the sadism it expresses, but it is never musically nauseating, because the expression, from deep down in Puccini's consciousness, fits the theme with that inevitability which, as I have already so often suggested, is one of the criteria of value in music. And yet I prefer *Salome* to *Turandot*,

E

because the seductiveness of Salome's music, however easily come by, is more palatable than the brooding sadism, wrought to perfection, of Puccini's masterpiece. Of course there is sadism of a sort in *Salome* too, but so superficially rendered that no one could be disturbed by it.

§ 4

Of Strauss' other operas, *Rosenkavalier* is one of the three works (with *Tristan* and *Aida*) by any composer that I have heard oftenest: and how performed! Before 1915 it was almost as great a rarity as *Feuersnot*: Beecham conducted it at an off-season in 1913, with Claire Dux, beautifully lyrical, as Sophie, and I was to hear it only once or twice again, with Eva van der Osten as Octavian, till my second active period of concert- and opera-going, the 1926–1936 decade. That was the *Rosenkavalier* time above all times, and I doubt whether there can ever again be such another. It was not at Covent Garden, as a matter of fact, that I first heard it during the period in question, but in the recovering Berlin of 1926, when Kleiber was in charge there. Strauss conducted, and Frida Leider sang the Marschallin: but fine though she was, even in a part that gave less scope for her special magnificence than that of Isolde or Brünnhilde, my memory of her in this role has been overlaid by what rapidly followed. For on the opening night of the Covent Garden season of 1927 Bruno Walter conducted *Rosenkavalier* with Lotte Lehmann as the Marschallin, Elisabeth Schumann as Sophie, Delia Reinhardt as Octavian and Richard Mayr as Ochs.

I have already mentioned, as supreme among the operatic performances I have heard, the Destinn–Caruso–Dinh Gilly *Aida*, the Destinn–Tetrazzini–Zenatello *Ugonotti*, and the Leider–Lehmann-etcetera *Walküre*. I must now add the 1927 *Rosenkavalier*, and shall presently be adding, to complete a quintet, the 1930 *Fledermaus*, which I can hardly wait to catch up with but do not want to catch up with either, it would be such a delight to linger indefinitely with *Rosenkavalier*. And this is the place to say a word about the perfection, comparable in a wholly different way to Destinn's, of Lotte Lehmann and Elisabeth Schumann. Both were of most gracious personality: both had voices of ravishing freshness and beauty: both phrased with a flawlessness they might have been born with: and both sang with a lovely Viennese bouquet that was all but devoid in the one case, and completely devoid in the other, of Viennese *Süsslichkeit*.

Lotte Lehmann's vocal expressiveness was extraordinary. To take
the first act of *Rosenkavalier* alone, who that heard her will ever forget the hint of smiling regret in her 'Einmal', as she recalls how the
Feldmarschall once returned with disconcerting unexpectedness? Or
the start of fear, but still that of a lady who never loses her head, in the
way she sang 'Quinquin, es ist mein Mann!'? Or the sudden change in
her tone to one of careless gaiety at 'Herrgott, das ist der Ochs'? Or
the kindly contempt of her 'schlechte Kerl' when the Baron has left
her? Or the shades of rebellion and resignation in passage after passage
that follows: 'Die alte Frau, die alte Marschallin!', 'Das alles ist
geheim, so viel geheim', 'Es is ja schon vorbei'; and then the wondering 'Die Zeit, die ist ein sonderbar Ding', and the beautiful kindness
of 'Und wenn ich fahr, und Er hat Lust', and the moment of final
despair in 'Ich hab' ihn nicht einmal geküsst'. I remembered all this
the other day as I sat listening to Regine Crespin at that performance
I have mentioned, for the critics had praised her so highly that I had
decided to venture down. Her performance was in many ways charming,
and her voice full of beauty; but when I thought of Lotte Lehmann's
discretion and lack of any exaggerated self-pity I could not enjoy her
successor.

As to Elisabeth Schumann, no one will ever forget, either, the soar
and leap of her voice at the presentation of the rose. Imagine silver as
pure as young happiness and as true as steel, and you have an idea of it.

These have never in my experience been equalled as the Marschallin
and Sophie, nor has Mayr as Ochs. The point in his case was this: the
voice was so ample, had such reserves in it, that the singer had only to
decide what at the given moment he wanted to express and the expression was there, with nothing to struggle against. And something
should be added. You often hear it said of Herr X or Mr. Y that "for
all his vulgarity he never forgets he's a gentleman". This is usually
quite untrue, but in Mayr's case it was exact.

Finally Delia Reinhardt's Octavian, though it has certainly been
equalled and perhaps surpassed, was delightful for the sort of roguish-
ness that I associate nowadays with Christa Ludwig.

To open the grand season with *Rosenkavalier* became almost
traditional, with few if any changes in the cast. Gitta Alpar sang
Sophie in 1929, and Adele Kern, with Kipnis as Ochs, in 1933; but
Lotte Lehmann was I think invariable. Of course we heard Marschal-
lins elsewhere, notably Germaine Lubin in Paris; but we thought of
them as all wrong, excellent though their singing might be—mere
substitutes for the real, the living Marschallin.

I must append a footnote. In 1926 we went to the old Tivoli music-hall in the Strand. There were three items in the programme: (1) The Tivoli Animated Review of Topical Events; (2) The Haunted Houses of Great Britain, featuring Gabriel Norton; (3) The Screen Version of Richard Strauss' Famous Opera *Rosenkavalier*. The orchestra was 'under the personal direction of Dr. Richard Strauss (composer of the Opera)'. By the orchestra was meant the Tivoli orchestra: the film was a silent one, and the sounds that should have emerged from the open mouths of the gesticulating singers were dovetailed into the score. "The advent of Richard Strauss' visit to London," says a note in the programme, "to direct the Orchestra at the Tivoli has aroused an extraordinary amount of interest amongst orchestral musicians, lovers of opera, and particularly those frequenters of the Cinema to whom music is as important a factor of the entertainment as the picture which is being exhibited." There is a comment on this visit, or similar ones, in the 1929 Grove: "One feature of his character," writes Alfred Kalisch, "which cannot remain unnoticed is his keen business sense, which indeed is sometimes carried to excess. When during his first visit to America he conducted concerts in a large drapery store he was severely attacked for his inartistic behaviour in so doing, but he replied to his detractors that the conditions under which he gave his concerts were perhaps even more artistic than those in ordinary concert-halls, and it was better to earn money honestly than to complain to those who do. But he cannot be absolved from all blame in some later incidents, as when he rearranged the score of *Rosenkavalier* to fit a film and himself conducted the performances with inferior orchestras in cinemas."

We had an encounter with Strauss closer at hand a few years later. Staying at Munich for a week or so we had gone in for lunch to Walterspiel's, then reputedly the best restaurant in Europe east of Paris, or the best, some said, without qualification. Next to the table we were taken to sat a big prosperous-looking man, whom I recognised with awe at second glance as the composer, not so much of *Rosenkavalier* but rather—for this was above all why I reverenced him—of *Elektra*. If I had been my present age I should probably have paid him my respects, but I was far too shy for that in the nineteen-twenties. I was able however to do so indirectly, though at great expense. He had finished his meal and ordered a cognac just as, after the incredible hors d'œuvres, every item a chef's masterpiece, we were starting on the day's speciality, namely a duck, or maybe goose, cut up into pieces and cooked inside a number of trepanned melons. When we in our

The Tivoli

Im Festspielhaus

Der Rosenkavalier

Komödie für Musik in drei Aufzügen von Hugo von Hof-
mannsthal — Musik von Richard Strauß

Dirigent: **Clemens Krauss**
Inszenierung: **Lothar Wallerstein**
Bühnenbilder: **Alfred Roller**

Feldmarschallin Fürstin Werdenberg	Lotte Lehmann
Der Baron Ochs auf Lerchenau	Richard Mayr
Oktavian, genannt Quinquin, ein junger Herr aus großem Haus	Margit Angerer
Herr von Faninal, ein reicher Neugeadelter	Hermann Wiedemann
Sophie, seine Tochter	Adele Kern
Jungfer Marianne, Leitmetzerin der Duenna	Carola Jovanovic
Valzacchi, ein Intrigant	Hermann Gallos
Annina, seine Begleiterin	Gertrud Rünger
Der Haushofmeister bei der Feldmarschallin	Viktor Madin
Der Haushofmeister bei Faninal	William Wernigk
Ein Polizeikommissär	Viktor Madin
Ein Notar	Karl Ettl
Ein Sänger	Karl Hauss
Ein Gelehrter	Emanuel Haller
Ein Flötist	Ludwig Verlik
Ein Friseur	Karl Nowak
Dessen Gehilfe	Emilie Köcher
Eine adelige Witwe	Gisela Fiedler

turn had finished I also ordered a cognac, and the waiter brought me a list. I waved it aside: "Give me," I said, "the cognac you gave Dr. Strauss." It cost me just on a pound.

My feelings about *Rosenkavalier* have been constantly changing over a period of fifty years. Sometimes I have found it ravishing: sometimes I have found it sickly, sickly with the sweetness of decay. In sum, I should give it an alpha minus, not a pure alpha and still less an alpha plus. The nervous wiriness of *Wozzeck* is now more to my taste than the lusciousness of *Rosenkavalier*.

§ 5

Of such other of Strauss' operas as I have heard—*Arabella, Ariadne, Die Schweigsame Frau, Die Liebe der Danae* and *Capriccio*—the only two I really care for are *Arabella* and *Ariadne*. The second of these has a sense of elusive mystery in some of its music that is new to Strauss, and my Italianism is gratified by the coloratura in the second act. But this must be sung perfectly, as it was sung by Maria Ivogün in those Charlottenburg performances under Bruno Walter, for an easy perfection is the whole point of it: and Bacchus must have a certain depth and gravity in the closing scene, particularly when he is heard 'off'—tenors are inclined to bawl in this role.

Arabella I have heard less often, and cannot know whether in time I should tire of it: but with Lisa della Casa, whose voice and style are as winning as her presence, and with Hermann Ude or Fischer-Dieskau, both pre-eminent Mandrykas, I have enjoyed it more of recent years than *Rosenkavalier*. As for *Capriccio*, I should have been inclined to say, on the evidence of the Munich performances at Covent Garden in 1953, that it must be the worst of all music-dramas: for everything depends on understanding the words (this is a veritable thesis), I could rarely catch them, and the effort to do so made me deaf to the music. But I am told that the text came over perfectly at Glyndebourne, and that the music is exquisite.

§ 6

Inseparable from the Bruno Walter *Rosenkavalier* is the Bruno Walter *Fledermaus* of 1930. One of the rarities of operatic literature is the 'appreciation' by Walter that was slipped loose into the programmes, and I happily reproduce it in full; for it is instinct with the loving enthusiasm that was characteristic of his approach to such diverse composers as Johann Strauss and Gustav Mahler:

"*Die Fledermaus* shared the fate of Bizet's *Carmen*, and of many other musical works which failed to achieve success on the first night on which they were performed. The reason for this is probably that it had been announced as an operetta, and that lovers of this type of work rightly perceived that it was anything but an operetta. The fact is, *Die Fledermaus* is no more an operetta than it is an opera. It is a work of art unique in its kind, occupying a unique position even in the works of Johann Strauss, the King of the Waltz. I should, however, immediately add that it is a piece of good fortune for the theatre that success came immediately after the first performance, a success which *Die Fledermaus* still continues to achieve. It apparently possesses for all time a kind of magic virtue which ensures for it the love and enthusiasm of the whole world, not merely of the world which fills the theatre, but of everyone connected with the stage. I particularly recall a never-to-be-forgotten performance which took place under the direction of Gustav Mahler at the Court Opera House, Vienna, assisted by artists of leading rank. All the great artists of the theatre took part in the chorus in the second act, and everything had been personally prepared by Mahler with a view to achieving an outstanding performance. This brings to my mind the wonderful performances conducted by Nikisch, and many others, at Salzburg, Munich, Berlin, etc., which were brilliantly rendered by singers of outstanding merit.

"What then are the qualities to which the exceptional place occupied by this work is due? They are beauty without heaviness, levity without vulgarity, gaiety without frivolity, and a strange mixture of exuberant musical richness (somewhat resembling Schubert) and popular simplicity. That is how I try to explain the charm of the work, whilst bearing in mind that all magical attraction—and happily so—remains inexplicable, simply because it is magic. Eisenstein, the gay deceiver and the gay deceived, satisfies his Rosalinde and all her questions, complaints and accusations by the explanation: 'It is the fault of the champagne'. The intoxication of this work may be compared with that of a very slight intoxication from champagne. It causes human errors to assume the appearance of delightful misunderstandings, and life in its entirety that of a fugitive paradise. Happiness flows from this work, and this happiness, this slight intoxication as of champagne, is contained in the immortal melodies of this most typically Viennese of geniuses. He is not a true musician who has not experienced the desire to render his music sparkling with the most eloquent expression of this happiness. In degrading the work to the level of an operetta, the danger exists of destroying the exalted spirit of the whole; and no work has more to fear than this from habitual routine, which without the most delicate purity in the style of execution would result in an unintelligible dance phantasy. *Die Fledermaus* insists and deserves that the best artists, the most brilliant orchestra, and a setting deeply imbued with the spirit of the work should be allied to a conductor who directs the work with a view to achieving the maximum of accuracy in its rendering. Given such conditions, it will always stand out as one of the finest jewels in our artistic treasury, a worthy link in that chain of works to which we are indebted in the theatre for transporting us into the beautiful realms of the unreal."

'The best artists, the most brilliant orchestra, and a setting . . .'. It is typical of me, I suppose, that I do not remember the setting of our 1930 *Fledermaus*, and all I remember of the orchestra is that, conducted as Walter conducted it, the champagne it vouchsafed us was not mere ordinary champagne, any champagne of any variety at any time anywhere, but the very Idea of champagne, champagne in a summer garden at noontide. As for 'the best artists', I shall give myself the pleasure of setting them out here with the spaciousness they deserve:

Gabriel von Eisenstein .	Willi Wörle
Rosalinde . . .	Lotte Lehmann
Frank	Waldemer Staegemann
Orlofsky . . .	Maria Olczewska
Alfred	Karl Jöken
Falke	Gerhard Hüsch
Blind	Heinrich Tessmer
Adele	Elisabeth Schumann
Frosch	Eduard Habich
Ida	Norah Gruhn
Conductor . . .	Bruno Walter

Before the Third Act, the 'Blue Danube' waltz will be played.

INTERLUDE

I SHALL GET OUT of the way now the few words I promised myself in the last chapter about the Callas-Zeffirelli *Tosca*, with the further opportunity it provided for an assessment of Zeffirelli's operatic stage-craft. But first let me repeat what I actually said about this whole controversial matter, for I have been grotesquely misquoted. I did not say that even the most elaborate production was necessarily incon-sistent with the musical-dramatic genius of a given work: on the contrary I specifically denied it, and cited the Visconti *Don Carlo* as proof of the opposite. My complaint was twofold. I complained, first, that "the current enthusiasm for elaborate production tends to divert attention from the paramount necessity of providing the essentials—namely great or at any rate good singing, fine orchestral playing finely directed and a satisfactory ensemble. . . . It is a question of priorities—your heart, over the field as a whole, will be where your treasure is. And I complained, secondly, that "certain kinds of fashionably elaborate production do fight with the musical-dramatic genius of the work in question." It was in the latter connection that I introduced Zeffirelli, giving by way of examples his *Falstaff* and *Don Giovanni*.

How then did Zeffirelli measure up to *Tosca*? In his direction of the singers, admirably (the knifing of Scarpia, if it was he who inspired it, proves him, in point of purely theatrical detail, a genius) : in some particulars of the stage traffic, equally so. As to the sets (executed by another hand, but his in conception) those for the first two acts were at any rate better than the old ones, and I specially liked the height of the scaffolding from which Cavaradossi sang 'Recondita armonia', with the Attavanti's portrait in full view. But in the third act that mania of his for high staircases, effective though they are in their old-fashioned way, betrays him into betraying Puccini as he betrayed Verdi and Mozart. The directions in the libretto are quite explicit: we are on the 'platform' of the Castel Sant' Angelo, with St. Peter's and the Vatican facing us ('nel fondo'). At the edge of the platform is one of those breast-high parapets that are built on such eminences to prevent people falling over. And what did Zeffirelli give us? A dark, deep defile, with a high narrow staircase leading up to the battlements on the left. The object was probably, first, to emphasise the darkness of Cavaradossi's fate,

THE HAMBURG SET FOR *TRAVIATA*

THE HAMBURG SET FOR *FIGARO*

and secondly to provide for something really spectacular at the close—
Tosca leaping from the top of the staircase instead of just throwing
herself over the parapet. But the device failed on both counts:
Cavaradossi's fate is far darker if he sees 'tutta Roma' before his still
living eyes; and Tosca's run up the staircase, with Sciarrone and the
rest of them keeping their distance so as not to catch up with her as she
tries to entangle them in her scarf, was not spectacular, it was ludicrous. But there was something worse. There is another series of
explicit instructions in the libretto: at first, night; then the grey and
uncertain light that comes before dawn: and finally, with 'O dolci
mani', dawn itself. Now the sky music, the music of approaching daybreak, is far and away the best thing in the score: who was it who said
that between *Bohème* and *Tosca* Puccini had visited Paris, referring to
Debussy? But down there in that narrow defile subtleties of lighting
were impossible: you could see no change at all until 'O dolci mani': and
the music, to anyone unfamiliar with the work, was robbed of all its
meaning. This is surely intolerable.

Some photographs, it happens, have just been sent to me that are
very much to my purpose here. In the devastated Hamburg of 1946
nothing remained of the Staatsoper except the stage. But they put on a
season none the less, using the stage for all purposes: the front of it for
the audience (a dozen rows of chairs); the middle of it for a small
orchestra; and the back for the work itself. Two operas were done
that October, *Figaro* and *Traviata*: very well done too, with not a
singer in either cast known to me. The performances moved me as the
music-camp *Fidelio* had moved me, because of their intimacy; and
for something else too, for the courage they showed, the courage
of a defeated and suffering people. But the point I want to make
is this. To fit into the available space the sets had to be exceedingly
narrow, and the producer, Günther Rennert, might have chosen to
compensate for the lack of spaciousness by something as brilliant
and elaborate as possible. He chose simplicity, and the result was
beautifully satisfying.

Courage was the mark of Germany at that time: I was to find it
again in Jülich, which I visited after Hamburg. This was perhaps the
most ruined town in Germany: our bombers had gone over it one
night, and twenty minutes later 93 per cent of it was no longer there.
Everyone was living underground, five or six perhaps to a tiny hovel,
at the end of narrow inclines tunnelled in the earth. But the gentle
Stadtdirektor, Erwin Stadthagen, was cheerful enough. He turned out
to be a Social Democrat, and to have been 'on the run' continuously

from 1933 right up to what he still called the liberation. When he found me sympathetic he asked if he might come in my car as far as Düren (I was going to Aachen) so that we could talk a little longer. As we were leaving the rubble for the green fields I noticed a bungalow of wood that seemed somehow to gleam and glisten in that awful desolation: and over the door the words, in bold lettering, 'Hotel-Restaurant Kaiserhof'. I looked at my comrade with a gesture of enquiry, and he replied with a smile, half proud and half deprecating, 'Es beginnt' ('Something's beginning'). I got out to have a look. Two or three men were drinking a glass of beer in the vestibule-restaurant, and we sat and talked with them for a moment or so. Then we went down the corridor. The rooms that opened out of it on both sides were small, overcrowded and furnished with the minimum of necessities; but they were bright and clean, and the people seemed content. In one room there was a mother with the three most beautiful children I have ever seen. The Hotel-Restaurant Kaiserhof has nothing whatever to do with music, but life is life, and I shall reproduce here, for love of little Jülich, the picture I got my photographer to take of it, together with another that shows the way people were living there.

I feel ashamed to be getting back after Jülich to all the glitter and wealth of that *Tosca*, but want to say something about Callas herself. I remain more than ever convinced that she is the only great soprano, or indeed singer of any kind, now living. Her reputation has run a curious course. A dozen years ago almost everyone except the Tebaldi group thought her wonderful. Time passed, and people shook their heads: those shrieks, that unevenness of register! She shouldn't have slimmed: she was clearly finished. So conscious was I of this that when Peter Heyworth asked me who it was that alone among living singers I should call truly great, I answered, "I know I'm being highly controversial, but Callas", and only later, on his insistence, cut out everything except the name. And now the whole world raves again. That Tuesday was a real 'sensation' night: the place was packed with disagreeably unmusical people—on the evidence of one's ears—but with faces familiar in other connections. I had myself been excited in advance by a sense of occasion, but when actually sitting there I found myself hating the atmosphere. Nor was it a question only of the sensation-mongers: a critic, a sensitive and highly intelligent one, who had reviled the Callas Violetta, was talking in the crush-room of the Callas Tosca as if it were flawless.

But it was by no means flawless. She could still shriek, though with

JÜLICH: HOTEL-RESTAURANT KAISERHOF

JÜLICH: AN ALL-PURPOSE ROOM FOR SIX PEOPLE

a good deal more discretion than sometimes of late: and occasionally there was a disconcerting sense of skating over thin ice, doing the thing by a hair's-breadth. More important was her comparative failure in certain vocally crucial passages: her 'Mario' from outside the church lacked Destinn's magic thrill, the end of 'Non la sospiri' went for little, and her 'Vissi d'arte', judged by a reasonably high standard, was no more than passable. Her voice, moreover, gave the impression of being considerably smaller than before. I fear she will never equal her London Norma of 1950.

But, when all has been said, what a marvel this Tosca of hers is! Her softer singing in the middle register, particularly of shorter passages, and most of all in dialogue, has hung about me ever since: for quite apart from the beauty of her voice, there was a magic in the phrasing that made me again and again hold my breath. Then in variety of vocal expression she showed herself the equal of Lehmann herself. To give four examples: the gentle playfulness of her 'Ma . . . falle gli ochi neri' as she leaves Cavaradossi in Act I; the contemptuous forthrightness of her 'Quanto?' to Scarpia; the almost intolerable pathos of her 'Ecco, vedi, le man giunte io stendo a te!' as she pleads with him; and the agonisedly believing unbelief of her second 'Mario' as she kneels by Cavaradossi's body. Such achievements are only possible to the greatest.

And there is still something more. I go little to the ordinary theatre: apart from Shakespeare and a few other masterpieces I find even the best of spoken plays flat and tedious after music-drama, and my preference is for reading rather than seeing them (even Shakespeare's *Othello* moves me less than Verdi's); but speaking as an ignoramus I find Callas, purely as an actress, supreme. So my admiration for her amounts to worship, and I hope she will forgive me my criticisms.

I shall add a paragraph or two about Zeffirelli's *Rigoletto*, which followed his *Tosca*: Zeffirelli's, not Verdi's and certainly not Geraint Evans's, for the crowd that equally sold the house out for both sets of performances probably went to hear Callas even more than to see Zeffirelli but undoubtedly went to see Zeffirelli far more than to hear Geraint Evans, who, superb in parts that suit him, has not as yet reached the ears of the extra-musical public. The production was in my view deplorable. The crowded lavishness of Scene I, the solid statuary in Scene III, the "real" bulrushes in Scene IV struck me as of a singular vulgarity, and the pantomime disappearance of the walls in Scene II, to reveal a garden of Annigoni prettiness, made nonsense of the whole idea, which is that what is going on inside and out should be simultaneously visible. The costumes, too, lacked unity of style: Veronese in Scene I, Carlo Dolci for Gilda when she emerges in a sort of nightgown after being raped. And the interval after Scene I! Scene I, not Act I: a mere prelude twenty minutes or so long, to be followed as rapidly as possible by the exchanges between Rigoletto and Sparafucile and the love-music. I timed this interval, as I failed to do in the similar case of Zeffirelli's *Don*: it lasted just on half an hour and seemed to last all evening—because the elaborate sets for Rigoletto's house took all that time to erect. Moreover the Veronese stuff in Scene I was fatally distracting: the opening dialogue between Borsa and the Duke— exquisite phrases—was lost, and may even have been drowned at the première, to judge from one of the notices, by applause for the set; and 'Questa o quella', which should at once capture the audience for its revelation of the Duke's character, became a casual ingredient of the stage traffic and a less important one than the women it was sung to. But worst of all was an outrage like the *Tosca* one to Verdi's intention. When Rigoletto shambles up, or should do, to Monterone, making play with his bauble, the music mirrors exactly the physical jerking in his gait and the moral one in his mind. But, according to Zeffirelli, Rigoletto must advance to the front and pick up a luxurious robe with an immense gaudy train to it that happens to be lying about there: must put it on: must arrange a number of dwarfs under it: then must go half way up-stage, turn about to face the audience and, standing there more like an emperor than a hunchback, deliver himself of his musical insults, jerking the robe to uncover his dwarfs when he ought to be jerking at Monterone. . . . My own view is that Zeffirelli does not really care for music, like the first fiddle who excused himself with words to that effect when Mengelberg asked him, at a London rehearsal, whether he was feeling ill.

CHAPTER X

WHEN I MENTIONED *Orfeo, Elektra* and *Pelléas* as the three great experiences of my gallery days, I added that I had an idea of why *Fidelio* was not in the list. The reason may have been one, or a combination, of several. The work was hardly ever performed at that time: I certainly heard it only once, and this may well have been for lack of opportunity. The performance I did hear was in the same Beecham season of 1910 that gave us *Salome*. Miss Gleeson-White was the Fidelio, that fine baritone I have already mentioned, Clarence Whitehill, the Pizarro, and Joseph O'Mara, quite famous in his way as a leading member of the Moody-Manners Company, the Florestan. The entire cast indeed, though it sang in German, was English (or Irish or American) and so was the conductor, Percy Pitt, whose appearance at the rostrum was nearly always a sign that the night was an 'off' one. (He was in fact an excellent musician.) All this may have spoiled my pleasure in advance, for in the atmosphere of family talk— the Marios, the Jean de Reszkes, the Christine Nilssons—I may have thought the whole affair a bit off colour. Or the performance may actually have been a poor one. But the main reason for my lack of appreciation was probably something quite different. This was the first opera I heard with spoken dialogue, and both my *Italianità* and my Wagnerism may have been shocked by what I must have thought of as an impropriety. But the odd thing is that the music should not have conquered me, for Beethoven and Mozart were already my favourite composers, and my favourite Beethoven was the Leonora number three.

Since that first imperceptiveness I have heard *Fidelio* in many cities, many circumstances and many types of performance. It has always seemed to turn up for us at the right moment. We arrive late in Venice, and go strolling early next morning in the Piazza. We come on a Fenice playbill, announcing *Fidelio*: we hurry up to it, fearing it may be out of date. No: the performance is for that very evening. We arrive in Frankfurt, where I am to receive the peace prize, and within the hour we are taken to *Fidelio*. I believe in this sort of coincidence: it is connected with holism.

I have heard brilliant performances and indifferent performances,

and have enjoyed the worst almost as much as the best. Of my Leonoras
—Helène Wildbrunn, Lotte Lehmann, Rose Pauly, Gré Brouwenstijn
and Sena Jurinac among them—no one has been perfect, not even
Lotte Lehmann, for she could not really manage the big top notes in
'Abscheulicher' with sufficient ease. But she was Lehmann, and had the
Lehmann magic; and some of the others have come close to her. I ought
also to mention Elizabeth Crook, who sang Leonora at some of the
concert *Fidelios* conducted by Colin Davis at Oxford and Cambridge
in the earlier days of the Chelsea Opera Group: she was one of the best
Leonoras I have ever heard, with finely ringing head-notes, and I hope
that one day she will emerge again. (The C.O.G. has produced a
number of beautiful but little-known singers, such as the amateur
Richard Gandy, whom I heard in *Idomeneo* at the Oxford Town Hall,
and was later to hear in Berlioz' *Te Deum* at a music-camp reunion in
Stepney.) Then there is Elizabeth Fretwell at Sadler's Wells, which is
also getting together a remarkable team: for instance Rae Woodland,
Elizabeth Harwood and Joyce Blackham, the last a Carmen of rare
excellence.

If perfect Leonoras are non-existent, good Florestans are exceedingly
rare: but Julius Patzak was magnificent, and Jon Vickers, though too
noisy, was and is movingly impressive. Good Roccos have been
commoner, with Paul Bender outstanding; and a Marcellina who
remains in my memory is Lotte Schöne, at a Bruno Walter *Fidelio*
in 1927. There have been two performances of the work as a whole,
apart from the music-camp one, that stand out for me above all
others: Franz Schalk's with the Vienna troup in Paris[1], and Klemperer's
at Covent Garden quite recently. In spite of the Paris cast, Klemperer's
was perhaps the finest of all.

Of *Fidelio* itself I shall say nothing. It is a work to be accepted as
supreme, and that is the end of it: others abide our question, Beethoven
is free. The heart of the work for me is the coincidence of trumpet-
call and pistol in the dungeon scene: for to repeat what I said earlier,
it reveals with final genius what to my ordinary human thinking is the
ultimate meaning of life, namely that our existence 'here below' is not
so much the vale of soul-making that Keats imagined it to be, but—
which may come to the same thing—an opportunity for co-operation
between God and man. This was an idea that we know from other
sources was precious to Beethoven. At the end of his arrangement of
Fidelio Moscheles had written "Fine. With God's help", but Beethoven
added "O man, help thyself". And just as he emphasises the human side

[1] See p. 47.

in that footnote, so he chooses one of the loveliest of his melodies to emphasise the divine side: the solo passage in the prisoners' chorus, 'Auf Gottes Hülfe bauen'.

And yet for years now my pacifism has raised a troubling question after performances of *Fidelio*. As we were leaving Covent Garden one night long after Hitler's war my wife asked me, in reply to a scruple I could not help expressing, "But was Leonora wrong to threaten Pizarro with the pistol? She saved her husband's life." And I had to answer "Yes, she was wrong." To interpose her own body, of course this was right: to threaten with the pistol was far better than just to have been indifferent, just to have done nothing about it: but to retaliate against violence with violence—this, absolutely, was wrong. And the absoluteness is everything. I do not believe that you can approximate to Christian ethics: that is why Christ told us, not merely to love our friends and do no injury to our enemies but positively to love our enemies, and not merely to be as good as we could manage to be but to be perfect as our Father is perfect. The question is not one of degree. You cannot be more or less of a Christian, just as you cannot be more or less of a lover. You either love or you do not. When absoluteness is reached, you are suddenly a Christian; before, however close you may have got, you have not been a Christian at all. And this absoluteness is the only possible road to the Kingdom of Heaven: it is the Kingdom of Heaven itself.

That anyhow is the climate of my mind, a climate for which the ultimate evil of Nazi violence is itself responsible: good, not evil, I have thought ever since I first heard Hitler on the wireless, is the answer to evil like that. And yet doubts will always come creeping in, particularly after performances of *Fidelio*. For, apart from all other considerations, *Fidelio* explicitly rejects pacifism: and Beethoven, whatever his doctrinal beliefs and however unseemly, on this occasion or on that, his behaviour may have been, was a far better Christian than I could ever hope to be.

§ 2

There is a point of detail in the presentation of *Fidelio* that I should like to discuss: I refer to the playing of the Leonora number three at the end of the dungeon scene.

The practice of playing it at this point, as Mahler was the first to play it, unless I am mistaken[1] (in Vienna at the beginning of the century), is now commonly condemned as illegitimate, inartistic, mere repetition, an anticlimax. I do not blame people who talk like that if they are judging by recent procedure at Covent Garden. When I saw *Fidelio* there round about 1950 the curtain was brought down after the Leonora and Florestan duet; there was much applause; the artists took several calls; and then Mr. Rankl raised his stick, and the overture began. This is horrible; the spell is broken, and the overture, with applause at the end of it before the final scene, is nothing but an unwarrantable intrusion. But played as Mahler meant it to be played and as I have heard it played, that night in Paris and often at Salzburg and even, under Bruno Walter, at Covent Garden itself, the overture is not only a piece of great music but a piece of great opera as well, for all that the invention was Mahler's and not Beethoven's. You have been watching and listening as the scene in the dungeon has run its course. Doomed Florestan has sung his hymn to the wife, the 'Engel Leonore' whom he sees with the faithful clarity of imagination while his body hungers and thirsts; the real Leonora, disguised as Fidelio, has come down into the deep and the cold—'das ist natürlich! Es ist ja so tief'—and has dug with Rocco her husband's grave; Pizarro has raised his dagger to strike; divine grace and human freewill have co-operated to save Florestan; and he and Leonora have sung their duet of love and rapture. But the curtain does not fall immediately. As the lovers go slowly up the dungeon steps, with the torchlight of freedom now shining from above, we hear the opening chord of the Leonora number three; and only when a few more bars have been played, and the lovers are nearer the sky, is the curtain very slowly brought down and the music left, wholly self-sufficient, to continue to its end. Played in this way the overture, summing up everything we have been living through, and proceeding from Florestan's song and by way of the trumpet calls—'ja, ja, es ist eine Vorsicht!'—to a paean of thanksgiving which again and again you think can never mount higher and yet again and again, with the incessant enriching of the strings, it does—played in this way the overture provides a climax far more moving even than the lovers' duet, though that had seemed at the time to reach the limit of musical expression. Beethoven, in the last movement of his last symphony, broke into human speech, and no one understands Beethoven who does not understand why; but when I hear the Leonora number three

---

[1] Perhaps I am. Mahler's priority is generally accepted, and has Klemperer's authority: but according to Harold Rosenthal Sir Julius Benedict anticipated him at Her Majesty's Theatre decades earlier.

greatly played, not as an interlude between two rounds of applause but as an integral conclusion to the whole long scene of fidelity and salvation, I have the feeling, not merely that the human drama is being superbly summed up, but that by the silencing of speech and song what was before experienced as greatly human is now experienced as an immediate and final reality which includes and rests in the human, but transcends it.

People who dismiss this procedure as blatantly inartistic might do well to ask themselves, was Mahler inartistic? Was Bruno Walter? Is Klemperer?

§ 3

I have had several remote encounters with Beethoven that it is a pleasure to recall. When I was in Hamburg shortly after the war a body of journalists asked me up to their club on the outskirts, for they wanted to thank me for what I was trying to do for their people. The starvation was at its height: I had seen human skeletons dying in hospital, and a man so swollen with hunger oedema that his testicles reached the ground. (It was at this time that the Burgermeister and Senate entertained me at the Rathaus. We had herrings for dinner: and after we had finished the Burgermeister pushed a bell, and a dignified old man, very much the stage butler, walked slowly in. The Burgermeister nodded to him, and he walked out. Then we took our places at a series of round tables: and presently the old man came in again, this time with a dozen bottles of wine, which we sipped happily for the rest of the evening. I have never enjoyed wine so much: it was a very precious Rhine wine, which the butler, an eager socialist, had hidden from the Nazis. The Bremen Senate had come over for the occasion, and had brought with them a photograph of a tablet commemorating my grandfather, who had once been a guest *chazan* at the synagogue there: it was almost the only thing in the building that had survived our bombing.)

To return to the journalists: when we had arrived at the club one of them made a little speech, to the effect that they could not entertain me as they would have wished (and indeed the fare was meagre, a biscuit or two and some chemical lemonade), but that, knowing I loved music, they had something in another room that they thought might compensate me: would I follow him? I did so, and there, as we entered, I saw a sort of high catafalque, with a man standing at each of the four corners, their faces outwards and as if with rifles reversed. The spokesman led me to the catafalque, and pointed to what looked like a large piece of parchment lying on top of it. "This," he said, "is

the Heiligenstadt Testament. You may know that it was presented to
the City of Hamburg by Jenny Lind's husband: we buried it deep, and
it survived the bombing. We got permission to bring it here, as we
thought you might like to see it." I shall leave it at that: there are
moments that are better left undescribed.

It must have been a dozen years later that we found ourselves in
Vienna, and thought it would be a good idea to explore the Beethoven
quarter. After a few enquiries we found the house—Probusgasse 6—
where he had written the Testament. So Ruth sat in the courtyard on
a dustbin and painted, while I strolled about: for a good couple of
hours, though I was limping quite badly, for only a month before I
had broken my ankle. I daresay I was being very subjective when
I felt, as my eye caught 'Eroicagasse' and other commemorative
street-names, that a peace as of the Elysian Fields arose quietly from the
place to welcome me: or may it be that men and women of the intenser
sort really do leave their impress on the places they have lived in—and
inner peace was as surely an essential element in Beethoven's make-up
as inner and outer turbulence? Or perhaps there was nothing to it but
the freshness of a beautiful morning: for it was in the morning, of
course, that we were there—in the evening the place would have been
hideous with the noise of heuriges.

I had in the meantime had another of my 'remote encounters' with
Beethoven: in 1950, when we were staying at Bonn as guests of
President Heuss. We had told the President at dinner that we should
be visiting Beethoven's *Geburtshaus* next morning; and he must have
done something about it (he was a man of beautiful courtesy, and we
had got on very well, telling each other Jewish stories through an
interpreter), for when we got there at half-past ten the custodian was
ready for us. We first went up to the birth-room itself: a small attic,
with what might have been a crib of beaten earth on one side. Next
we spent an hour or so examining the exhibits: and I recall my rather
wry amusement as my eye caught a poster announcing the 1822
revival of *Fidelio*, with a huge 'Schröder-Devrient' and an insignificant
'Beethoven'. Then, as we were about to leave, the custodian asked
me whether there was anything else he could do for us. Now one
of the things he had made a special fuss of was a piano by Graf, a bit
smaller than the modern sort, inside a heavy glass case: it was one
of the pianos, he told us, on which Beethoven had composed. So I
said rather hopelessly "Unlock that case and let me touch the key-
board". He shook his head decisively and said "No". Then he smiled,
said "Wait a minute" and went off. He was gone for half an hour:

PROBUSGASSE 6

returned with a huge bunch of keys: unlocked the case: and said "Bitte". So I touched a single note, without pressing it down; and that was that. I asked him afterwards why he had changed his mind: "I got special permission," he answered, with a certain pride in his voice, "from the President." I suppose he meant that he had telephoned the President's office.

§ 4

As I do not know whether, as things appear to be shaping, I shall ever get to the second part of this memoir, designed to be as long as the first and to deal with music other than operatic, I think I shall try to single out here what, out of everything written by Beethoven, I hold dearest.

Not the C sharp minor quartet, opus 131, though until a decade ago I should have put it above any other music known to me, and when I came to compile my anthology *A Year of Grace*, which is really a record in other people's words of my own experience, I reproduced the opening phrases of the fugue immediately in front of the first section. And I still think or feel that serenity—not personal or human serenity, nor unreflecting serenity as with Gluck, but the serenity, it might almost be said, of existence as such, existence that has learned to face itself—has nowhere else been expressed with such a perfection as can give ordinary human beings a distant glimpse of it.

Not the Grosse Fuge, which I put very close to the opus 131 for two reasons. Its sheer intellectual power, the power of a man who is also a titan, gives the promise that ordinary human intelligence is as yet but in its childhood: and it bodies forth, as nothing else does, the idea, or rather the reality, of that union of contraries which is at the root of what is often called mystical, but is really common-sense, philosophy. I feel very grateful to Felix Weingartner for his performances in the twenties or thirties of an orchestral version prepared by himself. Such tamperings are commonly disastrous: we used to hear some of the Brandenburg concertos with full strings at the promenade concerts, and this put me off them for years, for I found them too rich. But the Grosse Fuge is another matter: Weingartner's version really did clarify the complex structure. Not that I should want to hear the work done like that now, for I know it well enough to dispense with such aid. We in fact went to the Festival Hall recently to hear Klemperer do what I suppose was Weingartner's version, but magnificently though he conducted and the Philharmonia played I did not greatly care for the result.

Not the Hammerklavier Sonata, though in intellectual power it rivals the Grosse Fuge itself, and moreover achieves throughout the beautiful length of its Adagio a miracle unparalleled, so far as I am aware, in artistic expression—mind and spirit, and, bound up with them, a wondering awe are experienced as indistinguishably one. I have heard but a single pianist who could reveal it to the full for what it is, namely Artur Schnabel. This was a pianist who played Beethoven with an almost terrible gravity, and with an intellect that met the music in so absolute a unity that we seemed to be assisting, not at Schnabel's interpretation of Beethoven but at some new and inevitable act of joint creation. In sixty years or more of joy in music, I can remember very few experiences that can compare with those performances of Schnabel, and with his attack, in particular, at the opening of the Hammerklavier.

Not the *Heiliger Dankgesang* in the opus 132, though I think of it as the ultimate expression of thanksgiving. It has its forerunners in the Pastoral Symphony and in the phrase of simple gratitude that rises so solemnly from the orchestra immediately after the trumpet-call in *Fidelio*: but now the deep worshipfulness of Beethoven's nature finds its perfect expression, a flowering of everything that has gone before.

Not the B flat quartet, opus 130, despite the cavatina: because the finale that Beethoven wrote for it to replace the Grosse Fuge brings it down, in my view, from the heights. There is a struggle in that quartet between the near-horror of the presto and the peace of the cavatina, and, within the cavatina itself, between the heavenly tune and the *beklemmt* or 'anguished' passage that interrupts it: a struggle that the Grosse Fuge resolves, but not the present finale.

Not even that movement from the E flat major quartet (I forget where it comes) in which, amidst celestial harmonies, time like a dome of many-coloured glass is truly seen as staining the white radiance of eternity—or call it an apotheosis of the many in the one:

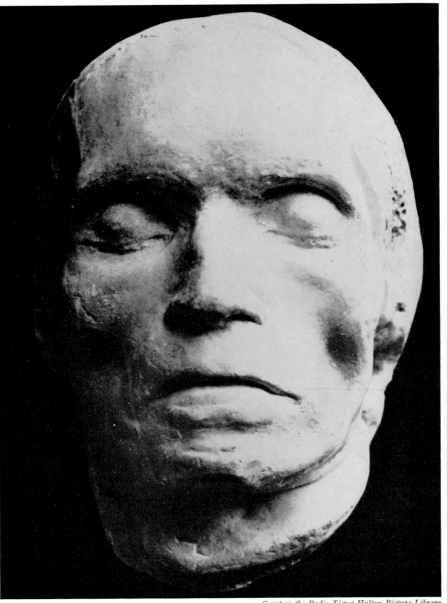

BEETHOVEN'S DEATH MASK

SCHNABEL PLAYING BEETHOVEN

REPRODUCED FROM EDMUND KAPP'S ORIGINAL LITHOGRAPH 'SCHNABEL
AND THE CONDUCTOR' BY COURTESY OF THE ARTIST. AUTOGRAPHED
BY SCHNABEL FOR THE WRITER

No, it is none of these that I love best, but one of two others, and I can never choose between them. Either the slow variation in the last movement of the Eroica, which does more than express uniquely the idea of transcendence: for a moment you are lost with it, as you listen, in the Transcendence itself. Or the quartet in F, opus 135. Where else, in music or painting or poem, can you find such an embodiment of ultimate faith as in the spiritual gaiety of the closing dialogue THE VERY DIFFICULT RESOLUTION? Whether or not the immediate occasion for it was a problem put by Beethoven to his cook or by his cook to Beethoven: or a mean amateur's importunity: or even the 'difficult resolution' of a purely musical dilemma—all this is irrelevant: 'eternity in a grain of sand...'. Underneath it all the dying Beethoven is contemplating death: broodingly he asks, with terrible stridencies every time he breaks off, 'Must it *be*?': there is one of those pauses that seem expectant on the peak of eternity: and then—words cannot say it, no use talking of confident rapture, or even of a child's spontaneity as it begins to welcome life—the cry 'It *must* be! It *must* be!' I know few things so moving in the whole realm of art.

The opus 135 was Beethoven's last complete work. Soon after finishing it he was on his deathbed, shaking his fist at the thunder-clap. The acceptance in 'Es muss sein' and the rebellion in the shaking fist are the two aspects, two in a unity, of the greatest human being, with one exception, who so far as we know has ever lived among us.

CHAPTER XI

Beethoven, it may be remembered, was not the only composer that I had unexpectedly failed to include among the supreme benefactors of my early operatic days: not a single work by Mozart was in the list. I think, however, that I shall keep him, with *Die Meistersinger*, for the Salzburg chapter, where he properly belongs, and use the present one for cleaning up the rest of pre-1915 Covent Garden. But *Idomeneo* was revived at the Wells last night (January 29th), and I cannot resist writing about it immediately.

The look of the place was infuriating. It was decently filled, but by no means to overflowing, and what is its capacity anyhow—about half Covent Garden's? The crowd that flocked in for Callas's *Tosca*, and regularly flocks in for anything spectacular or fashionable, kept well out of the way, if it had even so much as heard of *Idomeneo* or its promised performance last night. This is another example of the lamentable conditions in which music is given today, unless they have always been lamentable.

For this is a work of the rarest delight. If musically *Tosca* is on earth, *Idomeneo* is in the stratosphere: and I always think, after hearing it, that I love it better than any other of Mozart's operas except *Figaro*. According to my imperfect records, I first heard it—*novità in Italia*—in 1947 under Vittorio Gui at the Fenice; transported thither by an aging gondolier who, if I understood him correctly, had once worked for Baron Corvo. But I believe I must have heard it somewhere before, as a good deal of the music, and not merely 'Placido è il mar', was familiar to me; and I have never missed an available performance since, except the magnificent ones, as my friends told me, at Glyndebourne in 1951, with Sena Jurinac, Birgit Nilsson, Richard Lewis and Leopold Simoneau in the cast. But last night's was excellent too. No one of the singers was less than adequate, and the Electra, Rae Woodland, was far more than that: though I do not know how she would sound at Covent Garden (but am told that a larger house, with its greater resonance, is often kinder to the voice than a small one), her singing, with its beautiful purity supported by at any rate adequate strength, had the authentic thrill in it peculiar to soprano voices at their best. The sets were appropriately simple, never demanding undue attention for their own sake; and Colin Davis conducted with a just combination of enthusiasm and restraint. This is a work that clearly means a great deal to him, and with which (not necessarily the same thing) he is specially in tune.

The first act, with the lengthiness of its opening recitative (but the version in use at the Wells may differ from the adaptation by Gui) could strike modern ears as old-fashioned; the third is dramatically rather miscellaneous; but the second, taken by itself, gets nearly as close to the ideal of music-drama as *Pelléas* itself. And how entrancing are the felicities scattered throughout, those owing something to Gluck as well as the more specifically Mozartian ones—the little duet that breaks in during Ilia's 'Quando avran'; Idomeneo's 'Eccoci salvi' as he finds himself safe on shore, with its gracious recitative and the beauty of its orchestral accompaniment; the musical background as son is revealed to father and father to son; Ilia's aria 'Qual benigno influsso', with that ravishing figure in the orchestra, a figure that continues as Idomeneo comes on stage; Electra's 'Chi mai del mio provò', the most beautifully accompanied music of all (and here Rae Woodland surpassed herself in the purity of her high singing); the horns in 'Placido è il mar', and the effect of Electra's voice breaking in on the chorus; Ilia's heavenly 'Zefirette lusinghieri'; and the quartet, with its magical opening—one of those pieces, like Verdi's 'Bella figlia dell' amore' (but how much finer!), in which the musician takes charge and reveals, in a way no ordinary drama could ever do, the emotional interplay of his characters! And as a background to all this, the orchestral music—bound together into a quasi-symphonic whole by a number of short phrases, some repeated and all of a similar shape and colour—is instinct with an Elysian serenity that calms our hearts and minds and gives them peace.

§ 2

Covent Garden before 1915, apart from Verdi and Wagner, predominantly meant Puccini.

Destinn was at the heart of such pleasure (a highly qualified one) as he gave me, and so far as Destinn was concerned the pleasure was exquisite. Butterfly, all in all, was probably her finest role: I hear her in it now as I sit here, for among all the great singers I have heard she is one of the only two (Lotte Lehmann is the other) who can still bless me, lacking a score or even a libretto, with an exact memory of innumerable nuances in quality of voice and manner of vocalisation. I have already mentioned the miracle of her opening note in 'Un bel dì': but comparable beauties had preceded it, and many others were still to come. The first of them was like a starling before the spring: the soaring of her voice behind the scenes, high and pure above those of her companions, as they come up the breast of the hill for the love-duet that her music presages. I used to think of this all day long before every performance, and wait in quiet expectation, as I took my seat, for the moment to come. Then there was the urgency of her passion in 'Oh! Quanti occhi fissi', but of a passion controlled (and here she far excelled Callas) by such a masterly technique at the perfect service of so ample a voice that not a hint of any strain or distortion marred the beauty of her singing; there was the freshness, as of a gently running stream, that she brought to her share of the flower duet; and there was the sad tranquillity with which she read the inscription 'Morir con onore' on her father's sword. And still I have conveyed no impression (by picking and choosing I may even have conveyed the opposite) of how ravishingly she sang every phrase and every note.

Her other Puccini role (apart from Tosca) was that of Minnie in *La Fanciulla del West*, and I of course attended the British première on May 29th 1911, with Dinh Gilly as Jack Rance and Vanni Marcoux as Ashby. Dick Johnson (the names!) was taken at the first performance by Commendatore Bassi, the Sigfrido of our Florentine holiday: Wotan's grandson and the Californian bandit faring very similarly at his lusty hands, or rather throat. At the second performance he was replaced by Riccardo Martin, by no means to be confused with Martinelli, who was as much Martinelli as Riccardo probably wasn't Riccardo: one of those Italianate tenors, hard and loud, that a lot of people greatly admire, not as good as Jon Vickers but rather like him. I cannot remember how Destinn sang in the *Fanciulla*, perhaps because I heard it only twice. It bored me at a first hearing, and not only for the wretched little waltz tune that runs through it, worse than the Redemption by Love or even the Dance of the Veils; and it bored me at a second hearing so dreadfully that I was willing to forego the pleasure of hearing Destinn for the pleasure of not hearing *La Fanciulla*.

I was to hear Destinn in opera only once after 1914. When on my return from Singapore in 1919 I became engaged, a summer season, in the 'grand' tradition, was in full swing at Covent Garden, and Destinn was down to sing Aida. For some reason or other (I cannot imagine what it could have been, for I was out of a job) I'd have been unable to turn up early enough to get into the gallery; but I had hung about Floral Street a day or two before the performance, and little Harris, the barber-tobacconist, had promised to keep a balcony stall for me if I would tell him definitely one way or the other within twenty-four hours. I havered and havered: the price was not far short of all the money I had, but then this, after so many years, was Destinn in *Aida*: on the other hand I shied at the idea of a balcony stall. Once or twice, when taken by my father, I had sat in the amphitheatre, but the gallery was where I belonged. . . . An hour or so before I had to make my decision I was walking with the girl I should soon be marrying over the bridge in Kensington Gardens, and the sun was very bright and we had no hats on and had joined hands and were swinging them to and fro and must have looked as happy as we were feeling, when Her Majesty Queen Mary passed by in an open victoria with outriders, and, caught by the sight of us, waved a salute. Ruth had eagerly argued in favour of my taking that ticket, being for enjoyment, as she always has been, before money, however dubious the financial outlook might be: but I was still in two minds till Her Majesty lifted her hand. That decided me: it was as if she were commanding "Do as the girl says". Anyhow, I went. I did not in fact enjoy it very much: Destinn was a bit off colour and this distressed me; I liked the luxury of my surroundings as little as I had expected to; and my heart was elsewhere.

I was to have a second 'remote encounter' with Queen Mary in about 1946, which it is almost as pleasurable for me to recall as my Beethoven ones. I had been campaigning a whole year for permission to send food-parcels to starving Germany, when the Government, which had been obdurate, suddenly collapsed: my friend John Strachey, the Minister for Food, sent for me and said "Get on with it: I've told them that you're a sentimental old fool—I'm sure you won't mind—but that support for you is growing so rapidly that it's no longer safe to refuse." Safe, he meant, for Government stability. He explained that the whole thing would have to be run from my office: prospective donors would have to go there, sign forms and get tickets for presentation at a post-office. The scheme was announced to start the following Monday at nine. I gave instructions that they should telephone up to my room directly the first applicant arrived, for I wanted to see who it might be. At three minutes to nine I was given the signal and ran down. A small uniformed page-boy was sitting on the chair. "Who do you come from?" I asked. "Her Majesty Queen Mary," he replied. I rang up Marlborough House, and asked if I might tell the press. The official replied that he would ring back. When he did so he said something like this: "Her Majesty would not wish to interfere with your perfect liberty to do as you please. If however you would care to refrain, this would give Her Majesty special pleasure." None of which has anything more to do with music than the Hotel-Restaurant Kaiserhof had, but what matter? If I refrain from giving a photograph of Her Majesty, that is because everyone knows what she looked like already.

§ 3

Destinn was partnered in her Puccini performances by many exceptional tenors and baritones: Caruso, John McCormack, Martinelli, Anselmi, Dinh Gilly, Scotti and Sammarco among others. The last was specially fine in a number of roles. His voice was sweet and full, and he had that power and poise in his top register that is the thrilling mark of a really good operatic baritone, with its assurance that he will never let you down. But as Scarpia I preferred Scotti—preferred him indeed to any Scarpia I have ever seen. His voice was lighter than Sammarco's, though never without adequate strength; but what appealed to me most in his Scarpia was its distinction of singing and manner alike, whereas Sammarco was forthright and bourgeois. There are two opinions as to how Scarpia should play and sing (just as there are two opinions as to how Ochs should play and sing): some think he should play and sing like a 'gentleman', and some think he should play and sing like a sadistic brute, the more sadistic the better. I incline to the former opinion.

As to the *Bohèmes*, these were mainly Melba nights, with Caruso or John McCormack (or Martinelli towards the end) as the Rodolfos and Sammarco as the Marcel, Vanni Marcoux occasionally playing Colline. I never heard Bonci, thought by many the best Rodolfo of all, because of his sweetness and particularly charming lyricism.

§ 4

We heard many admirable Puccini performances at Covent Garden after the first world war, with such Butterflies as Rosetta Pampanini and Dusolina Giannini, and such Toscas as Göte Ljungberg, Rosa Raisa and Iva Pacetti: Gigli, in partnership with the last of these, sobbing 'E lucevan le stelle' most effectively. Then there was Elisabeth

Rethberg as Mimi with Ezio Pinza as Colline: and though Melba's Violetta had been greatly excelled by her Mimi, which requires a far narrower range of vocal expression, even so I much preferred Rethberg, with the hint of Destinn in her voice. As to Pinza's Colline, his bass had just that extra bit of warmth in it that the coat song demands. But of course the great Puccini event of those years was the Scala première of *Turandot* in 1926, followed by the British première at Covent Garden a year later, when Bianca Scacciati created the title-part, as she had done in Rome a few months earlier. Later in the same season we had Florence Easton; and the following year Eva Turner arrived, and annihilated the memory of her predecessors. Her clean powerful voice, with its cutting-edge as of icy steel and its ability to remain pure and true under every pressure, perfectly fitted her for the part and gave her the ultimate perfection in it of Destinn's Aida, Lotte Lehmann's Marschallin and Chaliapin's Boris. It is improbable that her Turandot will ever be equalled, certain that it will never be surpassed.

We also heard the Puccini operas often in Paris: a pleasant *Butterfly*, for instance, with Fanny Heldy as the heroine, and an eternally memorable *Tosca* at the Opéra-comique. This was at the end of 1946 or beginning of 1947, when Léon Blum was provisional Premier-President of the fourth French Republic. Travel allowances were ineptly minute, and this made me miserable for two reasons: first, because we couldn't afford the opera, and secondly because Rachel and Prudence Low, daughters of a very dear friend, were there, and we could not think how, with hardly the francs for a drink let alone a dinner, we could worthily entertain them. Then one day we were summoned to the Elysée for tea with the Premier's wife, who had heard we were in Paris and may have wanted to honour a participant, however minor, in the Popular Front. We were considerably elated, not so much by the honour as by the prospect, if the tea should be lavish enough, of saving the expense of a dinner. The tea was adequate, though rather disconcertingly interrupted, every now and again, by Madame Blum's milliner. And then the miracle happened: "Would you care," asked our hostess, "to have the presidential box for *Tosca* tomorrow night? I hear it is not too bad." Yes, we replied, we would care very much. We left immediately, took an expensive taxi to our hotel, telephoned expensively to the Low girls, and asked them, with Madame Blum's casualness, if they would care to come with us. They answered as we had answered Madame Blum.

Next evening, with the two girls in tow, we presented the ticket to one of those tall-hatted men in evening dress who sit high, or used to, on a rostrum near the entry to the Opéra-comique, looking rather like auctioneers, which is indeed what they probably are when off duty. He tore off the stub and waved me to a tall-hatted confrère at another rostrum. I felt slightly alarmed, for I suspected that something had gone wrong, and I hate any sort of contretemps: but I obeyed, and handed over the mutilated ticket. "—— francs", he ejaculated: I don't recall how many, but a stratospheric number. Now I was in a real panic. "But it's a gift," I began; and then "Don," I stammered out in my abominable French, "Don de Monsieur le Président." "Taxe," he replied, impatiently shrugging his shoulders. I paid, seeing our holiday at an end; and indeed we had to leave two days later, but not without having bought at a shop hardly a stone's-throw from the Elysée itself a piece of old English pottery at a third of its value.

When we arrived at the presidential box we found it oddly located: only one of us could see anything at all by direct vision, the rest having to sit with their backs to the stage and stare into a long mirror expressly provided for the purpose. My wife and I did the staring throughout, and the Low girls did it by turns. As to hearing as distinct from seeing, whoever had told Madame Blum that the performance wasn't too bad had misinformed her: there was quite a scene after 'Vittoria! Vittoria!', with the gallery hooting and whistling.

(This placing of the presidential box may have had its uses, as facilitating diplomatic conversation on gala nights: Rose Macaulay once told me that she was extremely musical, and always wrote to an accompaniment of good music on a wireless turned low, especially when she wanted to concentrate.)

§ 5

I have never greatly cared for anything by Puccini except *Bohème*. You can enjoy pretty music for its prettiness, sparkling music for its sparkle, witty music for its wit, and even sentimental music, provided you do not get too much of it, for its sentimentality. *Hänsel and Gretel*, for instance, is pretty; *Don Pasquale* is sparkling; a good deal of Rossini is witty and sparkling as well; *La Belle Hélène* is pretty, witty and sparkling, all three; and *Le Jongleur* is sentimental (and short). All these I enjoy. But for music to give a higher sort of pleasure, not to mention the highest, there must be an element of what the Hebrews called 'Hīn in it: an untranslatable word, but meaning something like grace in the religious sense, or an inwardness of which sacraments are the outer manifestations.[1] (Not but that there may be '*Hīn* in music that might otherwise be dismissed as affording the lower sort of pleasure only: there is '*Hīn* in the sentimental prettiness of Micaela's music and a great deal of it in the wit and sparkle of *Fledermaus*.) Now *Bohème* is all prettiness and sparkle and sentimentality—Callas revealed the full measure of its sparkle at a concert recently, when she sang Musetta's aria as no one else had ever sung it before—and is highly enjoyable as such; and there is a freshness and lack of pretentiousness in it that are very appealing. For this reason, it is one of those rare operas that I find as pleasurable, if on a sufficiently intimate scale, in a rougher as in a more polished performance, for all its associations with Caruso and Melba: I have greatly enjoyed it at the Opéra-comique (from an ordinary seat) and with Joan Cross—who sang, I hasten to add, anything but roughly—at Sadler's Wells. When given a 'big' performance, however, with 'big' singers of the second rank I find it intolerable.

But in what other Puccini operas are any of these qualities present in a really compelling degree? There is a good deal of prettiness, no doubt, in *Butterfly*, but of a rather sickly kind, so that one rapidly tires of it: the Ping Pang Pong music in *Turandot* is packed with musical wit: and there are tunes in *Manon Lescaut* that are more than pretty, are even rather beautiful. But except in *Bohème* these qualities are not pervasive enough for continuous pleasure of the lower sort: and, as to the higher, where, except in the *Tosca* sky-music, is it to be found? In *Turandot*, undoubtedly: but I have already had my say about that.

Why then, it may be asked, have I gone to these operas so often? For two reasons: first, because *Tosca*, *Bohème* and *Butterfly*, at any rate, are superb vehicles for vocal display, and secondly because Puccini was a rare musical dramatist.

(1) To take the first of my reasons: I can see the sort of person who 'cannot listen to' anything later than Bach, often identical with the person

[1] '*Hīn* can also connote charity of mind, and I may perhaps be excused for appending in this footnote the best 'Jewish' story I know, for it beautifully illustrates this derivative meaning. A Rabbi was one day taking a walk with his twelve-year-old son, deep in learned discourse, when he noticed that they had just passed a beggar exhibiting a placard with 'Blind' on it. "My boy," said the Rabbi, "we have just committed an *avarah* (sin). It is not incumbent to give charity unless you are actually asked to do so, though that is advisable too: but if you are asked and refrain, that is an *avarah*. So go back and give the man this coin." The boy did so. When he returned his father said, "Now you have committed another *avarah*. When you give charity you should always raise your hat, to show that you respect the man you're giving it to. So go back and raise your hat." "But father," the boy replied, "the man's blind: he couldn't have seen me." "How do you know," said the Rabbi, getting angry, "that he isn't an impostor? Go back at once and raise your hat."

who 'cannot look at' anything earlier than Picasso, raising his tedious
eyebrows. But why, if there is really any music in him? The human
voice, particularly a woman's, is not only the most beautiful of musical
instruments but the most beautiful of all things on earth and probably
in heaven: and unless the music is quite intolerably bad, as most of
Mascagni's and Leoncavallo's is but not Puccini's, a composer who writes
perfectly for the voice can be a means to the revelation of what in its
own kind must be called supreme beauty. 'Vissi d'arte' is, heaven knows,
nothing of a masterpiece: but I am grateful to Puccini for having written
it, if this was the best he could manage, for he allowed Destinn to give us,
in that miraculous change of register, a moment of rapture that blotted
out the world. 'Recondita armonia' and 'E lucevan le stelle' are specious
enough—almost as hollow underneath their bravura as Leoncavallo's
vulgarities: but how they enabled Caruso to thrill us with his amplitude
and power and McCormack with his sweetness, and both with the
perfection of their control and their beauty of phrasing!

(2) When I say that Puccini was a rare musical dramatist I do not of
course mean that he wrote music-drama of the highest kind or anything like it: apart from all other considerations, the quality of his
music would forbid such a judgement. But he had a remarkable sense of
theatre, and, purely as theatre, his operas are always satisfactory and
sometimes exciting. Now I like the theatre, and if I have said anything
that seems to gainsay this I have expressed myself badly. Most plays, I
think I said, strike me as dull and thin after the greater vividness of
opera. But there is something else: spoken plays, other than such
rubbishily delightful ones as thrillers and the best farces, are often hung
about for me with an air of artificiality that induces at best a mild
queasiness and at worst acute embarrassment. To many, to the overwhelming majority in fact, this must sound outrageously paradoxical:
they think of opera as artificial to the point of silliness, and the spoken
play as convincingly realistic. But no paradox is intended. Perhaps
because music is my own language, for all my inability to play or sing
or compose, it is opera that I find the more natural, and spoken plays
the less closely connected with the reality of life; and if I am to see a
play, a play without music, at all, then I prefer a poetic one, poetic in the
narrower sense. Poetry provides the nearest approach possible, after
music, to ultimate reality, is an 'imitation', μίμησις, of that reality:
by way of it we get a glimpse of the meaning behind daily existence:
but any attempt to take us beyond daily existence by imitating this
existence itself is doomed, otherwise than in the hands of a really great
dramatist with really great actors at his command, to almost certain

failure. And let me add the following. I have come to believe in my seventy-first year that while opera is the highest form of drama, the highest form of art in general is not opera but 'absolute' music, as being the supreme μίμησις of reality. There is a single opera, however, that challenges this supremacy, because the reality it 'imitates' is specifically seen as divine-human or human-divine: I mean *Fidelio*. And, on second thoughts, I should perhaps add *Die Zauberflöte*.

There is another point I want to clear up about the supposedly undramatic nature of opera as I knew it in my boyhood, and again in the twenties and thirties. Somewhere in 'The Operas of Mozart' (which may well have been published the morning after one of those great *Aida* performances) Dent says something like this: "Current international productions are concerts in costume, and nothing more." He was referring specifically to Mozart, and there he may have been right: I shall come to that presently. But I rather think that he was cocking a snook at Covent Garden in general, and if so he could not have been worse informed. There were cases to support him, no doubt, as was all but inevitable during the course of a long season: I can remember such cases myself. But as a generalisation the quip was quite out of order. Not only were the *Traviatas* and *Aidas*, the *Toscas* and *Otellos* (and later the *Tristans* and *Rosenkavaliers*) superb as sheer drama, but so were many smaller works too: I remember with special vividness a dramatically thrilling *Louise* other than the Saturday night one I've mentioned. The fact is that even apart from what were in effect carefully rehearsed repertory performances, like the *Rosenkavaliers*, many of these great artists had sung together all over the world: they knew one another, musically and dramatically, to a tee: and their immediate interaction, even if there had been little rehearsal, produced an all but perfect, and sometimes a quite perfect, ensemble, so that talk about "a bevy of international stars gathered hastily together" was in most cases nonsense. Moreover the music itself, interpreted by such artists, carried everything along, with the result that, even when a merely experienced conductor, not to say a great one, was in charge, the possibility of anything halting or undramatic in the general effect was inconsiderable.

It must also be remembered that intrusive applause, which can ruin the dramatic effect of any opera, was rapidly dying out at Covent Garden by the time I had become a regular opera-goer: this was not the least of our debts to Wagnerian seriousness. Most of us thought the practice an abominable one, for all that many composers had sanctioned and even encouraged it, and if people began applauding we quickly shut them up. But the nuisance is now back again more virulently than ever. When Joan Sutherland left the stage after one of her arias in *Puritani* the other night the storm of clapping and shouting went on so long without response that I thought "Good, she's going to show them; she's going to stay where she is and refuse to make a concert of it." But I was wrong: she came on at last, bowed, and then returned to where she belonged. If she was going to do it anyhow why on earth couldn't she have done it sooner? In the second or third act there was an even sillier episode. Elvira is supposed to be living high up in a castle, and sings one of her biggest arias at the top of a Zeffirelli staircase before departing to her room. Another tumult in the auditorium: another interminable wait: and then the diva pops out again, comes tripping down the stairs, and goes off on the ground floor to a part of the castle that I gathered (not that I gathered very much) she had nothing to do with. And not only the gallery but the fashion appeared to regard all this as more than excusable, as obligatory: when I tried very mildly to restrain my neighbour he stared at me as if he thought me an outsider. I became one before the next act.

§ 6

So much for Puccini. I feel about such other post-Verdian operas as I have seen—*Fedora*, *Andrea Chénier* and so on—as I feel about Puccini, only more so. We went to *Fedora* in 1926 mainly to hear Jeritza, but I remember nothing of this beautiful and elegant lady except her beauty and elegance. I do remember of her Tosca, however, that she sang 'Vissi d'arte', with enhanced applause at the close, lying more or less full length on the floor.

§ 7

Apart from summarily recording a few odds and ends—the premières of *Il Segreto di Susanna*, *I Giojelli della Madonna* and *Tiefland*, and of three other operas which are as if they had never been, by the composers Leroux, Camussi and von Westerhausen respectively —I have nothing further to say of pre-1915 Covent Garden, except a word or two about Gounod's *Faust*.

This is a delightful work: the sprightly or flowing melodies are beautifully clean and fresh, with nothing about them to bore or satiate. It is French in the best sense, far superior to anything by Puccini except *Bohème* and *Turandot*; and its neglect nowadays is hard to account for, particularly as it is full of opportunities for the kind of good singing still available, the jewel-song perhaps excepted. People think of it as banal and lowbrow, but this was not always the case: Dickens wrote of it from Paris "It perfectly delighted me, but I think it requires too much of the audience to do for a London opera-house". There is another passage in Dickens that should make people understand what music-drama can be:

"Last night I saw Madame Viardot do Gluck's *Orphée*," he wrote to John Foster, also from Paris, in 1862. "It is a most extraordinary performance—pathetic in the highest degree, and full of quite sublime acting. Though it is unapproachably fine from first to last, the beginning of it, at the tomb of Eurydice, is a thing that I cannot remember at this moment of writing without emotion. It is the finest presentation of grief that I can imagine. And when she has received hope from the Gods, and encouragement to go into the other world and seek Eurydice, Viardot's manner of taking the relinquished lyre from the tomb and becoming radiant again is most noble. Also she recognizes Eurydice's touch, when at length the hand is put in hers from behind, like a most transcendant genius. And when, yielding to Eurydice's entreaties, she has turned round and slain her with a look, her despair over the body is grand in the extreme. It is worth a journey to Paris to see, for there is no such Art to be otherwise looked upon. Her husband stumbled over me by mere chance, and took me to her dressing-room. Nothing could have happened better as a genuine homage to the performance, for I was disfigured with crying."

Another great admirer of *Faust* was Arnold Bennett, who had excellent taste in music, and was often to be seen at Covent Garden during the twenties and thirties, particularly on Melchior nights. He had edited and titled the Ufa film, based on Goethe's play, for its English version, and turned up at the Albert Hall for the opening night in 1927. The event had been anticipated with a good deal of excitement, Yvette Guilbert and Emil Jannings being in the cast: for my own part I wanted to hear Sir Landon Ronald's score, for he had based it on a mixture of Gounod and Boïto, and I thought the conjuncture might be revealing. But when I arrived I found the position hopeless: a crowd was milling around the entrance, unable to get in. I was just about to go home, greatly disappointed, when Arnold Bennett was kind enough to recognize me from the other side of the big glass doors and to beckon me in. As we sat in his box he kept whispering to me, as the Gounod melodies turned up, how good the man was: but owing to the familiar hiatus in his speech it was often Boïto that he appeared to be praising. I should like to add that he was one of the kindest men I have ever known.

CHAPTER XII

Tʜᴇʀᴇ ᴡᴇʀᴇ ᴛᴡᴏ special seasons elsewhere than at Covent Garden (apart from those mentioned already, like the Beecham and Brema ones) in my gallery days: the first of them rather sordid, the second of overwhelming splendour. The first was at the London Opera House in 1911 and 1912: the second at Drury Lane in 1913.

§ 1

The London Opera House in Kingsway, afterwards the Stoll Cinema and now offices, was built by Oscar Hammerstein the First after he had sold his New York interests to the Metropolitan, with a pledge that he would give no more opera in the United States for ten years. It was a cold, harsh building, repulsive as an opera-house to anyone who knew Covent Garden; and its spiritual rawness, as against Covent Garden's richness in tradition, made us sniff at it from the start. Our relation to Covent Garden, it must be remembered, was a highly personal one: we felt jealous for her, and not unreasonably, for her endorsement or rejection could still at this time make all the difference to a singer's career. Even the Scala was no more for us than the first of other opera-houses, with Vienna the second: to the Met we gave hardly a thought. We were critical even of changes at Covent Garden itself: I was distressed when the old curtain was replaced by a brighter one—curtains mean so much in an opera-house, they are mediators between the ordinary shadow-world and the real one on the stage—and angry when so many of the boxes disappeared, for an opera-house should look as if, apart from gallery and stalls, it consists of nothing but boxes: that is part of its historic charm, a charm still retained, in this respect, by the Fenice and other opera-houses abroad. As bad was the disappearance of the horseshoe,[1] for it was by the

[1] In the Covent Garden of those days there was a broad passage between the stalls and the ground-floor boxes on either side, and between the last stall and the ground-floor boxes at the back. There was also an additional row of seats hard up against the boxes at the back: and these might be extended down either side of the house on a crowded night to form a horseshoe with arms of varying length. See diagram opposite.

number of seats in it that we used to estimate the size of the audience as soon as we arrived in the gallery. Nor is it true that people can get used to anything: I always have the feeling nowadays that there is something a little wrong with Covent Garden—that she is too fresh, lacks atmosphere, looks like what any ordinary theatre might be expected to look like. I console myself by examining those fabulous programmes that line the semi-circular promenade beyond the entrance, and I particularly enjoy the gala ones on silk: though a programme of any kind, if old enough and particularly if lettered in the Victorian or Edwardian mode, gives me intense satisfaction.

(My few remaining political intimates will be shaking their heads and wondering whether I have become a Tory. No: I am a traditionalist in things that do not ultimately matter, such as the look of an opera-house, a Jacobin in those that do.)

Anyhow, the London Opera House *was* bleak and cold, and the performances far from pleasing. Only two of the artists had names that were known to me, Maurice Renaud, an exceptional baritone, and Lina Cavalieri, a woman of great beauty, who had sung as a girl at café-concerts. I heard her as Giulietta in *Tales of Hoffmann*, and a few days later went to hear her again, this time as Salome in Massenet's *Hérodiade*, for she was very beautiful. There was also a contralto, Marguérite d'Alvarez, who made an immediate hit, and deservedly, as Herodias. Others may have sung finely: I do not remember. But the performances as a whole were of a crudity that did more than distress me, it troubled my artistic conscience; for it made me wonder whether the people who found opera ridiculous might not be right after all. (I was often worried at this time by the suspicion that a day might arrive when I should find opera artistically indefensible and should have to forego it altogether; and when my cousin Arthur Friedlander, a

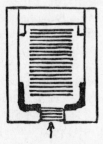 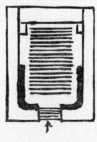 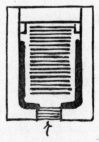

| The Horseshoe on a 'fair' night | The Horseshoe on a 'big' night | The Horseshoe on a 'very big' night |

musician devoted to Bach, made fun of my enthusiasm for it I felt outcast and desolate.)

Only a vague impression of that season remains with me, but the general picture I see is of people advancing to the footlights for the finish of their arias and flinging up their arms and gazing raptly aloft, as if to enquire, in the split second that must elapse between the culminating shriek and the applause, "Now what did you think of that?" There were even encores. In other words, ensemble was non-existent: these really were the concerts in costume Edward Dent was to complain of, and inferior ones at that.

Noise for its own sake, because quality is lacking; a combination of the second-rate with the gaudily pretentious: this can make opera almost detestable, and that is my impression of what Hammerstein gave us, in spite of a certain amount of fine singing. And I got the idea that this was the American way, so that when I went to the United States in 1948 for the first of many visits I was reluctant to visit the Met, though I knew that their array of fine singers was unrivalled. I soon discovered my mistake.

Not that I have heard much music of any kind in New York—business harries me there too insistently. But two performances stand out. One was of the Choral Symphony conducted at Carnegie Hall by Toscanini on his eightieth birthday in aid of a cancer research fund. It was the most moving performance of the work I had heard up to then or have heard since. Something in the way Toscanini drew the music out of his orchestra made it sound as if it were coming not so much from his players but, as a kind of emanation, from the hall itself and so from the world outside and the sum of things. The other event was of a different kind. We had gone to hear *Four Saints in Three Acts*, described however as in four acts and labelled 'an opera to be sung'. The libretto, if that is the word for it, is by Gertrude Stein and the music by Virgil Thomson. The cast was a Negro one. People came on, sang "And Saint Ignatius, Saint Ignatius" or "And Saint Teresa, Saint Teresa", and went off again. But I never discovered whether it was meant to be funny or serious in a very modern way or both. I managed to behave myself till towards the end of the first act, but then failed to stifle a guffaw. A few people took it up, but comparatively little damage was done, as the curtain fell almost immediately. After an interval that sobered me—I drank a couple of those lemonades they provide for you in flimsy containers, with no alternative—we took our places: and then, just before the curtain went up, the place started rocking with laughter, and this continued

SIR JOSEPH BEECHAM'S SEASON
OF
RUSSIAN OPERA AND BALLET
(Organised by M. SERGE DE DIAGHILEW)

OPENING PERFORMANCE OF SEASON
To-night, Tuesday, June 24th, at 7.45
FIRST PRODUCTION IN ENGLAND OF

BORIS GODOUNOV

Music Drama in Three Acts and Seven Tableaux
(after Pouchkine and Karamzine)

BY

M. P. MOUSSORGSKY

CAST

Boris	...	M. CHALIAPINE
Fedor (his son)	...	Mlle. DAWIDOWA
Xenia (his daughter)	...	Mlle. BRIAN
A Nurse	...	Mme. E. PETRENKO
Prince Chuisky	...	M. NICOLAS ANDREEW
Pimene (an old monk)	...	M. PAUL ANDREEW
Grigori (a young monk, afterwards the false Dmitri)	...	M. DAMAEW
The Hostess of the Inn	...	Mme. PETRENKO
Varlaam ⎱ Monks	...	M. BELIANIN
Missail ⎰		M. BOLCHAKOW
An Idiot Boy	...	M. ALEXANDROWITCH
Chelkalow (a Noble of the Duma)		M. DOGONADSE
A Commissary	...	M. ZAPOROJETZ
A Noble	...	M. ALEXANDROWITCH
Two Jesuits	...	⎰ M. SEMENOW
	...	⎱ M. STROBINDER

Nobles, Populace, Soldiers.

Conductor ... M. EMILE COOPER

Opera produced by M. ALEXANDRE SANINE
General Stage Director, M. P. STROBINDER.
Chorus of the Imperial Opera House of St. Petersburg, under
the Direction of M. D. POKHITÓNOW.
Stage Manager, M. O. ALLEGRI.

SIR JOSEPH BEECHAM'S GRAND SEASON
OF
RUSSIAN OPERA and BALLET
(GENERAL MANAGER · · DONALD BAYLIS)

LAST PERFORMANCES
To-night at 7.30
LA KHOVANTCHINA
Music Drama in Three Acts and Four Tableaux
BY
M. P. MOUSSORGSKY
Orchestration by RIMSKY-KORSAKOV
CAST

Dositheus (Chief of the Old Believers)	M. CHALIAPINE
Prince Ivan Khovansky (Chief of the Streltsy)	M. PETROV
Prince Andrew Khovansky (his son)	M. ROJDESTVENSKY
Chaklovity (a Nobleman)	M. PAUL ANDREEV
Marfa (a young mystic, one of the Old Believers)	Mme. PETRENKO
The Scribe	M. NICOLAS ANDREEV
Emma	Mlle. BRIAN
Varsonofiev (follower of Khovansky)	M. BELIANIN
Kouska (a Streltsy)	M. ERNST
Three Streltsy	{ M. BELIANIN / M. VARFOLOMEIEV / M. GOULIAEV
Suzanne, an Old Believer	Mlle. NICOLAEWA

The Persian Dance in Tableau III. composed and arranged
by M. ADOLF BOLM

Mlles. TCHERNICHEVA, KOPYCINSKA, FOKINA II., WASSILEVSKA,
GOULIOUK, MAJCHERSKA, MUNINGS, PFLANZ, KONIETSKA,
BARANOVITCH, LARIONOVA, HOKHLOVA, RAZUMOWICZ, DOMBROV-
SKA, DORIS, JEZERSKA.

Conductor - M. EMILE COOPER

Opera produced by M. ALEXANDRE SANINE.

Stage Manager, M. CHARLES WALTZ

Assistant Stage Manager, M. P. STROBINDER

CHORUS OF THE IMPERIAL OPERA HOUSE, MOSCOW.

Scenery and Accessories by THEODORE FEDOROVSKY

Costumes by THEODORE FEDOROVSKY, executed by MAISON
TALDYKINE of Moscow.

Chief Costumier M. NEMENSKY.   Wigs by F. GRIGORIEFF

till we slunk away. I still wonder whether the fourth act really existed, or whether a muddle had occurred between Saints and Acts.

Why did I keep on going to the London Opera House (for half a dozen performances or so) after experiencing what it was like? Because I wanted to hear some Massenet—and quite enjoyed, in a queasy sort of way, the Fugitive Visions and Meditations and other mawkishnesses; because I was insatiable for Verdi, and *Traviata* was in the repertoire; and because I had heard *Louise* less often than I should have liked and wanted to know it better. Or say simply that I could hardly ever keep away in those days from opera of any kind.

There was a rarity, even maybe a *hapax legomenon*, at one of those Hammerstein seasons, namely *The Children of Don*. This was a 'Cymric Music Drama in Three Acts and a Prologue', by someone described on the programme as 'T. E. Ellis', who turned out to be Lord Howard de Walden, and with music by Josef Holbrooke, whom we knew already from his 'Three Blind Mice', often played at the proms. Arthur Nikisch conducted, perhaps because Holbrooke had a considerable reputation in Germany. The work was very Wagnerian: there were gods and mortals in it, with names like Nodens, Lyd, Math and Gwydion (and Gwion and Goewin and Govannion, which was very confusing): and the cast also included a Sacrifice and a Demon.

§ 2

If the Hammerstein place was not far from hell, Drury Lane in the summer of 1913 was the seventh heaven. The Russian opera season opened there on June 24th, with Chaliapin as Boris.

Excitement had been steadily rising, ever since the first rumour of what the astonishing Beecham now intended had got about. Even the backwoodsmen had heard of Chaliapin, but hardly anyone had heard him: so this was the sort of event a first visit by Sarah Bernhardt might have been, and attendance was compulsory unless you wanted to be left out in the unfashionable cold. But it was also a musical event of rare importance: a question not only of Chaliapin, though rumour had it that he really was superb, but, quite as much, of *Boris*, which although already famous (it had been produced in Paris and at the Scala a few years before) was unknown to London. As a result, the sense of anticipation in the gallery that night was keener than at any performance I had ever attended, the première of *Elektra* not excepted. And the unusual surroundings somehow gave a special flavour to the atmosphere: everything was new and strange after Covent Garden, and I retain the curious impression of having felt myself unfamiliar with myself, of experiencing myself as shut up in that gallery with a mass of excited aliens, awaiting, as one of them, a wonderful but rather outlandish experience.

And it truly was wonderful. Production! Yes, this was production, with every detail at the faithful service of the musical-dramatic genius of the work. Nothing could have been more lavish, more blazingly rich with imperial colour, more exotically costumed; yet you never got the impression that the tiniest fleck of paint was extraneous, the merest scarf out of place. As to the choral singing, by the chorus of the Petersburg Opera, I was to hear nothing like it until a day, three or four years ago, when I happened to be twiddling with the wireless in the hope of hitting on something worth while. Suddenly a chorus came through, so beautiful that I caught my breath. They turned out to be singing in a Bayreuth performance of *Lohengrin*, and while nothing could have been more different in point of music or style they reminded me, after so many years, of the choral singing in *Boris*. They had been trained by the Wilhelm Pitz who afterwards created the Philharmonia Choir for Walter Legge.

As to Chaliapin himself, that walk of his across the stage on his entry —"and surely never lighted on this orb, which he hardly seemed to touch"—at once marked him as one of the great actors of this or maybe any time, as great in his way as Callas is in hers. You might perhaps have thought that it was not acting at all but superb natural dignity, had it not been for the scene with the chiming clocks, and for the death scene at the close.

(In case anyone should be puzzled by "and surely never lighted on this orb" etcetera, it is a quotation, with the necessary change of gender, from the greatest passage of English prose in the rhetorical style that is known to me, namely the reference to Marie Antoinette in 'Reflections on the Revolution in France' by Edmund Burke: "It is sixteen or seventeen years since I saw the queen of France, then the dauphiness, at Versailles, and surely never lighted on this orb, which she hardly seemed to touch, a more delightful vision. . . . I thought ten thousand swords must have leaped from their scabbards to avenge even a look that threatened her with insult. But the age of chivalry is gone. That of sophisters, economists and calculators has succeeded it, and the glory of Europe is extinguished for ever." The passage is always in my mind on appropriate occasions, for to recite it with as much inflation as possible was one of the tricks I used to amuse my young children with at Saturday lunch, as an extra after an 'exhibition': which consisted of climbing on a chair and letting a thread of treacle descend as precariously as I could on to the pudding below, with a lot of gurgling and giggling if I missed. All of which was a far cry from my father's exposition at Sabbath lunch of why Edouard de Reszke was far superior to Jean, and Plançon to Caruso.)

That passage from the *Reflections* really does describe exactly how Chaliapin walked across the stage in *Boris*, though it omits something: there was a legato about his gait, as if he were moulding, by nature rather than by art, a beautiful phrase.

I have written of Chaliapin's acting first because his voice is less easily describable, and can anyhow be heard on the gramophone. I have been trying to think of some image that could evoke it, but with little success. The smell of burning logs in the distance; of wood violets; of earth after an April shower: there was something of all these in his singing, and something too of the look of a flame rising high and steady but with a little smoke about it. Or think of autumn at its gravest and most beautiful; of words deep with compassion; of Casals' cello—that above everything: for Chaliapin had all the qualities of a great singer and something extra as well, something I have found, among musical executants, in Chaliapin's singing and Casals' playing almost alone. Take a number of great singers of a particular class—tenors or basses, contraltos or sopranos—and you will probably find that differences within the class are analysable into differences of power, range, feeling for a phrase and so on. You cannot explain Chaliapin by such an analysis. Some unanalysable residue in his voice and way of singing made him unique.

But the glory of that season and the following one did not end with *Boris*. We had *Khovantchina*, with Chaliapin: we had *Prince Igor*, again with Chaliapin (doubling the roles of Galitsky and Konchak) and, for additional splendour, a corps de ballet in the Polovstian dances headed by Tchernicheva and Bolm, whose great leap to the footlights chimed so perfectly with the leap of the music that you could hardly tell one from the other: we had Stravinsky's *Le Rossignol* and Richard Strauss' *The Legend of Joseph*. And we had the Russian Ballet, not only as an integral part of some of the operas but all by itself too. I shall say little of the Russian Ballet in this memoir, contenting myself with a bare mention of some illustrious names, in addition to those of Bolm and Tchernicheva: Karsavina, Cechetti, Nijinsky, Fokine; with an extra word of homage for Anna Pavlova, whom, dancing with her own company, I admired most of all (I was specially excited by her performance with Michael Mordkin in the Glazounov Bacchanale, and was one of those who stood all afternoon at the London Opera House on Tuesday October 7th 1913 to bid her farewell). And if I leave it at that, this is because what mattered to me, far more than the most exquisite dancing, was the music, for which the choreography and décor seemed no more, to my happy ears, than a beautiful excuse. I think particularly of *Pétrouchka* and *L'Oiseau de Feu*. I loved them immediately and have loved Stravinsky's music, with few reservations, in all its subsequent phases: for its sharp cleanliness, its rhythmic piquancy and vigour, its economy, its strength, and its great tonal and melodic beauty, sometimes of a very subtle kind. I do not think of him as musically Russian, for he is universal: but if I did, I should call him my favourite Russian composer.

We were to hear Chaliapin several times again between the wars. He sang *Don Basilio* at Covent Garden in 1926: and in the crescendo of *La Calunnia* managed to suggest the oiliest malice without the smallest sacrifice of tonal beauty. The same year he sang *Mefistofele*, also at Covent Garden, and two new roles at the Albert Hall, in concert productions organised by C. B. Cochran: Salieri in *Mozart and Salieri* and Varlaam in some scenes from *Boris*. What a range—a musician, a Tzar, a coarse buffoon, and a sophisticated scoundrel! In 1928 he was back at Covent Garden, singing Boris again. Then, in 1931, Beecham (who in the meantime had been Conductor-in-Chief of the Philharmonic and of the Hallé and London Symphony Orchestras, had founded a municipal orchestra in Birmingham, and, through the Beecham Opera Company, had produced such novelties as the Puccini *trittico*, Bizet's *The Fair Maid of Perth* and Ethel Smyth's *The Boatswain's Mate*) took the Lyceum Theatre for the 'Opéra Russe à Paris', an enterprise of Zeretelli and de Basil. Chaliapin sang Boris and Prince Igor, and we were back in a less resplendent Drury Lane.

We were always seeking him out at this time. It must have been about 1933 that we went specially to Paris, for he had been billed there to sing Boris, and we were anxious to hear him yet again in the finest of his roles. When we got to the Opera—in *tenue de soirée*, which was still, if I remember rightly, *de rigueur*, or at any rate customary, on nights like that for the seats we had booked—we found ugly strips, with the word *remis* on them, posted askew all over the playbills. On enquiring at the box office, to which we had eventually pushed our way, we were told that Monsieur Chaliapin was triflingly indisposed, and

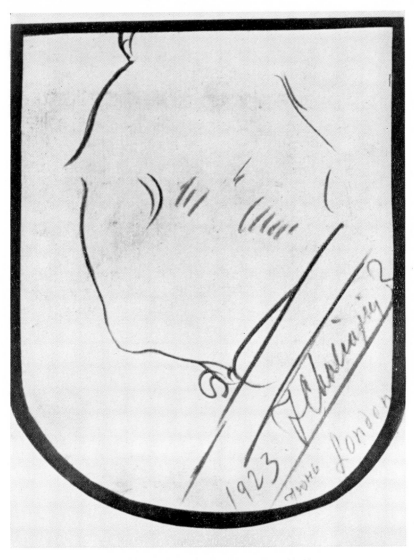

DRAWING OF HIMSELF BY CHALIAPIN

SKETCH OF VARLAAM BY CHALIAPIN

that our tickets would be valid for . . . . (about a fortnight thence), when the performance would surely take place. So we went off to Florence, which seemed nearer than London—there were no aeroplanes then, and my wife is an indifferent sailor—, and returned on the due date. Again we dressed, and I was irritated, as we got out of our taxi, to find that the strips were still there: typical French cheese-paring! But a crowd was again milling around, and it didn't look the right sort of crowd, a crowd anxious to get in and be seated with the minimum of delay: part of it was moving in the wrong direction. So I rushed up the steps, to find that the strips were in fact new ones, pasted across new play-bills with a new date on them. Chaliapin, a man as *large* in private intercourse as anyone I have known, was a notorious disappointer.

A year or so earlier I had published his autobiography 'Man and Mask', and he had allowed me on several occasions to give him lunch at the Savoy. I frequent the place, as most journalists appear to know; and I have always believed that the special deference I receive there is due, not to my lavish expenditure on authors or (if they virtually compel it) literary agents, but to the gossip of elderly waiters about Chaliapin and me. The autobiography was not a success. There is a good deal of misinformation about publishing finance, so I shall give the figures, which I got from my counting-house this morning. We paid Chaliapin an advance against royalties of £500, equivalent now to about five times as much; and by an iniquitous tradition, fostered by literary agents, an author is not obliged to refund any such part of his advance against royalties as his book may have failed to earn, the only one who has ever done so, *faisant le gentil*, being Rose Macaulay, a great lady for all her musical barbarism. We printed 3,000 copies: sold, after lavish advertising, 1,338: remaindered the balance for a few pence two years later: and should have lost heavily anyhow—even apart, that is, from the unearned sum of £349 12s. 3d. that remained with Chaliapin. The fact that the book was a rather bad one is irrelevant, or, if relevant, then relevant in the opposite direction. However, I shall continue to publish books about music: notwithstanding that, unless they are narrowly educational, the demand for them is as wretched as it has ever been. Only two out of the many on my list have sold decently, Henry Wood's 'My Life of Music' and 'The Musical Companion'; and though the Bacharach volume has long been a major 'best-seller', Wood's autobiography had reached a figure years after publication far lower than that achieved the first month by several specimens of the high-brow pornography so fashionable today.

We have heard several Borises since 1914, including Vanni Marcoux,

Silveri, Christoff and Ronald Stear (in the English production at
Sadler's Wells in 1935). Of these I have liked Vanni Marcoux best (in
Paris in 1922); for the union of darkness and a ringing tone in his bass,
and the natural dignity of his bearing, equipped him so pre-eminently
for the role of Boris that anyone who had never heard Chaliapin would
have written him down as its ideal interpreter. Christoff, too, was
superb in his way, but time somehow diminishes a little the impression
he made of vocal and dramatic grandeur. It does the opposite in
Chaliapin's case. His Boris has never really been approached: it remains,
with van Rooy's Wotan, Destinn's Aida, Lotte Lehmann's Marschallin, Frida Leider's Isolde and Callas' Norma, one of the supreme
operatic achievements of our time.

CHAPTER XIII

EVERY WRITER MUST have experienced hours or days when he has found himself unable to get on with the work in hand. It is not a question of a 'block', as people sometimes call it: rather the reverse. The fact is that one is on the threshold of something crucial or particularly precious, and that, anxious to do as well with it as possible, one hesitates to take the plunge.

I have been feeling this the last day or two, for the present chapter will be about Salzburg (and Mozart and *Die Meistersinger*), the flower of the precious seed my father planted in me when he took me to *Traviata* fifty-six years ago; and I tremble at the thought—I really do inwardly tremble, though with happy anticipation as well—that I may knock the bloom off it.

§ 1

Our first Salzburg year was 1930, and we went every subsequent year till, and including, 1936. I shall defer anything about the programmes till a little later, for I want to begin with more general memories.

Newest, most freshly delightful to us was the regular conjunction of music with those meals in the open air—or, if the open air has been impossible, by a window overlooking a pleasant expanse—that have been such a happiness to me all my life. I think of the restaurant on top of Danieli's, with tinges of green creeping over the water after the flaming of San Giorgio at sunset; of Valadier on the Pincio, with St. Peter's and half Rome in the distance—one Christmas, the time we heard the *pifferari*, it was so hot we had to move into the shade; and, better even than these, of lunch in the window of the Savoy on a blazing summer day, with the Festival Hall over in the distance beyond the leafy Embankment. (And yet the happiest of the Savoy ones was on a first day of spring, which happened to be my birthday. Two American friends sat in the sun there with Ruth and Livia and me: we had smoked salmon, asparagus from Lauris and strawberries from California, and drank champagne with the asparagus and Château Yquem with the strawberries and cream.) Then there were lunches at Ledoyen, with the chestnut-trees in blossom, and petrol smelling faintly, and the cars, smooth and muted, on their way to the Etoile or the Place de la Concorde; and a special sort of cheese, capped with cinnamon, that we eat one July afternoon at a window with another sort of prospect, the courtyard of the Hôtel de la Poste at Avallon. Only last year we had gone to see the Villa Mediciana, which we had never heard of, on top of a hill near Florence, and found to our pleasure that the old stables had been converted into an informal restaurant run by the gardener and his wife. There was no menu: we were just asked whether we would have the chicken or the veal. The woman insisted that it would be too hot in the open, but we laughed at this and lunched wonderfully at a little table outside for almost nothing. I fear, however, that the place will become fashionable: when we went a second time an English-speaking party had taken possession of the little restaurant upstairs, equipped with their own hampers and champagne.

But such occasions have been, and are, unconnected with music: at Salzburg they were all mixed up with it. During our whole seven years there we could not have lunched, dined or supped more than a dozen times or so indoors, and there was always music just before or just after our meals. We would lunch either on the terrace of the Österreichischer Hof or at a little inn near Aigen. In the earlier days, that is before the Toscanini time (when fashion deserted Estoril and irrupted into Salzburg), you could get an admirable *Suppe mit Huhn* at the Österreichischer Hof for an Austrian schilling, or possibly two, that is to say for about sevenpence or double: not *Huhnsuppe*, which is chicken soup, but *Suppe mit Huhn*, which is soup with a great piece of chicken in it, quite enough for an ample meal in itself. But we preferred the inn. This was fifteen minutes or so by car from Salzburg: an unpretentious little place, with an old-fashioned umbrella-stand in the vestibule. But it was not an ordinary inn: across the road it had an orchard, and there, also for a schilling or so, we used to lunch under the apples, or, a little deeper in, under the plums. Bruno Walter was often at a neighbouring table.

And then for dinner, or more usually supper, there was the Mirabell. It was at this end—at the end opposite the Schloss—of the Mirabell Gardens, and to the left of them; and its own garden (no one would have dreamed of dining or supping indoors except on dripping nights, which were rarities) was part of the larger one. Kasznár, the Hungarian proprietor, ran the place much as Mr. Abel used to run the Ivy: slowly perambulating the tables, he would nod to and even take a cup of coffee with the customers he preferred, and raise his eyebrows as he passed those he thought less of. The head waiter, who looked rather like Gobbi in the less sinister moments of *Tosca*, was in the habit of suggesting, with a hopeful inflexion, either paprika chicken or what he called paprika gooze: and he usually carried me with him, for I am ancestrally addicted to the *Salzgurken* that accompanies such dishes. (This is something very hard to get at English restaurants, even at the Savoy, though immediately obtainable in Soho or at any delicatessen; and if you do get it what they bring you, as often as not, is a mingy little affair, with none of the rich liquidity to it that is its whole meaning. The fact is that the English have never understood cucumbers, nor apparently the Italians either: I have been trying for years to make successive Pietros at the Savoy Grill prepare the things properly, but though they promise they never perform. For a good salad the slices have to be sprinkled with salt, left to lie for a couple of hours and then be drained: the result is as different from the hard ungracious stuff you usually get as an egg to your tea is from an egg at breakfast.)

The Mirabell is associated for me with one of those magical visitations, as Shelley called them, that occur, if they occur at all, but once or twice in a lifetime. This was in 1932. Sigle, my favourite Lynd, daughter of Robert and Sylvia, was staying with us, and among others in Salzburg were Robert Nichols the poet and Stella Churchill, a Jungian psychiatrist whom I greatly loved and who greatly loved me, until she quarrelled with me years later because she thought me wrong for not hating the Germans. I had arranged a supper party for the five of us one evening in Kasznár's garden after the performance, and had taken special pains with the menu, conferring with Kasznár himself, and inducing him to grant us a very special wine that I knew he possessed, Imperial Tokay he alleged, to sip with our sweet. The weather turned out to be almost tropically breathless, of the kind I had known in Singapore, and everyone had been more than usually happy all day: so that when we arrived at Kasznár's we were in tune with grace. Just as we had taken our places Bruno Walter, who had been conducting, came in, and I got up and went over to greet him. I do not remember for sure what he had been conducting, but it was almost certainly Mahler and probably *Das Lied von der Erde*, for it was this that he began talking about with the quiet homage he always accorded his master, and a look on his face as of a man seeing visions. He went on and on, standing there in his battered old raincoat, and people gradually got up and surrounded him, with Kasznár hovering about the empty tables; and such a paean of praise and devotion came singing from him

—from musician to musician, from friend to friend—that time, and what divides human beings, were annihilated. Then we all went back to our places and had supper.

I can best describe what happened as we sat there in the words of Shelley himself:

"We are aware of evanescent visitations of thought and feeling, sometimes associated with place or person, sometimes regarding our own mind alone, and always arising unforeseen and departing unbidden, but elevating and delightful beyond all expression: so that even in the desire and regret they leave, there cannot but be pleasure, participating as it does in the nature of its object. It is as it were the interpenetration of a diviner nature through our own; but its footsteps are like those of a wind over the sea, which the coming calm erases, and whose traces remain only, as on the wrinkled sand which paves it. These and corresponding conditions of being are experienced principally by those of the most delicate sensibility and the most enlarged imagination; and the state of mind produced by them is at war with every base desire. The enthusiasm of virtue, love, patriotism, and friendship is essentially linked with such emotions; and whilst they last, self appears as what it is, an atom to a universe."

And there is a passage in Swedenborg's description of Unity in the dwelling-place of the Beatified:

"Heaven is so full of delight that, viewed in itself, it is nothing but blessedness and delight: for the Divine Good proceeding from the Lord's Divine Love constitutes heaven both in general and in particular with every one there; and Divine Love consists in desiring that all may be saved and made happy from their inmost being and in full perfection. So that it amounts to the same thing whether you say heaven or heavenly joy. . . .

"How great the delight of heaven is, may be seen from this fact alone, that it is delightful to all in heaven to share their delights and blessings with others; and since all in heaven are of this character, it is plain how immense is the delight of heaven; for in the heavens there is a participation of all with each and each with all. Such community of life results from the two heavenly loves which, as was said, are love to the Lord and to the neighbour, and it is the nature of these loves to communicate their delight to others. Love to the Lord is of this character because the Lord's love is the love of communicating all that He has to all mankind, for He desires the happiness of all. There is a similar love in every one who loves Him, because the Lord is in them; and so the angels share their delights with one another. That love to the neighbour is of a similar character will be seen in what follows. It is evident, therefore, that it is the nature of these loves to share their delights with others. . . ."

I ought to add that I think all five of us except my wife and myself were technically atheists.

Next morning we all got presents from Robert Nichols. Each of the girls got a rose: I got a copy of the paper-back I had published at Benn's. The writing on the front, which has become rather faint, is as follows: "To V.G. remembering his party Aug 16th 1932, Salzburg. 'Hush! hath not the world now become perfect? What hath happened to me?' Zarathustra. Noontide. Book IV (which is for the Initiates)." The passage from Nietzsche runs like this:

"And Zarathustra ran and ran, but he found no one else, and was alone and ever found himself again; he enjoyed and quaffed his solitude and thought of good things—for hours. About the hour of noontide, however, when the sun stood exactly over Zarathustra's head, he passed an old, bent and gnarled tree, which was encircled round by the ardent love of a vine, and hidden from itself; from this there hung yellow grapes in abundance, confronting the wanderer. Then he felt inclined to quench a little thirst, and to break off for himself a cluster of grapes. When, however, he had already his arm outstretched for that purpose, he felt still more inclined for something else—namely, to lie down beside the tree at the hour of perfect noontide and sleep.

"This Zarathustra did; and no sooner had he laid himself on the ground in the stillness and secrecy of the variegated grass, than he had forgotten his little thirst, and fell asleep. For as the proverb of Zarathustra saith: 'One thing is more necessary than the other'. Only that his eyes remained open—for they never grew weary of viewing and admiring the tree and the love of the vine. In falling asleep, however, Zarathustra spake thus to his heart: 'Hush! Hush! Hath not the world now become perfect? What hath happened unto me? . . .

"'O happiness! O happiness! Wilt thou perhaps sing, O my soul! Thou liest in the grass. But this is the secret, solemn hour, when no shepherd playeth his pipe.

"'Take care! Hot noontide sleepeth on the fields. Do not sing! Hush! The world is perfect. . . .

"'What hath befallen me: Hark! Hath time flown away? Do I not fall? Have I not fallen—hark! into the well of eternity?'"

(Only once have I had another such experience, and then it affected only two people, my wife and myself. We were walking one morning up the Champs-Elysées in winter sunshine, when we were lost:

"Our spirits grew as we went side by side.
The hour became her lover and my bride."

An eternity encompassed us, without distinction of time or place or persons.)

§ 2

That year of our Salzburg visitation, 1932, is memorable to us for a second happening as full of horror as the first had been of grace. We had hired a car to take us home, and were idling a little at Munich to see a *Figaro* at the Residenz Theatre, a place almost as exquisitively rococo as the music itself. Strolling one afternoon to the *Alte Pinakothek* we passed the Brown House. Guards, with steel helmets and bayoneted rifles, were standing on the pavement; and as we hurried away I had a feeling of naked contact with bestiality such as I had never had before and have rarely had since, except when reading of executions. We left next morning, and stopped first at Rothenburg, loveliest of mediaeval cities; for we had been told that a clock-tower played a series of pretty melodies at midday there, and we wanted to hear them. Anxious to be home as soon as possible, we lunched on the pavement opposite at half-past eleven, so as to be off without a minute's delay when the performance was over; and were so hungry by the time we got to Stuttgart that we had a second lunch at the Hotel Marquardt. Back in England, I found the manuscript of Edgar Mowrer's 'Germany Puts the Clock Back' on my desk: I rejected it, as far-fetched and war-mongering. A few months later Hitler was in power, and I bought Brimpton, for my youngest daughter was a baby and I knew that war was coming. I ought to have been warned at the time by what we saw at Munich.

§ 3

The previous year, 1931, had been equally full of adventure, not on our way back from Salzburg but on our way out there. I had heard that at the Villa d'Este on Lake Como you had all your meals by the

George Jung

A SERENADE AT SALZBURG

THE AUGUSTAN BOOKS OF
POETRY

ROBERT
NICHOLS

[handwritten inscription:]

To I.G. remembering his party
May 16th 1937. *[signature]*

'Hark! hath not the world now
become perfect? What hath
happened to me?'

Zarathustra. Venice
Book IV / which
is for the individual /

LONDON: ERNEST BENN LTD.
BOUVERIE HOUSE, FLEET STREET

waterside, dinner (with little candles) as well as lunch, and thought it would be a good idea to stay there for a week or so before going on to the Festival. But I did not like the atmosphere; the puritanism in me overcame my love of luxury. So we took a car to Verona, and again were deceived. It was high summer, there had been a drought for three months, and the heat was intolerable. Sitting at midnight in the amphitheatre at an open-air performance of *William Tell*, with a huge orchestra and a flock, equally huge, of bleating sheep, we sweated horribly; so we asked next morning whether a car might be available to take us to Meran, which we thought would be cooler. A racing motorist, who had broken the record in some contest or other the previous week, was glad to oblige us, and turned up with a very long and very low car that appeared to be made entirely of wood. Parts of the structure flew off halfway to Meran, and the driver had to turn back and recover it; but in spite of this he told us, when we arrived at the Meraner Hof, that he had broken his own record, and I was not at all surprised.

It was the dead season at Meran, and we were alone in the gigantic hotel. But the town was adorable—more beautiful, I thought, than any small place I had ever been in, except perhaps Bibury or Winchelsea. The day we had intended to spend there lengthened into a week and then into a fortnight. In the early morning, before breakfast, I would walk barefoot on the hotel lawn, to feel the dew between my toes. For lunch we would sit alone at a little table on the veranda. In the afternoon we wandered in the cool shade of the pines down the long Tappeiner Weg, or in the cobbled and arcaded streets; and at tea-time we paraded in the square for the town band, in the company of half Meran and (in patent-leather shoes) Sir Thomas Beecham. We would gladly have prolonged our stay there till winter, even at the cost of missing Salzburg. We did in fact miss three or four performances.

Once we had decided to be off I was in a frenzy (characteristic, I am told) of impatience. I kept urging the chauffeur to go faster, but he insisted on slowing down every time he approached a pair of railway lines, pointing, when I protested, to *Halt wenn ein Zug kommt!* We arrived late, rushed to the Festspielhaus without washing, and were allowed to stand at the back. Lotte Lehmann was singing 'ein sonderbar Ding' just as we got in. But the journey had been too much for my wife, who nearly fainted, and was given brandy in the women's cloakroom by one of the Sitzkissen girls.

§ 4

Music in the open air is even better than meals in the open air preceded or followed by music, and this is another of the pleasures I had been looking forward to when contemplating Salzburg. Parks—'the country' as I called them; for my father had a low opinion of the other kind and rarely took us there: 'parks are good enough for me', he used to tell us—parks, and Hyde Park in particular, had initiated me into open-air music when I was six or seven: I would stand and listen to the band 'with the sweet and curious apprehensions of the world I had as a child', while the smell of cigar-smoke hung mingling with the summer heat. It was on these occasions, I think, that I first acquired my love of cigars, though I was not to smoke one till the night before my fifteenth birthday. My parents had a great friend called Arthur Klingenstein, a cigar importer who lived quite near us but far more grandly. He had a passion for his calling, and had converted a large room into a humidor: it looked like a library with its rows of cigar-boxes on all four sides from floor to ceiling and its library ladder on little wheels. Mr. and Mrs. Klingenstein (who were also fond of music and alleged that they had once heard Grisi in Berlin, which was impossible) were kind enough to take a special interest in me, and often asked me to dinner all by myself. I was there that night before my fifteenth birthday, and Arthur suddenly asked me "How old are you, Fiktor?" I replied "Fifteen tomorrow." "It is time," he said, "that you learned to shmoke a cigar. Come with me." So he took me to the humidor, which had a kind of double opening to protect it from the atmosphere, stood thinking a moment, wheeled the ladder about, brought it to rest, climbed up it, stretched his arm out, took a box, took a cigar from it, returned the box, descended, and handed me the cigar. "Here is fone," he said. "It is a little bit shmashed: I fould not offer it to anyone except you."

The next thing in open-air music after Hyde Park was the White City, which I shall have something to say about in Part II, if I ever get there; and since then my pleasure in it has never waned. The Embankment Gardens for a few minutes before lunch, with the Blue Danube just catching your ear as you approach the band-stand; *Otello* in the courtyard of the Doge's Palace; Berlioz's *Symphonie Funèbre et Triomphale* in Regent's Park, with the roses afterwards; the town band in the middle of the Piazza San Marco, maybe with a whole act from *Traviata* and an occasional rarity, something from *Le Villi* perhaps;

chamber-music in the courtyard of the Pitti about the time of the flower-show; even strolling musicians, like the man who entertains me with a concertina every Sunday at lunch-time—they all please me, irrespective of quality in the music or skill in the performance: I just like the sound of pleasant noises in the open air, especially if it comes from a distance.

Then there are 'German bands' (now unhappily almost extinct); barrel-organs (the same applies); Salvation Army bands; and, as I heard once but once only, musical glasses: as well as casual noises of several kinds, such as the cloppity-clop of horses' hooves (ubiquitous in my boyhood and still to be heard most mornings in Eaton Place, when mounted soldiers ride down to some barracks); the whirring of a Bentley in Hyde Park; Cunard sirens both in harbour and at sea; and the puffing of smoke from the engine at the beginning of a railway journey. (The pleasure inherent in such noises lies at the bottom of *musique concrète*, or rather of the theory that produced it: but the misunderstanding that hideous barbarism reveals is typical of a lot of so-called modernism, for casualness is of the essence, and this is lost, or worse, perverted when called into the service of a deliberate composition.)

In a similar category are musical toys of any kind: miniature pianos that open and play a tune; a Turkish clock we once had at Brimpton that played a dozen, including 'Là ci darem', but was always getting out of order; the collection of birds sitting on trees in glass cases that Moshe Oved used to house in a back parlour at Cameo Corner, with an electrical device that allowed him, got up in his velvet frock, to set off the whole lot of them together; and to continue with birds, a bird-in-a-box that Rose Macaulay once gave us, and that sang a pretty tune when you pressed a button. We were distressed to discover one

morning that it refused to pop up and sing, for the last man who knew how to mend them, a Swiss, had recently died; but my wife, who is good with her hands, took the whole thing apart—there were hundreds of pieces, including a miniature bellows—and put it together again; and the bird, though its wings are now rather bedraggled, having been applied after an accident with glue, has sung unfalteringly ever since.

Open-air music at Salzburg was deficient in quantity but superb in quality, for it consisted of Mozart serenades played by candle-light in the courtyard of the Prince-Archbishop's Palace at nine o'clock in the evening. The programmes were delightfully varied: we had quartets with the Mairecker people in 1935, and the Vienna Philharmonic, in such things as the Haffner serenade and the one in D major for two violins, viola, bass, two oboes, a bassoon, two horns and two trumpets in 1930.

I think that of all the concerts at Salzburg these were the ones I enjoyed most, though you could hardly call them concerts, you just sat there and assisted: I may even have enjoyed them more than those resplendent operas with the wonderful casts that were the principal raison d'être for our being there. I was about forty: and the tendancy that had begun to develop in early manhood and was to end by making me even happier with the Schubert octet than with his 'great' symphony, and prize Beethoven above all for some of his trios and late quartets, was growing stronger and stronger in me.

Apart from the serenades, the only open-air music at Salzburg was an occasional performance of *Bastien and Bastienne* in the Mirabell Gardens with the Schloss as a background. But open-air talk about music, almost as good as the thing itself, was another matter; for we would often hang about the whole morning in the garden of the Café Bazar, to read the notices of last night's performance or look out for celebrities or gossip with friends. Stephen Spender might be there, eager and handsome (he was writing or had just written 'Forward from Liberalism'); so might Toscanini's brother, at sight of whom my daughter Diana, about twelve at the time and just learning about *café complet*, used to mutter 'Maestro brother complete'; or Clemens Krauss, who 'mixed' more than any other of the conductors except perhaps Bruno Walter; or Madame Sukerkandel, who invariably asked us whether we didn't think it had been a wonderful performation; or Madame Homburg, in a pink linen costume and wearing a huge floppy hat, who was in the habit of crying at Mozart's Mass in C minor; or the woman, no one knew her name, who used to follow Bruno

Walter all over Europe and the United States; or those social go-betweens, Kommer of Czernowitz and Olga Lynn. And Sidney Loed would certainly be there. This astonishing man, who looks younger than most men of seventy but is in his very late eighties, must be the last surviving link with Wagner's Bayreuth: his wife is Hans Richter's daughter, and when she greeted me at that *Tristan* performance with Birgit Nillson I felt a thrill of positively pro-Wagnerian awe. Sidney Loeb is invariably kind: he has recently given me, from his marvellous collection of photographs, one of Destinn's grave.

For the rest, there would be St. Gilgen to visit, our favourite excursion; or St. Wolfgang, with the Michael Pacher altar-piece; or one of the more distant lakes. It was near one of these that we encountered our shepherd. He was sitting by the roadside and put his hand up as we passed, so we stopped and told him to get in. He had never been in a car before, and asked me innumerable questions about how it worked, which I could not have answered even if I had fully understood him; and he giggled all the way, and more than giggled when to his enquiry as to where we lived I replied 'London'. You might have judged from his paroxysms of laughter either that he placed it on the other side of the moon or that he thought I was lying.

Another special delight at Salzburg was music at eleven in the morning. Can there be anything more like heaven than this? Your proper business, all at once, is to be a cherub and hear the angels quiring: at the very moment when at ordinary seasons the muddy vesture of decay—working out costs, drafting advertisements, etcetera—doth most grossly close you in. For now 'love's a duty'. I have always felt like this at the Edinburgh festival, to which, I must shamefacedly confess, my general attitude has been rather mixed: the theatre is so inadequate, the weather usually so dreadful (not only by rumour but in fact), the beauty of Prince's Street and its public gardens so wretchedly diminished by all that belching smoke; but on the other hand the hospitality is so warm-hearted and the generosity of the Scots as a people so overwhelming. But for one thing I have always been grateful, even on the wettest and smokiest days: namely for the concerts at Freemason's Hall—the Archduke, the *Geister*!—at that same improper hour of eleven in the morning. Materially improper, I mean: it is indeed its impropriety in the material sense that gives it a supreme propriety in the spiritual one.

§ 5

For seven years in succession we went to Salzburg, as I have said, but the seventh, 1936 (memorable for the production of Hugo Wolf's exquisite concert-opera *Der Corregidor*), came abruptly to an end. On our first visit we had put up at the Bristol, but had soon moved to the more spacious Österreichischer Hof. We had a magnificent bedroom on the first floor, with great windows looking on to Hohen-Salzburg, and Ruth would paint there in the late afternoon while I lay on a sofa in the bay reading a detective story. The general atmosphere had been rather worrying us for some time: Sigle Lynd, for instance, had been invited to a reception by local bigwigs, and had been asked to bring along anyone "except Jews". As Isaiah Berlin was of her party she declined—tho' I don't really know why I bring Isaiah into it, for being a morally sound and highly intelligent creature, as well as a very beautiful one, she would have declined, if given that proviso, anyhow.

But now, in 1936, things seemed tenser, for already, before the Anschluss, Austria had been declared a German State. It was either this year or the previous one that we went to some performance at the little Stadttheater, and felt horrified when Prince Starhemberg arrived with a large body of storm-troopers, who occupied the place till he left.

After a week or so of our 1936 visit my wife began to look tired, and to nod during performances. She shook her head when I asked whether she felt ill, but when I insisted she came out with it. An antinazi had just been smuggled out of Prague and murdered: I was by then a prominent antinazi: Salzburg was on the German frontier: our bedroom door was never locked (I am slightly claustrophobic): and might not someone break in when I was asleep and kidnap me? So she at least would not be caught unawares: she would keep awake all night and take care of me. Of course we left three or four days later, and have never been back, for from what I hear we should not greatly care for the Festival nowadays. It turned out afterwards that a prominent employee of a leading Salzburg hotel was one of the top Austrian Nazis, so my wife's fears had not been unjustified.

§ 6

I come to *Die Meistersinger*, which, as readers may remember, I have been saving up for the present chapter, the reason being this: it was at Salzburg that my *Meistersinger* experience came to exquisite flower.

SALZBURG FROM THE OESTERREICHISCHER HOF

The twenties and thirties had already been, and even apart from Salzburg were still to be, a great *Meistersinger* time for us: I doubt whether, during the period in question, we missed more than half a dozen Covent Garden performances, and those we heard were of the quality that makes one reluctant to criticize occasional defects. Lotte Lehmann was the dominant figure, though she was replaced by Delia Reinhardt for some performances in 1926, by Göte Ljungberg in 1928 and by Tiana Lemnitz in 1936, as well as once at least by Elisabeth Schumann. I hesitate to say that Lotte Lehmann's Eva was one of the greatest of her roles, as of course it was, for great suggests overwhelming and that paints a wrong picture: say rather one of the most lovable. There were a number of Sachses—Emil Schipper, Hans Nissen, Friedrich Schorr and Rudolf Bockelmann: all were fine, but Bockelmann was specially moving, for his Sachs had the same natural graciousness as his Wotan, a graciousness that never verged on the self-consciously benevolent. Alexander Kipnis, with his noble bass, was so good a Pogner that one always waited for 'Das schöne Fest, Johannis-Tag' as if it were the most beautiful melody in the whole work, as I often think it is. Eduard Habich was the usual Beckmesser, and never exaggerated in the kind of way that so often makes the clownishness of the man almost intolerable. The tenors were decent enough. Bruno Walter conducted mostly till about 1932, and then Beecham. Both were peculiarly fitted by temperament to give exceptional rendings of the score, Walter a beautifully flowing and gracious and Beecham an immensely exciting one.

So we were particularly expectant when *Die Meistersinger* was announced for Salzburg. Would the London performances be surpassed, almost impossible though that might seem? How would Toscanini compare with Walter? With Beecham? We must have been optimistic in the way we answered ourselves, for we booked for the whole series of performances that were to be given during our visit.

I do not recollect what year it was: I do not recollect the cast, even to the extent of a single name, though I suspect that Lotte Lehmann sang Eva: I remember only that the second act was so beautiful in the inevitability of its orchestral flow, so ravishing in its combination of countless felicities with unity of texture, that never, I thought, had I heard anything like it in a symphonic piece of that length. I still think, after thirty years, that my judgment was a sober one.

We went to the whole of only the first of the performances we had booked for: in the case of the others we arrived for the second act and left at the end of it. The reason was that we wanted our ears to be absolutely fresh for the beginning of that symphonic marvel, and were equally anxious that the impression should remain undisturbed when it was over. Eccentric, no doubt: but as a result we had a musical experience almost certainly unique.

(Why do not people deal more often like this with the hearing of music? When you visit a picture gallery you do not go steadily through the rooms and look at every exhibit: you linger before a few pictures you have wanted specially to see again and then leave. I am going to take a season-ticket for the proms this year, my first since 1914, so that I can stroll in from time to time and hear anything I want to: there are a lot of such items now that William Glock has taken over. Besides, it will be a pleasure to share the floor again with the kind of people I used to listen with in my boyhood.)

But of course we missed a great deal by leaving after the second act of those *Meistersingers*. I remember an experience of the third act many years later—about 1950 or 1951, under Beecham. From the opening bars of its prelude, played, as I had never heard it played except under Toscanini, with that justness of time in which all great conducting so largely consists, I was lost. With what a prodigal outpouring is beauty made present to us in those two closing scenes! And how perfectly it was realised that night—Eva's pretty confusion about *links* and *rechts* while she stands with her foot imprisoned on Sachs's stool, and her break into confident rapture as Walther von Stolzing, all ready in his knightly clothes, appears on the balcony opposite: Beckmesser at Sachs's desk, the *Preislied* within an inch of his nose, and the orchestra, *piano*, telling us just that and nothing more—no device could be imagined of a rarer intellectual beauty, and no better example of what the leitmotif system is capable of, however boring its creator's misuse of it may so often be in the way of endless repetitiousness. And then, best of all, the quintet! Yet the scene still to come is a true climax. Apart from all the special things—the *Preislied* at last in its continuous perfection, the homage to Sachs, the chaplet on Sachs's brow—a luxuriance of elaboration in the intermingling of motifs shows the overture, which now comes to mind again after a five hours' interval, not as the anticipatory summing up it had then appeared to be, but merely as a starting-point for further development. I hardly slept all that night; I seemed to be asleep, but I knew when I woke up that my brain had been alive every minute of the time with the glorious bustle of the closing music.

Not that I would wish to pretend that I enjoy every quarter of an hour of *Die Meistersinger* as I enjoy every minute of *Pelléas* and

Figaro, of *Orfeo* and *Falstaff*. I persist in thinking of the Tabulatur business as intolerably *langweilig*, with its inaudible, mock-comical words (how right Walther is: 'Hilf Himmel! Welch endlos Töne-Geleis'!'); of David as insufferably callow, a sort of lower-middle-class brother to the young Siegfried; and of the humour, or much of it, as embarrassingly arch. Then, in the second act itself, there is Sachs's interminable heartiness as he cobbles under the elder: it is as tedious, this four-square melody, as Siegfried's at the forge, with which it could easily be interchanged, and I have a good deal of sympathy with Eduard Hanslick's description of it as ostensibly comic but actually reminiscent of a peevish hyena rather than of a merry cobbler. But these defects, as I think them, hardly affect my enjoyment, my more than mere enjoyment, of the work as a whole; nor is it open to the objections I feel nowadays to *The Ring* and even to *Tristan*. There is no "too-muchness" about it, nothing cloying, nothing over-ripe: on the contrary it is forever fresh and happy, forever like an English morning in spring. Even the march has an inwardness, an irresistible *Hin* in it, that makes it unique among examples of the kind in Wagner's music. I must find a word to sum it up, this work that, for all my antiwagnerism, I have never ceased to love: let me call it heavenly.

§ 7

The rest of the music at Salzburg may be divided into Mozart and non-Mozart. I shall deal with non-Mozart, and with Mozart's non-operatic music, first.

Perhaps it will be best to give the barest details of what we heard (apart from the Mozart operas) in two typical years, 1930 and 1935; and if I call them typical, this is, first, because every year was typical, and secondly because I have the programmes for those years, and nothing but memory to rely on for the rest.

In 1930, then, we heard an exceptional *Fidelio*: exceptional not because Lotte Lehmann was singing Leonora—this was almost routine —but because Richard Mayr was singing the Minister. That was what things were like at Salzburg. In the great Paris performance I wrote about earlier he sang Pizarro, the principal baritone part; but at Salzburg he sang the smallest part of all, one that appears only as the work nears its end. I have already referred to that wonderful phrase 'es sucht der Bruder seine Brüder' as crucial, for it expresses in the simplest human terms the divine message of the trumpet-call; and

Richard Mayr, his mouth slightly askew, sang it with a perfection of phrasing and purity of emotion that made it for me the most beautiful moment in the whole work.

Then there was a *Rosenkavalier* at the Festspielhaus with Lotte Lehmann, Richard Mayr, Margit Angerer and Adele Kern; and a *Don Pasquale* down at the little Stadttheater, with Maria Ivogün as Norina and Richard Mayr as the Don. Bruno Walter conducted a delectable performance, for he was as fond of Donizetti's masterpiece as of *Fledermaus*, and could bring out the charm of its melodies as no one else in my experience has ever been able to do. For concerts, we had a Mozart one conducted by Schalk; another conducted by the same, and specially enjoyable for the freshness of its music—Rameau, Lully, Ravel, Honegger, Roussel and Rabaud; and a Johann Strauss one conducted by Clemens Krauss. This was an annual event: it used to intoxicate us all, particularly at the moment when Krauss began fooling about with the Perpetuum Mobile.

Finally there was Bruckner's Mass in F at the Cathedral, and we went to serenades in the courtyard of the Prince-Archbishop's Palace two evenings running.

1935 was a year of years, and I feel abashed at being the chronicler of its splendours. There was an array of conductors such as could never before have been gathered together in a single city; Weingartner, Kleiber, Bruno Walter and Toscanini. There were *Falstaffs* and *Fidelios* under Toscanini, the former even better than Walter's at Charlottenburg, the latter at least as good as the great Vienna one in Paris. There were *Cosìs* and *Dons* and *Seraglios* and *Figaros*, which I shall come to presently: a Lotte Lehmann recital with Bruno Walter at the piano: a C minor Mass (Mozart's, the Costanze one) at St. Peter's; several serenades; a Cathedral concert of music by Bach, Handel and Mozart (the Coronation Mass); other concerts conducted by Kleiber and Bruno Walter—Mozart and Bruckner one Sunday morning at the Mozarteum, Dvořák and Schubert at the Festspielhaus; and all within less than a fortnight. Quite likely there were some odds and ends too that escape me: perhaps a *Bastien* in the Mirabell gardens; a concert I seem to remember at Linz; certainly Kasznár's gypsy fiddler playing into our faces, particularly my wife's, at lunch or supper.

§ 8

Mozart.
I think I know the reason why nothing of Mozart found a place

among the great operatic experiences of my boyhood. First, performances were comparatively rare, except in one of the Beecham winter
seasons when my money had run out. Secondly the singing may have
been poor, though there was a *Don Giovanni* with Destinn as Donna
Anna and McCormack as Ottavio, and another with Scotti and a third
with Forsell as the Don. But most of all, and here my recollection is
clear, the productions were so wretched that I really did think, in this
case if in very few others, that Dent's jibe about concerts in costume
was justified. And this offended my feeling for music-drama: I did not
want to go and see things that played into the hands of the anti-
operatic enemy.

Vocally, the performances at Covent Garden between the wars were
outstanding. We had a *Don* with Frida Leider, Lotte Lehmann, Elisabeth Schumann and Mariano Stabile; a *Figaro* with Lotte Lehmann,
Elisabeth Schumann, Delia Reinhardt and Richard Mayr; and a
Seraglio with Maria Ivogün, Elisabeth Schumann and Paul Bender.
Such casts were indeed more than outstanding: by present standards
they seem almost incredible. There was a regular Mozart cycle at the
Old Vic, too, with Joan Cross revealing anew her astonishing versatility
as Donna Anna and Pamina; and Bruno Walter conducted an otherwise rather undistinguished *Zauberflöte* at Covent Garden in the early
nineteen-thirties.

But whether or not the production in these cases was in fact un-
satisfactory, and though my enjoyment of Mozart as an operatic
composer grew and grew (though *Seraglio* has always been less to my
taste than the others: I find it lacking in freshness and like best the lilting
vaudeville that ends it), I was still vaguely troubled by the 'concert-in-
costume' aspect of Mozart performances, and remained so till we went
to Salzburg. There everything came wonderfully right. Nothing
obtruded, as nothing ever should, so I can give no details, though it
was at Salzburg, unless my memory is at fault, that a happy use of
curtains solved the almost insoluble problem of *Don Giovanni*: it is
simply that, as never previously (there was to be no Glyndebourne
till 1934), I experienced these operas as fully dramatic works, comparable from the stage point of view with the best of Verdi's, and
musically their superior. And I should like at this point to amend
something I said to Peter Heyworth: namely that in most operas
(and I failed to include Mozart among the exceptions) great singing
must always come first. In the case of several operas by Mozart,
great singing and satisfactory production are of equal importance,
above all in that of the *Don*: satisfactory not meaning lavish (I have seen

horrible results from lavishness applied to *Zauberflöte*) but more often the reverse. The reason lies in the episodic structure of such works as *Zauberflöte* and the *Don*. But if I had to choose between poor singing with good production, and good singing with poor production, I should still choose the latter: Mozart inadequately sung is hardly Mozart, while Mozart greatly sung is, in Gounod's word, divine.

The Mozart singers at Salzburg were mostly of high excellence (though I cannot pretend that any single cast equalled the best of the Covent Garden ones): such as Jarmilla Novotna and Adele Kern in *Così*, Lotte Schöne in *Seraglio*, and Dusolina Giannini, Dino Borgili, Emanuel List and Ezio Pinza in the *Don*. But what counted was the excellence, very near to perfection, of the performances as a whole. We sat there in the certain knowledge that there would be nothing amiss, nothing unworthy of the composer's genius; and we left with an emotion of happiness even greater, more serene, than our normal one at Salzburg. And Mozart, being not only a genius but the genius of the place, was always with us. When we were there, and whatever thoughts of Verdi might creep in afterwards when we remembered Toscanini's *Falstaff*, Salzburg was Mozart.

About the operas themselves there is little to say. *Zauberflöte* ranks very close to *Fidelio*: as exquisite in its basic simplicity as Christ's parables, it uncovers, with an amazing variety of musical and dramatic expression, the divine meaning of human existence. Yet *Figaro* perhaps surpasses it. If it were not for another passage in the same work I should say that the 'Contessa, perdono' in the closing scene is Mozart's greatest moment. But there is a moment even greater: I mean when Susanna comes quietly out from the unlocked door as they all expect Cherubino. There is a sense in that music of everything working for charity, of a providence that always provides in the end. *Fidelio* is shot through with just this feeling: but Mozart's harmony steals on us with a beautiful lightness that eases the heart as well as uplifting it. There are moods in which I think that, with the slow movement in the clarinet concerto, this is one of the two loveliest things in all Mozart.

PART TWO

My secretary tells me that I have already written eighty thousand words, and my publisher warns me that I must not exceed ninety thousand. I disbelieve the first, and feel inclined to snap my fingers at the second. But it is clear that I cannot follow my original intention, which was that the second part of this memoir, designed to be about music other than operatic, should be as long as the first: for if I did the result would be as bulky, and therefore as unmanageable even in a crude physical sense, as some of the novels I am offered from time to time by American publishers. On the other hand I am unwilling to stop altogether at this point, for I have looked forward from the start to describing the flavour of at any rate my early approach to what I called at the *Traviata* time 'ordinary' music. So I shall do this: I shall write the merest sketch of Part II as originally planned, and shall keep the real Part II for another volume, if I can ever get down to it. I am consoled in this decision by my discovery, as I re-read myself, that I have already written a certain amount about music in general by the way.

§ 1

If throughout boyhood my cardiac artery for operatic music was the Baron's-Court-Covent-Garden tube, that in my earliest days for 'ordinary' music was the Edgware Road. But this hideous thoroughfare, as I now see it, was more than one that ended in my gateway to music, though that was its principal and its only Sunday function: in the eager romanticism of my 'looking forward' I thought of it as meaning real, grown-up life. I would often take a 'bus down it just for fun on holiday week-days; and first, as I emerged from the comfortable propriety of the Sutherland, Clifton and St. John's Wood Road districts, with Hamilton Terrace away on my left (I used to trundle my hoop there as a child, and pick up burrs for the museum my Aunt Minna had started for me with a necklace of cinnamon from the Sahara), I would come to the Grand Union Canal with the flower-women on its pavement (I think it was these, with their glorious

dahlias, that were to make the Parsifal maidens seem so bogus to me).
Sometimes I would get off at this point, and penetrate down those
leafy banks as far as Little Venice. Then I would resume my journey,
and all at once, for the intervening patch of no-man's-land was
inconsiderable, the real town would be on me: with eventually the
Metropolitan music-hall and its pictures of Marie Lloyd and Little
Titch on my right, and Chapel Street, which I got my suits from, on
my left. I loathed the Chapel Street tailor for two reasons: first,
because his jackets were so tight they hurt my arm-pits, and secondly
because his line of talk, as he measured me for alterations to his miserable reach-me-downs, was at once so reactionary and so unmusical.
(By the same token, my wife has cut my hair for forty-five years, once
every couple of months or so: I used to detest the Maida Vale barber's
hearty drivel.) But another feature of Chapel Street delighted me,
namely the Edgware Road Underground Station, and again for two
reasons. First, because it was dark and smoky and mysterious: and
secondly because it would so often be the starting-point for one of my
most exciting adventures—a 'pea-soup' fog, of the sort nowadays
unknown. I would sometimes spend the day at my father's office in
Aldgate as a treat: in the evening we would take the Underground
back from Aldgate to the Edgware Road, and then catch a 'bus home:
and it might happen in winter that a suggestion of fog hung about us on
our way to Aldgate Station. The question was, would it get thicker
and thicker, or, as foolish people said, worse and worse? I used to
worry about this all the way back, but might find, on coming up into
the open at Chapel Street, that 'you couldn't see your hand in front of
your face'. Then the real fun would begin. My father—we would be
walking, with the 'buses long since at a standstill—might decide, and if
matters were 'bad' enough almost certainly would decide, to bargain
with a link-man, and, provided his terms were not wholly outrageous,
or even, when it came to it, if they were, engage him to guide us home.
These linkmen were very attractive: they carried enormous flares,
smelling of acetylene, which streamed in the wind of their movement
like the strands of a woman's hair. Sometimes the link-men were not
men but boys; and this was more satisfactory, because then you could
hire them more cheaply. Streaming flares, muffled footsteps, mouths
tightly shut: a murky smell, lights suddenly looming, accidental
bumpings, scraps of conversation from people unseen: these were
enchantments, and each new enchantment was more ravishing than the
last. And the final one was still to come; for suddenly, as we felt a wall
with our hands, or peered at a name-plate by the light of our flare, we

might realise, my father to his consternation and I to my delight, that
we had missed our turning and were lost . . .

But the delights of the Edgware Road were endless. There was the
sickly-sweet smell of a food-shop near the Met., with a man in dirty
white overalls and a chef's hat cooking onions, and I suppose tripe, in
the window: and a mysterious street opposite, leading to a barn-
storming theatre where they played melodramas like 'East Lynne' with
seats at sixpence downwards. The posters—villains in top-hats; tall
ladies in trailing black dresses, handkerchiefs to their eyes; babies in the
ice and snow—entranced me: set to music by Mascagni or Leoncavallo,
with décor by a super-Zeffirelli, these vanished melodramas might still
draw the crowd to Covent Garden.

But the real thing about the Edgware Road was this: it ended in
Marble Arch, and beyond that lay the Albert Hall.

It was these I was making for when on Sunday afternoons in the
summer I would rush away early with my lunch half finished, and wait
for a 'bus, or a puffing green vehicle—propelled I think by steam, and
of a type that was soon to become obsolete—at the corner of Elgin
Avenue and Maida Vale, in the lull and remoteness of the deserted
streets; and the anxiety was, as I arrived at the hall and leaped two at a
time up the broad stone stairs to the topmost gallery, whether any free
places would still be vacant in the standing-room at the end of the
sixpenny seats. There were about fifty of these places, and if I was too
late I would spend a precious sixpence and, looking down at the
orchestra far below, divide my time between listening to the tuning
up, so heavenly a sound, and reading over and over again the programme descriptions. By some trick of memory there comes singing
into my mind now, to the exclusion of everything else, Tchaikowsky's
'Capriccio Italien', all mixed up with the Mendelssohn Violin
Concerto.

I usually walked home, through the park and up the Edgware Road:
partly to save money and partly because I loved the park and the streets
and walking; and always, when I got to Marble Arch, I would stop
and stand listening to the orators: sometimes for two or three hours,
taking part, if a Tory was speaking, in the heckling: but more often
hurrying off to the bandstand, where I would stand and listen, or sit
and listen if I could afford it.

When a little older I often went to the Albert Hall for performances
of the Royal Choral Society, but with a curious selectiveness that I cannot explain: I am sure, for instance, that I never heard the Elijah in
those days, nor do I believe I have ever heard it since. And yet I am far

from being prejudiced against Mendelssohn: the Italian Symphony, the octet, and some of the *Lieder* have always given me pleasure. Perhaps my father may have had something to do with it, for, as will already be patent, he greatly influenced my musical life, in spite of my recurrent hostility to him: I vaguely remember that he sniffed at Mendelssohn, perhaps because they were both Jews (though he adored Meyerbeer). In a similar way many Englishmen were in the habit, before the Britten vogue, of sniffing at any English music later than Purcell's, which they probably hadn't heard anyhow, and particularly at Elgar's—which I confess I used to sniff at myself (but it is better now. Not that I would put him at the head of recent British composers, for Vaughan Williams, I think, is more likely to survive. I base this opinion on only a very slight knowledge of his works: but the last movement of his sixth symphony, with its portrayal of spiritual entropy, could issue only, it seems to me, from a composer of genius).

I think it must have been at one of those Choral Society concerts, a little later than the time I have been speaking of but well before 1914, that I first heard Verdi's Requiem. It was little esteemed in those days by the generality, for the music, they told you, was operatic rather than religious. You still occasionally hear this glib nonsense: at a performance only a few weeks ago my neighbour mouthed at me the old wisecrack 'his best opera', and I might have been inclined to knock his silly head off were it not that I happen to prefer verbal to physical violence. What do these people mean by 'religious' music? Music somehow related to God? But all serious music, perhaps all music of any kind, is that (however unconsciously on the part of its creator), to the degree of its excellence; and it follows that all great music is great religious music. The greatest of all religious music in the narrower sense (the word narrower denoting a specific connection with the Church, with formal worship and so on) is Beethoven's Missa Solemnis; but it is no greater as religious music in the deeper sense than the opus 131 or indeed any of the late quartets. By the same token, the music of The Magic Flute or Orfeo (or Figaro or Wozzeck, for that matter) is greater as religious music in the deeper sense than say, not to mention anything contemptible, the music of a Parry oratorio. To equate religious music with Church music is indeed to misunderstand the very nature of music itself. The Verdi Requiem is essentially a religious work, and a supremely great one, but only by occasion a Church work: and it should always be performed in a concert-hall, however well it might sound in a Cathedral, because it is above all a consecration of the secular. On the other hand the Bach Passions should always be performed in Churches, the smaller the better.

And yet Verdi was far from being hampered, in expressing what he wished to express, by the traditional form, the form of a Requiem Mass, that in a Catholic country he necessarily chose for his purpose. The fact is that his attitude to Catholicism was not as simple as some have imagined. He quarrelled with the Church, of course (and there may be even churchmen who will not blame him when they remember what the Church was like in the Italy of his day): and on one occasion at least—when he heard of the death of Manzoni—he denied the existence of Divine Providence. Nor was he in any way a formally practising Catholic. On the other hand we have it on Boïto's authority that "he kept in his heart the great Christian Festivals, Christmas and Easter"; that "he bore witness to Christian truth in the observance of certain rites and the burial arrangements specified in his will ['two priests, two candles and a cross will be sufficient']"; and that "he retained for his early loss of a belief in miracles a poignant regret all his life". More-over, we have the testimony of Adalberto Catena, the priest who gave him Extreme Unction: "A long clasp of the hand, a meaningful look and a deeply serious expression assured me that he understood the religious significance of what I was saying"—which doesn't sound like the invention of a propagandist. The final verdict, so far as one can ever be given, will probably be that Verdi did 'believe in God' (to employ the loosest of formulae) except in such passing moments of bitterness and indignation as we all experience from time to time, after Hiroshima, for instance, or at the bedside of a friend dying from cancer of the spine; that he did not believe, after boyhood or early youth, in the dogmas of the Catholic Church; but that he regretted the loss of this belief, and hankered after a renewal of it, till the day of his death. Evidence for all this is to be found in his music: there is a quality of awe in the Requiem, and of hope in the Te Deum ('In Te, Domine, speravi'—at the end of his life), which, intensely religious anyhow, would be described I think by Catholic philosophers, and even by an outsider like myself, as specifically theological virtues.

I have heard the Verdi Requiem a couple of dozen times or more, I suppose, in half a dozen countries: and I have all but invariably re-sponded, according to the quality of the performance, with varying degrees of pleasure or joy. I remember particularly two or three Beecham performances—he was superb in this work; a rendering at the Paris Opéra in about 1935, with Ezio Pinza singing bass and Tullio Serafin conducting; and another in Vienna under Giulini only a few years ago, when Leontyne Price, the coloured soprano, suddenly carried me away with a hint of Destinn in her voice during the 'Domine Jesu Christe' and 'Libera me'.[1] The only time I have been unmoved, or worse, was at a Festival Hall performance a day or two after President Kennedy's assassination. There was a minute's silence at the start; no interval; no applause at the end. The atmosphere was insufferable in its churchiness: add that Dorati, the conductor, took a view of Verdi's phrasing altogether different from mine and my feelings may be imagined. In revenge, I tried what I could do with the Recordare myself when we got home, and this restored my composure, if not my wife's. I specially love the Recordare. It has been singing in my mind ever since I started writing a few minutes ago about the Requiem.

There was another recurrent occasion at the Albert Hall of those days: a series of ballad concerts Saturday after Saturday, year after year. Clara Butt, a magic name with the oratorio public, used to 'star' at them, and on the only occasion I went to one John McCormack sang ballads as exquisitely as he was in the habit of singing 'Il mio tesoro' at Covent Garden. However disastrously we may have fallen off in some other respects, such concerts would be impossible nowadays. But perhaps I ought to explain what ballads in this particular sense were, for I am told that the term will mean nothing to people of even a single generation younger than mine, not to mention the boys and girls of today. Ballads, then, were English or Scottish *Lieder* of a more or less, and usually more, debased kind, highly sentimental when the theme was love, musically starry-eyed, in the manner of 'Land of Hope and Glory', when it was a question of patriotism. They might be described, I suppose, as the 'pop' songs of their day, more exalted in intent than the ones we know, but even lower, perhaps, in artistic quality. I remember one my Uncle Assur used to sing in the Elm Tree Road studio: 'Bonny wee thing,/Canny wee thing,/Lovely wee thing,/

[1] I have just heard (April 22nd), as I am about to send the proofs of this memoir to press, a performance of the Requiem at the Festival Hall more moving, and at the same time more thrilling, than any I have ever heard anywhere. Giulini, who conducted, is now supreme among living interpreters of the work, and I doubt whether any of his predecessors have come up to him. Perhaps Beecham: certainly not Toscanini, who, great though he was, failed to make, on me at least, a comparable impact. Yet to single out Giulini is grossly unfair: for he could not have done what he did without an orchestra (the Philharmonia) or a chorus (also the Philharmonia) of superlative quality. Such playing and singing is what one dreams of, but rarely gets. I did not know which to admire most—the terrific attack, the heart-easing flow of the cantilena passages, or the glorious phrasing. All the soloists were excellent too; and if three of them had trifling defects, the fourth, Miss Bumbry, touched greatness.

Wert thou mine,/I would wear thee/In my bósom. . .'. (And now I'm suddenly afraid that this may be a fine old Scots folk-song.) Perhaps things of the kind still exist: but concerts that purveyed them to the exclusion of everything else have certainly vanished for ever.

One of those antique phenomena, however, survives to this day, though with diminished vitality: the operatic recital, complete, in the case of tenors, with sobs and intrusive h's.

§ 2

Perhaps a year or two after the earliest of my Sunday afternoons at the Albert Hall I bought a season ticket for the proms, and a month later was paying my first visit to the old Queen's Hall, which was soon as familiar as home to me. As I sit writing here with affectionate and not unhappy regret there hangs about my nostrils once again the peculiar smell of the hall and the refreshment-room and above all the downstairs corridor: it never varied, from the day I used my first season ticket for the opening night of my first proms to the end of 1939.

I should have thought it impossible to miss a night at the proms, except at first on Fridays, when I wasn't allowed to go, riding being tabu on Sabbath eve; and just as I had my own seat, B49, in the Covent Garden gallery, so I always stood in almost exactly the same spot at the Queen's Hall, about a couple of yards from the bank of flowers that hemmed off the orchestra, and a little to the left. It was the occasional operatic aria, and the Monday Wagner, that thrilled me most in my earliest seasons; the easier overtures, 'Coriolan' and 'Egmont'; the popular bits, such as 'Finlandia' and 'Peer Gynt' and 'Casse-Noisette'; the ballet music from 'Rosamunde'; one symphony, the Unfinished, which I was to put a few years later in the spiritual category of Orfeo; and, specially, the excerpts from Berlioz' Faust. But very soon the German classics were unfolding themselves and transporting me: Mozart and Haydn, Schubert and Beethoven; and I realised, with a sense of continual expectation, that day after day throughout the lifetime ahead of me there would be a whole new world to grow familiar with. The Beethoven symphonies were played one by one on Friday evenings, and this meant that I had to miss them till I broke the tabu: but I heard them at other concerts, such as the Philharmonic and London Symphony, which I was very soon frequenting against the promenade background, and there was a good deal of Beethoven anyhow on secular evenings. The Ninth Symphony, when I did come to hear it

at the proms, was invariably shorn of its choral section; the last movement was begun, but ended abruptly just before 'O Freunde, nicht
diese Töne'. So I was always looking for opportunities to hear it
complete.

But if Beethoven and Haydn and Mozart carried me away, I was in
rather different case with Bach and Brahms. Bach at the proms meant
for the most part the Brandenburg concertos, and I have already
explained why, orchestrated as they were, they had no great appeal
for me. But there was one piece of Bach, I recall, that made me think
'This is as good as Beethoven'. I imagine it must have been the violin
concerto in E; but I have nothing to jog my memory with, for of all
those programmes for the period up to 1914, whether of promenade
or other concerts, only two have survived. Why the particular two I
cannot imagine: they are for some Schumann centenary concerts in
April 1910, and for a London Symphony one the following January.
(But my retention of the latter is perhaps explicable after all, for I have
just been looking at it, and find one thing after another: the Ben-
venuto Cellini overture—Berlioz, whom I already worshipped; the
Eroica—Beethoven, and not only that, but the best for me of all his
symphonies; Hugo Wolf, sung by Elena Gerhardt, whom I shall be
coming to presently; 'Till Eulenspiegel', against which I can just
decipher the words in very faded pencil "Wonderful performance".
And perhaps I went to that whole L.S.O. series. They included Berlioz'
Faust, conducted by Hans Richter; parts of *Romeo and Juliet*, conducted
by the same; Elgar's violin concerto, which I remember wanting to
like and do like half a century later; and the whole of the second act of
Tristan, conducted by Nikisch. This series may have been a landmark,
for all my failure of memory, in my musical life.)

As for Brahms, I felt about him in my promenade days very much
as I feel about him now. Bernard Shaw changed his tone a little during
his years as a music critic. He began by saying that Brahms "takes an
essentially commonplace theme; gives it a strange air by dressing it up
in the most elaborate and far-fetched harmonies . . . and finds that a
good many wiseacres are ready to guarantee him . . . the true heir of
Beethoven . . . Strip off the euphuism from these symphonies and you
will find a string of incomplete dance and ballad tunes. . . . That is why
Brahms is so enjoyable when he merely tries to be pleasant and naïvely
sentimental, and so insufferably tedious when he tries to be profound."
But he ended, a few years later, by saying: "This [the first] symphony
is a wonderful feat of the young Brahms—a mere heap of lumps of
absolute music; but then, such magnificent lumps! Such color! such

richness of substance! one is amazed to find the man who dug them
out half smothering them with mere slag, and quite unable to
construct anything with them[1]." I have suffered no such change of
emphasis. My objection to Brahms's bigger pieces has always been
that they are too cloying and luscious, especially if played by a stream-
lined orchestra under a streamlining conductor. (One gets 'fed up' at
times with the mechanical perfection of those American orchestras
under conductors like X. I once told a friend of mine, after a concert by
one of them, that I was going to hear orchestra Y. under conductor Z.
Why? he asked. Because, I replied, the conductor is so feeble and the
orchestra so poor. And I was not speaking wholly in jest.) So, as in the
case of *Götterdämmerung*, I have often found myself longing for *Carmen*
after a Brahms symphony: it has been a question of the Latin sparkle of
Bizet drying out the richness of Brahms. But I greatly enjoy some of his
Lieder and chamber music, and, as I may presently relate, the horn trio
has played a crucial part in my life. . . . And now I suddenly find myself
repenting—a little—even about the symphonies and concertos: some
of those lyrical passages, after all, are rather lovely.

I must add a word or two about Henry Wood, the memory of
whom is inseparable from any thought of the proms. For half a century
he was all but unique as a benefactor of British music-lovers, his only
equal in this regard being Thomas Beecham. He educated, unless the
word is too forbidding, my whole generation. No one could have
called him a great conductor: but he carried 'usefulness' to the point
of genius. His resource, and what he could do with a minimum of
rehearsals, were phenomenal. But there was more to it than that. He
understood, as by no means every conductor understands, that a
concert should be an act of communion, with soloists, orchestra, every
member of the audience and the conductor himself participating in a
sacrament of unity. Or if he did not consciously understand this; if he
would not have put it that way himself: then his simple and unreflecting humanity, and his love of music and respect for his audience,
combined to produce an atmosphere akin to that of an early Christian
love-feast. We really did love everything and everybody on those
prom nights: the music, the performers, our neighbour and Henry
Wood.

I have had dealings of one kind or another with many famous men,
some of them greater, in the obvious sense, than Henry Wood: with
Bernard Shaw and Stravinsky, with Gilbert Murray and Theodor

[1] *Music in London.*

Heuss, and with three not inconsiderable Prime Ministers; but in the presence of Henry Wood alone have I felt, a thing that comes hard to me except at thought of a Beethoven or an Elizabeth Pilenko, a sense of awe. That is a measure of what I felt the man stood for and had done for me.

And I loved him as well, with the love not as for a friend but of gratitude. There are not many in the musical world of whom I could say as much, for some, like Beethoven, are unapproachable in their greatness, and others lack the special grace that alone can evoke it. My small number includes Verdi, Yehudi Menuhin, Bruno Walter, Lotte Lehmann and Elisabeth Schumann. It also includes Henry Wood.

And a word about the programmes. They were ordinary enough, with a minimum of 'novelties' and little that was specially adventurous. This to my mind was as it should have been. To grow familiar with the classics alone, not to mention other music of outstanding interest, would have meant going, in the absence of proms, to such a mass of concerts as, at even minimum prices, would have been impossibly expensive for the majority of inexperienced music-lovers: who, on top of that, would have had difficulty in finding their way about in the musical world. So you paid your precious pound and went to the proms with the specific purpose of hearing the basic music: and you were properly given it, with some 'lollipops' to lead the weaker ones on. Critics who complained at the time about the absence of novelties failed to realise that for the majority of promenaders, and particularly for the younger of them, almost everything was a novelty, more or less.

§ 3

The third of my musical homes before 1915 was the White City at Shepherd's Bush. I can give an exact date in this case. The place was opened in 1908: it was not quite finished when I started frequenting it: so I must have bought a season ticket that summer as the first of several. I would spend most of my day there during the school holidays, and then, after tea at home (raspberry-jam sandwiches on a sofa in the garden-room downstairs), would go off to the Queen's Hall for a prom, Covent Garden being over for the year.

The purpose of the place, which seemed to me enormous, a city within a city, was twofold: to house the Franco-British exhibition, and to provide a gigantic stadium for the Olympic marathon, starting from Windsor Castle, to finish up at. Galleries abounded for the exhibitors, full of showrooms and shops, into which you could wander freely; and some of these, with their French names and the smell of women's perfume that hung about them, seemed very *soigné* to my inexperience and made me long for Paris. There were mock-Venetian canals, with mock-gondolas on them: pretty gardens and refreshment rooms: fairy lights by night, for I would often stay till closing-time if the proms as well as Covent Garden had finished for the year: and—this is the point—bandstands everywhere, and, down at the far end near the flip-flap, a gramophone shop.

This description may inflate the reality, for I was looking with the eyes of a boy and memory enlarges the glory as it diminishes the agony of the past. Compared with the London Airport the place was not enormous but puny. The mock-Venetian canals may have been a single waterway and the craft not a number of mock-gondolas but a single ordinary boat. There may not have been bandstands everywhere. But the very minimum was this: two or three bandstands and a gramophone shop.

The bands used to play most of the afternoon and evening, not in rotation like the little orchestras on both sides of the Piazza San Marco but simultaneously; and I would wander from one to another picking out what I wanted to hear, for the programmes were put up at the entrances and it was a matter of calculating when a particular item would be ending somewhere and another beginning somewhere else. The operatic music I was on the look out for—always operatic, for nothing else was worth listening to on a military band—was of two kinds: pot-pourris of familiar works, and bits and pieces from, or more commonly overtures to, things I might never hear otherwise. These latter were again of two kinds: my father's 'fine old classics', such as the *Prophète* and *La Juive* and *Semiramide*, and the minor jollinesses, like *Zampa* and *The Merry Wives of Windsor* and *Le Pré aux Clercs*; and sometimes I would be lucky and get, in the unfamiliar category, not merely say the Coronation March from the *Prophète*, but even quite a long potpourri from *Semiramide* or *William Tell*. Not that I liked them all, not by any means: but I was interested in the history of opera, and wanted to hear everything I could.

In the other category, that of the familiar, it was only of course the things I took pleasure in that I picked out: but here I was recurrently troubled, to put it in a way that must sound ridiculous but faithfully describes what I felt, by a crisis of conscience. My scruple was this: that by hearing something precious too often I should grow tired of it, and that this would mean not merely to spoil my own pleasure, for the thrill of dawning recognition would be done for if the thing had become *too* familiar, but somehow to dishonour the music itself. And for how little: Covent Garden was one thing, a military band quite another! So I would hang about before taking the plunge and make a count: "*Traviata.* Heard it four times at Covent Garden: heard it three times on an M.B." I could not know in my inexperience that you can never grow tired of great music, or foresee that when Klemperer conducted the *Fantastique* at the Festival Hall a few nights ago it would thrill me more than it had ever done before. But anyhow my conscience always lost: when it came to it, I could no more resist the prospect of hearing the 'Libiamo' pealing out on an imitative cornet through the still summer night than abandon Covent Garden because my cousin Arthur made fun of me for going there.

But I must not give the idea that I was always listening, those three summers, to military bands. I would draw a lot of blanks: it might be ages before I could find something I wanted to hear: and I doubt whether, all in all, the time I spent listening to music on any one day at the White City came to more than an hour or so. Apart, that is, from the gramophone shop.

It was not quite a shop: rather a sort of showroom, very spick and span, with a highly knowledgeable salesman in charge and a lot of enticing horns and pictures of dogs all over the place. And the wonderful thing was this: the man would put on whatever I liked, repeat it as often as I liked, replace it by anything else I might like, and so on *ad infinitum*, without the smallest hint, by look or gesture or tone of voice, that I was doing anything improper. And indeed I was not. Comparatively few at that time possessed a gramophone or had access to one, and the H.M.V. people wanted to sell as many as they could: and what better way of selling them than by letting young enthusiasts have their fling? The salesman could not have known, or judged by my smart if ready-made appearance, that I could no more buy a gramophone than sing all those arias myself: besides, he loved music as much as I did, and we were quite conspiratorial at our sessions, smiling or giving little gasps at appropriate moments.

I spent hours in that showroom, and remember particularly Tetrazzini's marvellous polacca from *Mignon.* I think it must have been there, too, that I heard Plançon, whom I believed, until a few months ago, I had heard in the flesh, for I described him, in the first draft of my interview with Peter Heyworth, as the greatest, with Destinn, of all my Covent Garden singers, greater even than Caruso (Chaliapin being Drury Lane, not Covent Garden, before 1914). However I began to have doubts, and found, on investigation, that I couldn't have heard him at Covent Garden, for the dates didn't fit. But I still think I heard him, despite irrefutable evidence to the contrary: how, from a mere gramophone record of that date, could I have such a living impression, not only of his great bass, as wine-coloured as Homer's ocean, and of his glorious phrasing, but of his very presence on the stage? The official dates must be wrong: there must be an error in the Covent Garden records, a misprint perhaps of 1904 for 1908.

§ 4

This is the place for a short excursus on the gramophone. I have already explained, in that same interview, but only sketchily, why I do not possess a gramophone, or did not till a few days ago, and rarely listen to one. "The reason you may think rather peculiar," I said. "Though I hear a great deal of music, listening to it is always an occasion for me, and I don't want to be able to turn the thing on and off at my whim. Take works one can hear only once every so often, like the Missa Solemnis or L'Enfance du Christ or those late Beethoven 'cello sonatas: I like looking forward for weeks or months to hearing them." But that was only the half: space prevented me from saying all I wanted to, and even a bit of what I did say had to be cut. And now I find to my pleasure that Stravinsky agrees with me, or I agree with Stravinsky, or whatever is the humble way of putting it; for I have just come across the following in his 'Chronicles of My Life', and it exactly expresses not only what I feel and said, but what I equally feel and hadn't the room to say:

"In the domain of music the importance and influence of its dissemination by mechanical means, such as the record and the radio—those redoubtable triumphs of modern science which will probably undergo still further development—make them worthy of the closest investigation. The facilities that they offer to composers and executants alike for reaching great numbers of listeners, and the opportunities that they give to those listeners of acquainting themselves with works they have not heard, are obviously indisputable advantages. But one must not overlook the fact that such advantages are attended by serious danger. In John Sebastian Bach's day it was necessary for him to walk ten miles to a neighbouring town to hear Buxtehude play his works. Today anyone, living no matter where, has only to turn a knob or put on a record to hear what he likes. Indeed, it is in just this incredible facility, this lack of necessity for any effort, that the evil of this so-called progress lies. For in music, more than in any other branch of art, understanding is given only to those who make an active effort. Passive receptivity is not enough. To listen to certain combinations of sound and automatically become accustomed to them does not necessarily imply that they have been heard and understood. For one can listen without hearing, just as one can look without seeing. The absence of active effort and the liking acquired for this facility make for laziness. The radio has got rid of the necessity which existed in Bach's day for getting out of one's armchair. Nor are listeners any longer impelled to play themselves, or to spend time on learning an instrument in order to acquire a knowledge of musical literature. The wireless and the gramophone do all that. And thus the active faculties of listeners, without which one cannot assimilate music, gradually become atrophied from lack of use. This creeping paralysis entails very serious consequences. Oversaturated with sounds, *blasé* even before combinations of the utmost variety, listeners fall into a kind of torpor which deprives them of all power of discrimination and makes them indifferent to the quality of the pieces presented. It is more than likely that such irrational overfeeding will make them lose all appetite and relish for music. There will, of course, always be exceptions, individuals who will know how to select from the mass those things that appeal to them. But for the majority of listeners there is every reason to fear that, far from developing a love and understanding of music, the modern methods of dissemination will have a diametrically opposite effect— that is to say, the production of indifference, inability to understand, to appreciate, or to undergo any worthy reaction.

"In addition, there is the musical deception arising from the substitution for the actual playing of a reproduction, whether on record or film by wireless transmission from a distance. It is the same difference as that between the *ersatz* and the authentic. The danger lies in the very fact that there is always a far greater consumption of the *ersatz*, which, it must be remembered, is far from being identical with its model. The continuous habit of listening to changed, and sometimes distorted, timbres spoils the ear, so that it gradually loses all capacity for enjoying natural musical sounds.

"All these considerations may seem unexpected coming from one who has worked so much, and is still working, in this field. I think that I have sufficiently stressed the instructional value that I unreservedly ascribe to this means of musical reproduction; but that does not prevent me from seeing its negative sides, and I anxiously ask myself whether they are sufficiently outweighed by the positive advantages to enable one to face them with impunity."

There is an additional point. Every time you hear a particular record you hear precisely what you have been hearing before: whereas every time you hear a 'live' performance of that particular piece of music you hear something different, for a singer never sings a song and a conductor never conducts a symphony exactly as he has sung it or conducted it at a previous performance. The result is that half a dozen hearings of a record can satiate you with the music recorded, whereas you can hear a hundred 'live' performances of it and be ever more enthralled.

There is of course another side to all this. A big public has been given access by the gramophone to a lot of music it might never have heard otherwise: owing to laziness—but why should people as lazy as that be given music anyhow?; or to lack of time—going to a concert takes longer than turning on a gramophone; or even to lack of means—a machine with a few records is probably cheaper in the long run than going often enough to South Bank. This, however, is a double-headed argument: if you make it easy enough for people to keep away from concert-halls the 'live' performance of music may run into difficulties, and is indeed already beginning to do so, as anyone can discover for himself by taking a look at the Festival Hall on an 'off' night (by which I mean a night when there is nothing 'special' on), or even, for that matter, on an 'on' night too. You might have thought that more than a few hundred people would have turned up a fortnight ago for Stravinsky's own 'Symphony of Psalms'; but that was the number, and, even so, many of them, for instance a long row of schoolgirls, looked like paper.

Very well then: the gramophone has been a boon to the musical masses, or to lukewarm music-lovers, or to whatever you may care to call them; but I have never, after all, suggested abolishing it (I am no devotee of 'The Republic' in such matters), I have said no more than that it is not for me. For the musician, moreover, or the keen amateur, or even the keen ignoramus like myself, it can be useful in at least three ways. It can enable him to study the detail of a work, not too commonly heard, as performed or conducted by a master; it can enable him to make a meticulous comparison between a work, whether commonly heard or not, as interpreted by two or more leading execu-tants: and it can enable him to grow familiar with a work that he might not otherwise hear more than once.

It is this last type of consideration that has broken me down. I found myself wanting, at the end of last month, to refresh my memory of a few works for the purpose of this memoir, and a friend offered to lend me her gramophone, as she was buying a new one. She even offered to give it me if I found I could do with it permanently. I think I can: I have bought five or six records, and shall add slowly to this initial stock. But if I find myself succumbing to the almost inevitable temptation of abusing it I shall throw it out or get my wife to hide it away somewhere till I get too decrepit to stick to my present routine of concert- and opera-going.

Someone asked me at *Macbeth* the other night whether, if I knew I was going to be wrecked on a desert island and could take a gramophone with me, I should do so. The answer would depend on the probable length of my stay there. If it was going to be for life, of course I should: if for a year, it would be a matter of fifty-fifty: if for three months, certainly not. What joy, when I got back, to experience once more the familiar 'looking forward' after a doubtless salutary abstinence!

§ 5

Against the general background of Sunday afternoons at the Albert Hall, of nightly proms at Langham Place, and, in a minor way, of days at the White City, a few names stand out in the memory I have to rely on, with no programmes to help me, for everything before 1915: namely Pachmann, Paderewski, Elena Gerhardt, Julia Culp, Casals, Cortot-Thibaud-Casals, Ysaÿe, and Ysaÿe-and-Pugno.

Pachmann and Paderewski specially pleased me with their Chopin (I remember vividly the former's 'feathery' pianissimo, as Harold Schonberg[1] justly describes it) and with divers externalities: Pachmann with his familiar winks and idiotic mutterings and his antics at the piano-stool, and Paderewski with a nobility of look and manner similar to the 'red' Dean of Canterbury's, but probably more studied. Mature women reacted as hysterically to Paderewski as teenagers do to the Beatles, and he worked hard at his legend: "What with his private railway cars," writes Schonberg, "his chef and butler, his masseur and private physician, his tuner, his wife, and *her* aides, his tours . . . were royal processions." As to his playing, contemporary pianists thought less well of it than I did: "Yes, he plays well, I suppose," one of them is

[1] The Great Pianists, by Harold C. Schonberg, Gollancz, 1964

said to have remarked, "but he's no Paderewski." The other pianists I heard were undoubtedly greater than either Pachmann or Paderewski, though for some reason or other they meant less to me: Godowsky, Emil Sauer, Sapelnikoff, Moriz Rosenthal and, best of all, Teresa Carrēno, so magisterial and yet so tender.

Elena Gerhardt will always be the name that comes at once to my mind when I think about *Lieder*, for it was she who opened up for me a whole new world of musical delight just as I was getting deep into the operatic one of Covent Garden. I really do not know which I preferred: Covent Garden was far more glamorous and immediately exciting, but *Lieder*, as I penetrated an inch or two below the surface of that inexhaustible treasure-ground, appealed more to the other side of me: the side that loved rose-quartz and matrix of opal, and the smell of privet leaves, crushed between the fingers, from roadside hedges in London gardens, and the fragrance of mould, as evening came on after sunshine and shower, in my own birth-month of April.

I am not sure whether I first heard Elena Gerhardt, singing Hugo Wolf, at that L.S.O. concert in 1911: I rather think I had heard her the year before. After that I was to hear her often, by myself till 1914, and occasionally with my wife right up to 1935, when she sang the 'Zigeunerlieder' and 'Neue Liebeslieder' at a Tuesday Subscription Concert at the Queen's Hall. In the meantime we had heard her sing the 'Kindertotenlieder' in 1931, as well as two programmes of the normal sort in 1926, immediately after our resumption of concert-going. She was of course a very great *Lieder* singer, the greatest, many would say, of her time; and certainly her variety of tonal expression, her command of every vocal resource, and her ability to suggest a character or emotion with the subtlest of nuances were beyond critic-ism. And yet I did criticise her and still do, like a traitor, I uneasily feel: for it was she who made me understand what *Lieder* singing is all about. It is not merely that her voice was in itself of no great beauty: what mattered more was that there was just a hint of stuffiness in her singing. One realised that the qualities I have mentioned were those of a very great artist: and yet she lacked, it seemed to me, that highest art of all that results in an appearance of utter spontaneity. So one admired her singing this side of fanaticism, but did not really love it.

It was Julia Culp that I really loved in those years before 1915. She was as expressive and musically intelligent as Elena Gerhardt, but her voice, a rich contralto, was by far the more beautiful of the two: and there was no hint in her singing of the stuffiness I have ascribed to the other. Elena Gerhardt suggested the music-room, Julia Culp the open air.

The ones we loved in 1926 and after were Lotte Lehmann and Elisabeth Schumann. They may not have had all Elena Gerhardt's art in this or that particular: but in grace, in charm, in beauty of voice and above all in apparent spontaneity they were incomparable. Almost every year from 1926 to 1935 we heard one or other of them or both, and often at concert after concert. The greatest experience of all was Lotte Lehmann with Bruno Walter at the piano, for there was clearly a special rapport between them in their love and understanding of *Lieder*, and he accompanied her, he did more than accompany her he met her in a single act of joint interpretation, with a peculiarly smiling affection. We first heard them at Langham Place in 1926, and twice the same year at the Albert Hall; and were to hear them for the last time at the Salzburg concert in 1935 that I have already referred to. But there was an even happier occasion. She sang about this time at the Palazzo Pitti in Florence; and perhaps it was the contrast between a setting of such grandeur and the delicacy of her Schubert that made this concert, which hardly seemed a concert at all, the most moving of them all.

The prodigality of Lotte Lehmann's repertoire matched the amplitude of her voice and the generosity of her style. In one of those 1926 recitals she sang 'Morgen' with an exquisite refinement of vocal technique, but was equally successful in the closing scene from *Salome*. She sang the 'Frauenliebe und -Leben' as well as she sang Giordani, Monteverdi as well as she sang Brahms. At a recital in 1930 she ranged over five centuries and nine composers, including some early Italians, Gluck, Beethoven, Schumann and Liszt. And this was when she was singing the Marschallin and the Countess, Donna Anna and Sieglinde and Rosalinde, at Covent Garden! I doubt whether any singer has ever accomplished such a feat, before or since. Elena Gerhardt could never have managed Sieglinde, not to mention Rosalinde or the Marschallin, and even Destinn would I fear have bungled 'Die Forelle'; but Lotte Lehmann attempted a hundred styles, and excelled in them all. She was not the greatest soprano of the century, Destinn was that; but she was the most various and the most winning.

Or one of the two most winning. The other was Elisabeth Schumann, who, apart from this, came very close to equalling Lehmann in many particulars. If her voice was not as flowing as Lehmann's it was as limpid, and there was a beautiful compactness about it that gave it a solidity as of the finest silver. The cleanliness with which she sustained a phrase, and in particular an extended one that rose into the top register, was of a kind that delighted the mind, giving it a sense of security, no less than the ear: it was this as much as anything that made her a supreme Sophie in *Rosenkavalier*. She was as varied in expression as Lotte Lehmann; and if now and again she trembled on the edge of a Viennese archness, as Lotte Lehmann never did, she rarely went over it. Finally her range, if not quite as great as Lehmann's, was nearly so: she was as successful in Brahms as in Johann Strauss, in Mahler as in the Incarnatus from Mozart's Mass in C minor. Her brilliance in the elaborate cadenza of the last was as satisfying as her finish throughout.

Apart from Lotte Lehmann and Elisabeth Schumann, we heard Jarmilla Novotna, Sigrid Onegin, and once, to make up to me for never having heard Destinn in *Lieder*, Elisabeth Rethberg. That is about all, and it was enough. But I must mention, almost as a curiosity, a *Lieder* recital by Lauritz Melchior. This was a private affair at 21 Sussex Place. Rose Morley, an amateur often to be seen at the Queen's Hall, lived and entertained there, and was in the habit of taking people home after concerts, often to meet Weingartner, who liked changing on such occasions from tails into a flowered waistcoat. (He was as plain and simple as his conducting, with an air of quiet authority, however, that he sought to conceal behind a singularly gentle smile. He spoke fairly good English, but his inability to choose the appropriate rendering of a German word with several meanings often produced a charmingly comical result. Casals was once playing the Haydn concerto at a concert he was conducting, and half-way through the first movement suddenly stopped. There was a conference on the platform, then Weingartner turned to the audience and said: "Mr. Casals has the cramp. We shall play the symphony now, and Mr. Casals shall play the concerto at the end from the evening.")

Melchior sang that night a Schubert group and a Strauss group, the latter including 'Ständchen' and 'Traum durch die Dämmerung'. We had really gone out of courtesy to our hostess, a generous and lovable woman who was always very kind to us: for wouldn't that overpowering Siegfried be less than enjoyable in the most intimate of musical forms? No: he sang like a sucking dove, and we went home properly grateful. There was another excellent musician there that evening, or let me call him, for the unvarying self-effacement that did nothing to diminish the beauty and significance of his playing, a genius: Gerald Moore at the piano.

§ 6

There were three small concert-halls that I began frequenting about
1909, the Steinway, the Aeolian and the Bechstein: but it was only the
Bechstein that I thought of as possessing a distinctive personality, and
one more dear to me in a way than that of the Queen's Hall itself, for
if the Queen's Hall was my home the Bechstein was a precious room
away from it, of the sort one visits now and then as a special privilege.
It had a flavour of intimacy and at the last I have always liked intimacy
better than bigness; moreover it was in the afternoon that I mainly
heard music there, and music in the afternoon begins to attain, if it
never fully attains, the feel of music in the morning, a sense of the
spiritual trespassing on the material. And, perhaps because of the
intimacy of the place, a ritual familiar to all young concert-goers had a
special flavour there too, I mean the collection, as one waited in the
vestibule, of those shiny sheets of paper, sometimes complete with a
fine photograph, announcing coming events. At the Queen's Hall they
were rather lost, owing to its size: at the Albert Hall they have hardly
ever existed, so vast is the place and such a pigmy you feel in it: but at
the Bechstein they dominated the vestibule, you were in the very
midst of them. And, apropos, there was a peculiarity about my earlier
concert-going that is shared, I fancy, by many young people: I thought
more about the music that, as I had just discovered from these announcements, I should be hearing with luck in a couple of months' time than
about the music I should be hearing in five minutes. This was part and
parcel of the spiritual greed that I have already referred to: a greed
that was not to vanish (if it has wholly vanished even now) till my
illness in 1942, when I learned to substitute for the future the eternal
now.

Was it at the Bechstein Hall that I used to hear Ysaÿe-and-Pugno,
one of the two annual events of my boyhood? Until a few minutes ago
I should have been sure of it, and this is a measure of my affection for
the place, and of my instinctive certainty that if I heard any of the
smaller forms of music anywhere I heard them there. But my wife is
equally sure to the contrary, and it does seem probable that it was at the
Queen's Hall I heard them, for they were very famous, and must have
attracted a great audience.

They played all the Beethoven piano and violin sonatas at a series of
three recitals every year, always repeating the Kreutzer at the end of the
third. It could never have seemed possible that either of them should

affectionately

Yehudi

Photo David Farrell

THE BARN AT MUSIC-CAMP

be differently partnered in this music, but I suspect that the perfection of their ensemble derived more from the give and take of players in tension than from stylistic or temperamental similarity, as with Fournier and Kempe in the sonatas for piano and 'cello at the Festival Hall recently. For I can just remember Pugno as exquisitely Mozartian or Chopinesque in total effect, but Ysaÿe, with the utmost vividness, as fiery and passionate. And yet these adjectives are perhaps misleading. For what distinguished Ysaÿe above everything was a fullness and gravity of tone that made me think of Casals, whom I might be hearing a week later; and when I heard Casals I would think of Ysaÿe.

I was pretty familiar with Kreisler's fiddling at that time, and I doubt whether I have missed a single leading violinist from 1914 onwards: but only one among them all has ever equalled or even approached, in my judgment, the greatness of Ysaÿe, and that is Yehudi Menuhin. Any dullard can complain that Menuhin is sometimes far below his best, but so was Shakespeare, so was Beethoven, so for the matter of that, one is sometimes driven to believe, is the Almighty Himself. But the question one must ask oneself is this: what could Ysaÿe do, what can Menuhin do, that the others couldn't and can't? I do not mean in matters like technique or sweetness of tone—Paganini may have been unique, for all I know, in respect of the first and Kreisler of the second: I am thinking of more ultimate musicalities, and shall try to illustrate what I mean.

We first heard Yehudi Menuhin on November 14th 1929, a few days after his London debut, when he was twelve: he played the Brahms concerto at an L.S.O. concert conducted by Fritz Busch. He had long been famous in America, but we had also heard about him from Edmond Fleg, the French dramatist and poet, who was a friend of his family and an intimate of Georges Enesco, who, though not Yehudi's teacher, had often coached the boy on his visits to Europe. (Fleg and Enesco were collaborating at the time on a Shakespearian opera, and we were to hear Enesco improvise on themes from it at Fleg's apartment overlooking Notre-Dame.) So we were prepared for something more than the average prodigy, but even so he was a revelation, not as a prodigy but as a musician. We heard him whenever we could: playing the Mendelssohn concerto in 1930 and the Beethoven in 1931; and it was on this last occasion that what I prefer to call not a miracle but an inevitability happened. He was nearing the end of the first movement, and had played the cadenza with extreme but not unsurpassable brilliance; and then, as the second subject returned, there came a purity from his violin that was at once childlike and divine. I rank that moment with the very greatest of my musical experiences. It may be that there was something subjective about my reaction: that I was in the mood to outsoar earthly shadows and find divinity in his playing when perfect tone, perfect time and perfect phrasing were all that was there. I think far otherwise. But if so, all that is being said is this: that by these qualities, combined with a total lack of self-awareness and total surrender to what is in hand, the divinity of great music is itself immaculately revealed.

I had a similar experience with Yehudi Menuhin a few months ago. He was playing the Beethoven concerto at the Albert Hall with one of the Oistrakhs conducting, and not really intending to listen for more than a few minutes (I was drafting advertisements) I turned on the wireless. I of course listened to the end. I was familiar with every note of the music, more familiar even than I had been on that other occasion in 1931: but it dawned on me as fresh as heaven and earth on the day of creation.

The other annual event of my boyhood (alongside Ysaÿe and Pugno), namely Cortot-Thibaud-Casals, comes back to me as an emanation of Casals that allowed him to play trios without loss to his identity, and without loss to the identity, either, of Cortot and Thibaud, partners that came near him in greatness. But it was not till the early thirties that I was to become really familiar with the masterpieces of chamber-music and with some of the smaller pieces, Haydn quartets and Schubert trios and suchlike, that are in the same relation to the opus 131 as 'Shall I compare thee?' is to Hamlet. The Busch and Lener quartets chiefly instructed me, with nothing to choose between them, unless the Busch was perhaps a little more virile than the other: and both gave us the greatest of all such musical experiences as extend over a period, namely the whole series of Beethoven quartets, played not only with a (for the most part) perfect ensemble but with an individuality of interpretation that is nevertheless based on a firmly established tradition. The Busch people were often joined by Rudolf Serkin for piano quartets or quintets, and I once heard the Brahms horn trio played by Adolf Busch, Rudolf Serkin and Aubrey Brain: a composition that may have saved my sanity, for when during my illness in 1942 I was sleepless for twenty-two days my wife used to play it to me on a borrowed gramophone, this being one of the few pieces of music that seemed able, not indeed to give me sleep, but to soothe my tired nerves. Berlioz and Sir William Walton also helped to rescue me on that occasion. We were staying at the Nethybridge Hotel, Walton, my wife and myself, and he noticed, as I think no one else did except the hall porter (who recommended Vat 69, and sent me up a bottle 'out of his own pocket'), that something was wrong. So I told him about my insomnia, and how I always put off going to bed till the last possible moment, knowing that the tossing would begin all over again: and he replied that he had a private room with a piano in it, and would I care to go and sit with him any night I liked and as late as I like while he improvised a bit? I often went, and sooner or later always asked him for 'Voici des roses', which also soothed me. I bless him.

If I say that Aubrey Brain, who assisted at my salvation by making that Brahms record, was an orchestral player supreme in his kind, which everyone knows already, it is for the purpose of mentioning another, namely James Bradshaw, who till his retirement a year or two ago was tympanist to the Philharmonia. I am ignorant about drumming and can give no technical description, but my word will please be taken for it that in his whispering taps or beats; in the poise of his arm, like that of a great pianist's fingers—the sense of hovering and weighing—a second before committal; in his machine-gun fortissimi, with right arm racing over and hitting to left and left arm racing over and hitting to right; and in his phrasing, etcetera etcetera, he equalled Menuhin and Casals (which sounds extravagant but isn't) in the perfection of his artistry. I always took my opera-glasses along to watch him with, as I never watch a conductor, for I was fascinated by his every nuance. And there was another thing that made him unique: other tympanists occasionally put an ear to their drums for tuning purposes but he did so almost every second he wasn't playing, as if conscience forbade him to take a risk. For the same reason he arrived on the platform not only in advance of the other players, as many tympanists do, but almost in advance of the ushers.

I had gone behind one evening after Klemperer had been conducting the Choral Symphony and was talking to the old man when Bradshaw, whom he had summoned, came in. Klemperer thanked him for his work in the symphony, and I added a superfluous tribute: whereupon Bradshaw showed signs of considerable emotion. So he must be a very modest man: one of those however who, unlike the eminent politician in the Winston Churchill story, have a hell of a lot to be immodest about.

Before leaving the subject of chamber-music I should like to chronicle a special occasion. In the concert-hall of Broadcasting House round about 1934 we heard the Kolisch Quartet play the opus 130 with the Grosse Fuge in its proper place as its finale: an overwhelming experience that is unlikely to be repeated.

II

Apart from chamber-music and *Lieder* singing, I see our resumed concert-going of 1926-1936 as centring in a group of composers and executants, some of whom I have touched on already. I shall now run rapidly through the rest, and then finish.

§ 1

The composers were Stravinsky, Mahler and Berlioz.

1. The Stravinsky years were 1931 and 1934. In 1931 we saw and heard him twice; and the first of these concerts was not only memorable to musicians and music-lovers in general, for this was the first British performance of 'Capriccio', with the composer at the piano, but specially memorable to us, for he conducted our own 'L'Oiseau de Feu'. But the second concert, later in the year, was even more eventful: he was again conducting, this time the 'Symphonie de Psaumes' and the violin concerto. Neither had been heard in England before, and the second had had its first performance anywhere (in Berlin) less than a month earlier. Samuel Dushkin, to whom the composer records his indebtedness on the first page of the score, was the soloist.

It is difficult to disentangle first impressions of music from subsequent ones: but I remember being greatly moved by the solemnity of the coda to the Laudate dominum in the Psalms, and delighted (I was hearing a lot of Wagner at the time) by the economy of the concerto. The composer had spoken of this in an interview.[1] "The duration of a composition nowadays," he said, "can no longer be measured by those of the past. For a Mozart the invention of the themes represented, if one may say so, the maximum effort; all the rest was made up in great part of a certain formalism, or, at least, technical skill had the upper hand over creative fantasy. It is understood that, as he was Mozart, the skill is always great, but at the same time it is always distinguishable from the pure lyrical moment. With the development of the theme, the

[1] *The Daily Telegraph.*

repetitions, refrains, and necessary *cadenze*, the half-hour was soon reached. But now that in a scholastic sense this development of the theme no longer exists, and still less repetitions (I am speaking, of course of my own music), now that every bar is the result of an enormous condensation of thought, so that sometimes in a whole day's work I just manage to write one or two; proportions have changed, and a concerto of fifteen minutes is already a monumental work. Naturally, it would be easy to lengthen the duration, but what would be added would be nothing but padding, inert matter, sound, but not music."

But the climax of those Stravinsky years was to come in 1934, when he conducted the British première of *Perséphone*, with Ida Rubinstein speaking the name-part and René Maison singing Eumolpe.

Perséphone is performed far too rarely. André Gide's poem touches the profoundest issues of human destiny and of existence itself; and Stravinsky has made of it an intensely moving expression of the *lacrimae rerum*, and, above that, of a hope that does not merely strive with despair but lies at the heart of it. I suggested when I was discussing Gluck's *Orfeo* that only three other works for the stage were marked by so consistent a purity. The ones I had in mind were Monteverdi's *Orfeo*, Berlioz' *L'Enfance du Christ* (if that can be called a work for the stage) and *Perséphone*: which in its variety of expression betokens not only a great musician but a man of the widest human sympathies, just as the unity in which this variety is enclosed, without for a moment breaking it, betokens not only the same but, by reason of the spiritual purity that pervades it, a man of deep religious faith. Rythmically it is irresistible: and its melodic beauty time and time again touches the heart. Its economy, moreover, argues a rare self-restraint: from the simplicity of the opening chorus to the tension between agony and acceptance at the close not a note is wasted. I do not understand how anyone who knows *Perséphone* can regard Stravinsky as other than the greatest living composer, or deny him a place among the great composers of any age.

2. It was at a Courtauld-Sargent concert in 1930 that I first heard *Das Lied von der Erde*, which I had missed at its performance in England, at the beginning of 1914, under Sir Henry Wood. Bruno Walter conducted, with Rosetta Anday and Jacques Urlus as the singers.

Bruno Walter worshipped Mahler, as my anecdote about that evening at Salzburg will have made clear: Mahler the musician and Mahler the man; and it was inherent in his generosity that he could never spare himself as a conductor or rest quiet in conversation till beauty and value as he saw them had got their due. I met him often, and doubt whether on a single occasion the name of Mahler did not somehow crop up. I once ineptly complained after a performance of *Rheingold* that one of the horns had bubbled, and he replied that this might always happen: "even Mahler couldn't prevent it".

He loved *Das Lied von der Erde* best of all Mahler's works, and anxious that everyone else should love it too wrote the following note for the programme of that 1930 performance:

"'The Song of the Earth' is a cycle of six songs, of which the sixth bears the title 'The Farewell'. This title could appropriately be applied to the whole cycle, for its composition was inspired by the thought of parting.

"The hand of death had already been laid on Gustav Mahler when this music was written; a serious and unexpected affection of the heart which he had acquired in his later years soon made the composer intimately familiar with the thought of death. He was well prepared to meet it; a man who believed in God, and who always had lived in God, deeply inclined to the mystical, and always full of thoughts, feelings and presentiments of eternity, the atmosphere of death now filled his soul more and more.

"We have few works of art which come from such an atmosphere, surely none which brings this vision of the sunset—the beauty of the fading light, the clearness of the evening before the darkness descends—into music, with such moving truthfulness.

"In the first song, 'The Drinking Song of the Misery of the World', in the second, 'Loneliness in Autumn', and also in the fifth, 'The Drunken One in Spring', the volcanic power of a titanic nature like Mahler's is still alive, but the despair, the wildness, the scorn, the gloom—all have something in them which points to 'The End'. It seems as though somebody was saying 'With this I am giving my last word on that matter'.

"In the third and fourth songs, 'Of Youth' and 'Of Beauty', we see more clearly expressed the gravity and tenderness of the farewell, as well as the high serenity of the passing soul. In the last and principal movement of the work, 'The Farewell', we are led from the pain and sadness of parting to a serene and unearthly peace.

"Those who were fortunate enough to be personally associated at this time with Mahler will never be able to forget how his whole being continuously overflowed with affectionate emotion. 'The dear earth'—with these words the last part of 'The Farewell' begins, and this deep love for 'the dear earth' coloured every word, every look of Mahler's at that time.

"In the lyrics of the Chinese poet, Li-tai-po, a soul affinity greets the composer, over the distances of space and the centuries of time; and we may look upon it as a wonderful event that Mahler, pre-occupied with thoughts of death, should, in this moment, make the acquaintance of this far-distant, long-deceased friend, whose poems, created by the same vision, he is able to unite to his music.

"So a work of art, *sub specie mortis*, to vary the famous saying of Spinoza, was created, and the harmony between the Chinese poet and the Austrian musician shows clearly, by its wonderful example, that true art comes from the depths of the soul, where time and space do not exist.

"Mahler himself never heard this, his own most personal work, which is now very frequently performed. He died in May 1911, and the first performance was given in the autumn of the same year under my direction, in Munich. I know that I am not acting contrary to his wishes when I preface this performance in London of 'The Song of the Earth' with these lines.

"I am sure the work needs no explanation in words in order to be understood, but in view of its unique character it may be permissible to give this short note on the spiritual circumstances that went to its creation."

I feel presumptuous to be saying it in view of Walter's authority, but my own feeling is that there is a reference in this music to something wider than personal death. We in England were carefree before 1914, but on the Continent of Europe, and perhaps particularly in Vienna, there was anguished regret, as disaster approached, for a day that would soon be done: and it is surely this that sounds again and again in the heartbreaking sadness of *Das Lied von der Erde*. For years I could never hear its 'Abschied' without calling to mind, in a mood as regretful as its own, those long afternoons on the Cher in the summer of 1914. 'O Schönheit! O ewigen Liebens—Lebens—trunk'ne Welt!' 'O Beauty! O Eternal Love—Life—drunken World!' And then, at the close, two syllables so lingeringly repeated that you think they will never end: 'Ewig . . . ewig', 'Ever . . . ever'.

My attitude to the 'Abschied' (as to Mahler in general) has varied from time to time over the years. Most often I have found it full of tragic beauty, but have thought of it sometimes as over-ripe, over-romantic,

over-sensitive, over-expressive. But for one work at least by Gustav
Mahler I feel unreservedly grateful: I mean the supremely beautiful
eighth symphony, with its grandeur, its agony, the depths of its searching, the heights of its aspiration. I have heard it only once, but cannot
think I shall change my opinion.

3. We heard others works by Mahler, of course, including a specially fine performance of the second symphony, conducted by
Walter; but my impression is that he was far less often performed
during the period in question than he is today. The opposite is the case
with Berlioz. In 1936 alone we heard *L'Enfance du Christ*, conducted
by Malcolm Sargent; *The Damnation*, conducted by Beecham;
Romeo and Juliet (complete), conducted by Albert Wolff; the
Requiem, conducted by Hamilton Harty; the *Symphonie Funèbre
et Triomphale*, conducted by the same; and *Harold in Italy*, conducted I am not sure by whom. In other years we heard the Te Deum,
once without the final march and once with it, on both occasions
conducted by Beecham; several other performances of *The Damnation*; and one of the *Fantastique*, conducted by Monteux. Nothing
of this sort would be likely today—six works in a single year—except
at a festival specifically devoted to Berlioz.

§ 2

Our pianist was Schnabel.
I have already suggested one of the essentials in Schnabel's playing,
and shall not attempt a more general analysis here: I shall only say,
first, that in my opinion he was far and away the greatest pianist of our
age, as many but by no means all would agree (some could hardly
abide him, as some, often the same people and for the same reason,
cannot abide Klemperer): and secondly that, as not so many would
agree, he was as great in Mozart and Schubert as in Beethoven. We
heard him a couple of dozen times or more in the years 1929-1934,
his approach to an overwhelming climax being gradual. In the first of
these years he played concertos by Beethoven and Brahms: in 1930 the
Mozart concerto in A major: in 1931 the Diabelli variations and the
great Beethoven sonata opus 110; and in 1932 the lovely posthumous
one by Schubert in B major. During these years he had also played a
good deal of Schumann and Brahms.
Then, later in 1932, came the whole series of Beethoven's thirty-two

sonatas at seven recitals. This was an experience which, in point of varied musical interest and recurrent sublimity, has been equalled for me on few other occasions and surpassed on only two: namely when the Busch and Lener people played the whole series of Beethoven quartets. For thirteen days we lived in Beethoven's intellectual and spiritual world, recreated for us by the genius of Artur Schnabel.

What came after—his collaboration with the Pro Arte Quartet in the Brahms quintet, with Huberman in some of the piano and violin sonatas, and with the London Philharmonic Orchestra in three Mozart concertos—was not an anticlimax: this would have been impossible, Schnabel being Schnabel; but for anyone who was present on those afternoons and evenings in the winter of 1932 it will always be in virtue of what he did with the thirty-two sonatas that he must be thought of not only as a supreme pianist but, I shall dare to say, as Beethoven's partner.

We were privileged to know him fairly well, for we saw a lot, as we still happily do, of Dorothy and Robert Mayer, those benefactors of the musical youth, and they were among his intimates. They had a studio off Norland Square, to which, for talk and informal music, they would often invite a dozen friends or so on an otherwise musically blank evening; and Schnabel was always willing to play for us, sometimes alone, sometimes with a string trio or quartet. (Robert Mayer was one of the few whom Schnabel would see when he was dying from a particularly dreadful disease.) There was quite a different side to the man than the one he showed at the Queen's Hall, with its almost terrible involvement in the music and obliviousness to the public: he was easy with everyone, often light-hearted and wholly without a sense of importance. I ventured to rag him once about the way he snorted at the piano, and even went so far as to imitate him, but he did not mind a bit. I think I must add him to the small list of musicians I have loved.

§ 3

Among conductors of the decade in question Otto Klemperer meant little or nothing to us. There is a mystery about his first appearance in London. He assures me that it was at a Courtauld-Sargent concert in 1929 (at which we were present), when he gave a Bach suite and, for its first performance in England, Bruckner's eighth symphony; but in the programme of a B.B.C. concert at the Albert Hall in 1926, when Strauss conducted some of his own compositions, it was announced that 'Otto Klemperer, General Music Director at Wiesbaden' would conduct at a later concert in the series. I must leave the point to be cleared up by historians of music.

Anyhow, I must have been deaf on that evening of 1929, or the Bruckner may have sent me to sleep, as Bruckner occasionally does (and occasionally doesn't—I am highly ambivalent about him): for Klemperer, as it turns out to have been, made no impression on me at all, and I had no idea I had ever heard him at the time in question until, digging out material for this memoir, I chanced on that 1929 programme. But when suddenly, as it seemed, he turned up at the Festival Hall a few years ago, it was not a question, for anyone in his audience, of whether he made an impression, the question was what sort of impression he made. He affected a few disagreeably: the remainder discussed only the degree of his excellence.

For my own part I had no doubt on that evening, and have had no doubt ever since, that he has been surpassed as a Beethoven conductor by no other I have heard (and I have heard most of the conductors of my time) and equalled only by one, namely Weingartner. The reason, I think, lies in a number of intrinsically simple factors: justness of rhythm; sensitive phrasing, never distorted for effect; an understanding of "where the tune lies", without the smallest temptation to give it undue emphasis; and the power to bring out every detail in the score without damage to the totality of the design. In respect of the last, I am sometimes reminded of Klemperer's Beethoven by Sansovino's Libreria Vecchia in the Piazzetta. I reproduce it, so that the reader may decide whether I am being fanciful.

And then there is his sanity, which is the same thing as his refusal to exaggerate. Those who heard Furtwängler's Ninth Symphony will remember that he began it with a pianissimo so etiolated that you could hardly hear it. Klemperer's is a true pianissimo, but a positive one too, as it should be.

There are those who quarrel with his tempi, and particularly with the slow one in the Pastoral Sympathy. For me, on the other hand, such criticisms are out of order: if Klemperer does it like that, then that is how Beethoven would surely wish it to be done. This is not stupid hero-worship: I am as little a hero-worshipper as anyone. It is simply that for me Klemperer, in his reading of Beethoven, is his own sufficient authority for any point in it that others may query: he is one of those who correct an old tradition and create a new one.

Nor do I agree with people who, while subscribing to everything I have said, question his greatness in the interpretation of music other

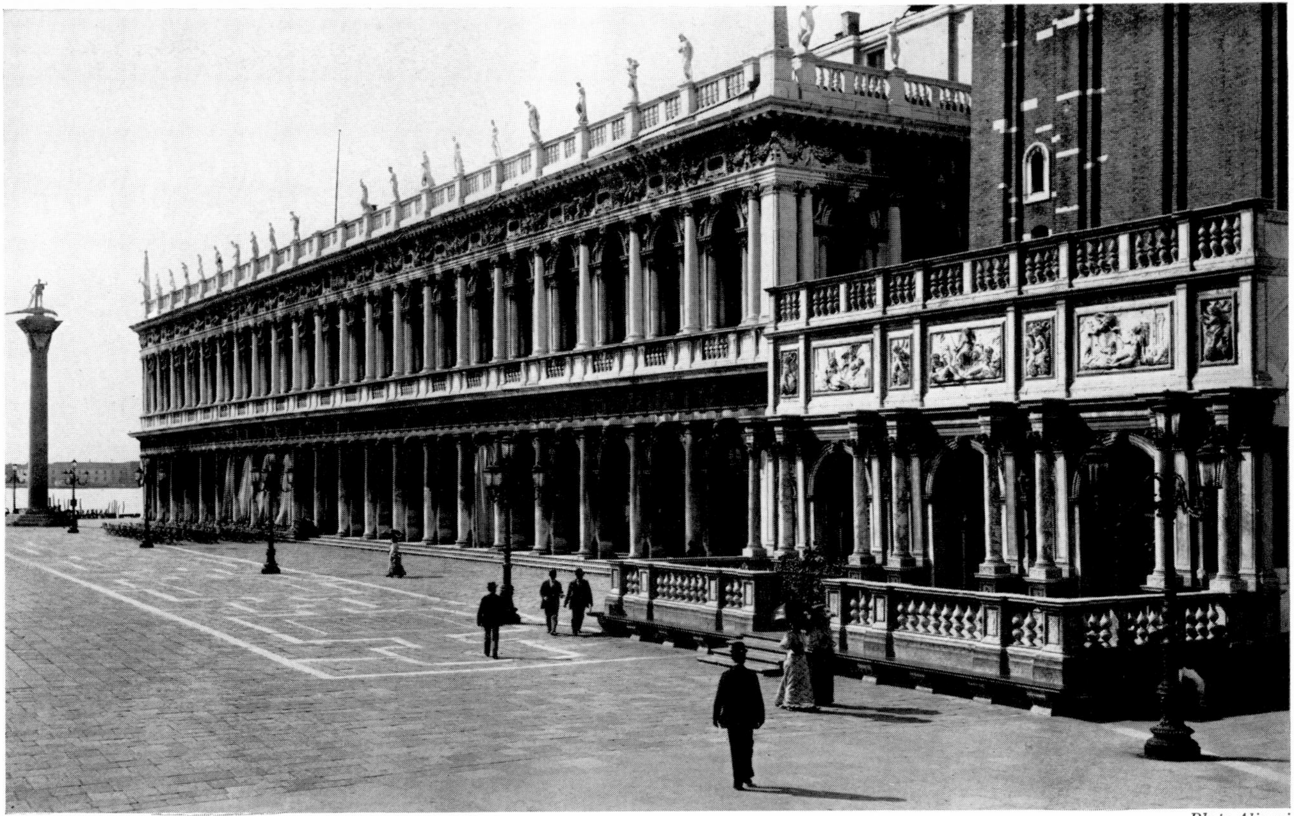

Photo Alinari

THE LIBRERIA VECCHIA

For
Mr. Gollancz
cordially
Otto Klemperer
1964

than Beethoven's. I think his Mozart superb; and his *Symphonie Fantastique* the other evening seemed bigger and more moving than ever before (his phrasing of the extended version of the motto was incomparable). In one case only have I felt critical: I thought his reading of the Schubert "great" symphony a little rigid, a little like a pianist playing Chopin without rubato. But for once in a way I am persuaded that I must be wrong.

Is there more in it than the narrowly musical qualities I detailed at the start, combined with sincerity, devotion to the composer and utter self-forgetfulness? Has his suffering, as great perhaps as Beethoven's own, something to do with it? I cannot say, but this I will say: that when I see that half-paralysed old man shuffling on to conduct a symphony by a stone-deaf composer, and know that heaven will be the result, I am comforted by the thought, dangerous though it is, that physical evil may be an occasion for the highest spiritual good.

But though we had no Klemperer in 1926-1936, or no Klemperer to speak of, the conductors we did have were good enough, and so, apart from our own excellent ones, were the orchestras. Furtwängler brought over the Berlin Philharmonic and Walter the Vienna Philharmonic, and Toscanini was frequently here. We heard him conducting Wagner at a B.B.C. concert in 1936 or 1937. After that we heard very little music, as I have said, till 1948, my preoccupation first with Hitler and then with Jewish suffering and German starvation forbidding it. But when Toscanini returned in the summer of 1939 to conduct the nine symphonies we could not keep away, and it was with 'Freude, schöner Götterfunken, Tochter aus Elysium' that my nights at the Queen's Hall, which had given me almost my first musical happiness more than thirty years before, ended for ever.

This memoir, begun accidentally, as I have explained at the beginning of Chapter I, and written throughout exclusively for my own pleasure, now lacks nothing but a concluding paragraph. I shall call in Heine to provide it:

"Now, what is music? This question occupied me for hours before I fell asleep last night. Music is a strange thing. I would almost say it is miracle. For it stands halfway between thought and phenomenon, between spirit and matter, a sort of nebulous mediator, like and unlike each of the things it mediates—spirit that requires manifestation in time and matter that can do without space.

"We do not know what music is."

Adagio.

APPENDIX

I F I WERE PUT in charge of a nine months' opera season, and were limited to twenty-seven operas—three a month, as many as ought to be attempted—I should chose the following:

Monteverdi: *Orfeo, L'Incoronazione di Poppea*
Handel: *Semele*
Gluck: *Orfeo, Alceste,* an *Iphigeneia, Paris and Helen*
Beethoven: *Fidelio*
Mozart: *Idomeneo, Figaro, Don Giovanni, The Magic Flute*
Berlioz: *Les Troyens*
Wagner: *Die Meistersinger*
Bizet: *Carmen*
Bellini: *Norma*
Verdi: *Traviata, Don Carlo, Aida, Otello, Falstaff*
Puccini: *Bohème*
Strauss: *Elektra, Ariadne*
Debussy: *Pelléas*
Berg: *Wozzeck, Lulu*

After hearing it, I might substitute *Moses and Aaron* for one of the Glucks.

INDEX OF NAMES AND PLACES

INDEX OF NAMES AND PLACES

Compositions will be found under the name of the composer, and opera-houses, etc., under the name of the city. E.g. 'Don Giovanni' will be found under Mozart, and the San Carlo under Naples.

Abel of the Ivy, 174
Abruzzi, The, 42
Ackté, 128
Adolphus, Gustavus, 113
Aigen, 174
Aix-en-Provence, 60
Albani, 60
Alboni, 20
Alvary, 88
Anday, 217
Angeles, de los, 24
Angerer, 188
Annigoni, 139
Anselmi, 156
Arditi, 116
Arnaud, The Abbé, 117
Avallon, 174

Bach, J. S., 30, 35, 147, 159, 188, 197, 200, 205, 221
Bacharach, 171
Bahr-Mildenburg, von, 71, 125
Baklanoff, 70
Bardi, Giovanni de', 99, 100, 101, 122
Barzun, Jacques, 41
Bassi, 87, 154
Basil, de, 170
Bayreuth, 78, 80, 84, 98, 99, 116, 168, 183
Bean, Ernest, 37
Beatles, The, 208
Bechstein, Hans, 71, 80

Beecham, 40, 59, 72, 77, 87, 89, 115, 125, 127, 130, 141, 164, 167, 170, 179, 185, 186, 197, 198, 201, 220
Beethoven, 141-151 et passim
Bellini, 23, 25, 50, 59, 60, 65, 74, 95, 139, 162
Bender, 80, 125, 142, 189
Benedict, 144
Bennett, Arnold, 163
Berg, 29, 78, 102, 133, 196
Berlioz, 24, 33, 36, 37-42, 45, 48, 89, 91, 127, 142, 180, 199, 200, 204, 205, 214, 215, 217, 220, 223
Berlin, Isaiah, 184
Bizet, 28, 89, 114, 117, 129, 134, 142, 159, 170, 201
Blackham, Joyce, 142
Blake, William, 121
Blum Léon, 157
Blum, Madame, 157
Bockelmann, 88, 89, 125, 185
Boïto, 163, 170, 197
Bolm, 169
Bonci, 156
Bonn, 146
Borgioli, Dino, 190
Borkh, 129
Borodin, 169
Botticelli, 39
Botting, Cecil, 53
Bradshaw, James, 215
Brahms, 34, 200, 201, 209, 210, 211, 214, 215, 220, 221

Brain, Aubrey, 214, 215
Braque, 29
Brema, 115, 116
Bremen, 145
Britten, 33-37, 111, 124, 196
Brixton Theatre, The, 114
Brouwenstijn, 142
Bruckner, 188, 221, 222
Bumbry, 198
Burke, Edmund, 168
Busch, Fritz, 213
Busch Quartet, The, 214
Butt, 198
Buxtehude, 205
Byndon-Ayres, 128

Cairns, David, 38
Callas, 24, 50, 52, 71, 95, 124, 126,
  136, 138, 139, 152, 154, 159, 168,
  172
Calvé, 114
Camussi, 162
Cantelo, 41
Carrěno, 209
Carl Rosa Company, The, 114
Caruso, 22, 27, 66, 70, 73, 90, 95, 156,
  159, 160, 169, 204
Casa, della, 24, 133
Casals, 169, 208, 211, 213, 214, 215
Catena, 197
Cavalieri, Lina, 165
Cechetti, 169
Chaliapin, 22, 24, 157, 167-172, 204
Charlottenburg, 72, 95, 133
Charpentier, 22, 85, 120, 167
Chelsea Opera Group, The, 142
Chopin, 65, 223
Christoff, 24, 172
Churchill, Stella, 175
Churchill, Sir Winston, 78, 215
Cigna, 93
Cochran, C. B., 170
Coleridge, S. T., 34, 105
Coliseum, The, 78, 115

Como, Lake, 178
Cornelius, Peter, 71
Coronet Theatre, The, 73, 114
Corri, 92
Cortot, 208, 214
Corvo, Baron, 152
Covent Garden, Queen's Hall, Albert
  Hall, Festival Hall, Sadler's Wells,
  etc. etc., passim
Cox, 92
Crespin, 43, 131
Crook, 142
Cross, 92, 95, 159, 189
Culp, 208, 209

D'Albert, 162
Dalmorès, 70
D'Alvarez, Marguérite, 165
D'Annunzio, 111
Davis, Colin, 37, 40, 48, 142, 153
Dean of Canterbury, The 'red', 208
Debussy, 22, 36, 69, 102, 117, 120-124,
  137, 141, 153, 186
Delius, 128
Délibes, 72, 129
Dent, E. J., 74, 161
Destinn, 22, 27, 64, 66, 69, 70, 73, 78,
  88, 90, 93, 114, 130, 139, 153, 154,
  155, 156, 157, 160, 172, 189, 198,
  204, 210, 211
Dickens, 163
Dickinson, Emily, 63
D'Oisley, 128
Dolci, Carlo, 140
Donizetti, 65, 67, 74, 75, 158, 188
Dorati, 198
Dvořák, 188
Drury Lane Theatre, The, 167
Dushkin, 216
Dux, 130

Easton, 157
Edinburgh, 50, 183

Edvina, 120
Elgar, 116, 196, 200
Enesco, 213
Evans, Geraint, 139

Farrar, 27
Faure, Jean-Baptiste, 60
Ferrier, 116
Fiat Company, The, 44
Fischer-Dieskau, 133
Fisher of Lambeth, Lord, 27, 66
Flagstad, 88
Fleg, 213
Florence, 87, 90, 174, 210
Fokine, 169
Forsell, 189
Fournier, 213
Frankfurt, 49, 129, 141
Franz, 70
Fretwell, 142
Freud, 104
Friedlander, Arthur, 165
Friedlander, Rosetta, 59, 115
Furtwängler, 89, 222, 223

Galilei, Vincenzo, 100
Galli-Curci, 73
Gandy, 142
Garden, Mary, 121
Gautier, Théophile, 61
Gay, 115
Gerhardt, 80, 200, 208, 209, 210
Ghiaurov, 24
Giannini, 93, 156, 190
Gide, André, 217
Gigli, 95, 156
Gilgen, St., 183
Gilibert, 22
Gilly, Dinh, 22, 70, 93, 154, 156
Giordani, 210
Giardano, 162
Giroux, Bob, 91
Giulini, 36, 197, 198

Glazounov, 170
Gleeson-White, 141
Glock, William, 186
Gluck, 45, 60, 69, 75, 79, 102, 113-119, 122, 141, 147, 153, 163, 196, 199, 210, 217
Glyndebourne, 133, 152, 189
Gobbi, 175
Godowsky, 209
Golz, 125, 129
Goossens, Eugène, 114
Gorr, 24
Gounod, 74, 120, 162, 163, 190
Grant, Elsie, 65, 120
Grieg, 199
Grisi, 20, 54, 180
Gruhn, 135
Gui, 152
Guilbert, Yvette, 163

Habich, 135, 185
Halévy, 23
Hamburg, 78, 137, 145, 146
Hammerstein, Oscar, 164
Handel, 19, 82, 117, 188
Hanslick, 187
Harewood, the Earl of, 80
Harris (barber-tobacconist), 21, 155
Harty, 40, 72, 220
Harwood, 142
Hatchard, 128
Hauk, 114
Haydn, 199, 200, 211, 214
Heine, 223
Heger, 88
Heldy, 94, 157
Heuss, Theodor, 146, 202
Heyworth, Peter, 32, 43, 46, 47, 70, 75, 95, 120, 189, 204
Higham, David, 48
Hindemith, 63
Hippodrome, The, 115
Holbrooke, 167
Holloway Theatre, The, 114

Homburg, Madame, 182
Honegger, 188
Hope-Wallace, Philip, 119
Hotter, 89, 106
Howard de Walden, 167
Huberdeau, 70
Hugo, Victor, 106
Humperdinck, 115, 158
Hüsch, 135

Ibsen, 113
Ivogün, 23, 72, 133, 189

Jameson, 81
Jannings, 163
Jarred, 116
Jeritza, 162
Jöken, 135
Journet, 22
Joyce, James, 23
Jülich, 137, 138, 156
Jurinac, 142, 152

Kalisch, 132
Karsavina, 169
Kasznár, 174, 175
Keats, 34, 142
Kempe, 213
Kern, 131, 188, 190
Kipnis, 88, 131, 185
Klee, 29
Kleiber, 130, 188
Klemperer, 24, 30, 37, 47, 62, 77, 89,
    127, 142, 144, 145, 147, 204, 215,
    220, 221, 222
Klingenstein, 180
Kobbé, 80, 81, 97, 99
Kolisch Quartet, The, 215
Kommer of Czernowitz, 183
Kousnietzoff, 73
Krauss, Clemens, 182
Kreisler, 88, 213

Lago, 116
Lammers, 125
Lassalle, 60
Legge, Walter, 168
Lehmann, Lilli, 88
Lehmann, Lotte, 23, 46, 47, 82, 87,
    88, 89, 91, 130, 131, 135, 139, 142,
    153, 157, 172, 179, 185, 187, 188,
    189, 202, 210, 211
Leider, 87, 88, 130, 172, 189
Lemnitz, 185
Lener Quartet, The, 214
Leon, Luis de, 63
Leoncavallo, 19, 115, 129, 160, 195
Leroux, 162
Lessing, 113
Lewis, Richard, 152
Li-tai-po, 219
Lieder, 24, 34, 80, 125, 196, 201, 209,
    210, 211, 216
Lind, Jenny, 20, 146
Linz, 188
Lipkowska, 73
List, 190
Liszt, 210
Litvinne, 71
Ljungberg, 129, 156, 185
Lloyd, Marie, 194
Loeb, Sydney, 183
London Opera House, The, 164
Low, Rachel and Prudence, 157
Lubin, 119, 131
Ludwig, Christa, 131
Lully, 188
Lunn, 70, 71, 76, 89, 115
Lussan, Zélie de, 114
Lutyens, 32
Lyceum Theatre, The, 75
Lynd, Sigle, 175, 184
Lynn, Olga, 183

Macaulay, Rose, 158, 171, 181
McCormack, 22, 72, 156, 160, 189,
    198

Maeterlinck, 113, 121

Mahler, 134, 143, 144, 145, 175, 209, 211, 216, 217, 218

Mairecker Quartet, The, 182

Maison, 217

Manzoni, 197

Marcoux, 22, 70, 120, 154, 156, 171

Mario, 20, 60, 141

Martin, Riccardo, 154

Martinelli, 22, 70, 91, 154, 156

Masaryk, Jan, 28

Mascagni, 19, 43, 115, 160, 195

Massenet, 43, 44, 128, 158, 165, 167

Materna, 88

Matters, 92

Maurel, 60

Maurier, George du, 52, *sqq.*

Mayer, Dorothy and Robert, 221

Mayr, 23, 47, 88, 130, 131, 187, 188, 189

Melba, 21, 66, 76, 88, 94, 156, 157, 159

Melchior, 24, 87, 88, 91, 163, 211

Mendelssohn, 195, 196, 213

Mengelberg, 140

Menuhin, 36, 92, 202, 213, 214, 215

Meran, 179

Metropolitan music-hall, The, 194

Meyerbeer, 22, 59, 60, 67, 72, 75, 196, 203

Michaelson, Assur, 65, 120

Michaelson, Selina, 65

Milan, 90, 91, 93, 114, 157, 164, 167

Monaco, del, 91

Monteux, 37, 89, 220

Monteverdi, 38, 102, 119, 120, 210, 217

Monte, dal, 45

Moody-Manners Company, The, 114, 141

Moore, Gerald, 211

Mordkin, 170

Morley, Rose, 211

Moscheles, 142

Mowrer, Edgar, 178

Moussorgsky, 22, 124, 167, 169

Mozart, 18, 19, 27, 30, 37, 41, 45, 65, 69, 74, 79, 89, 92, 102, 105, 109, 117, 121, 127, 136, 137, 140, 141, 142, 152, 153, 161, 173, 178, 181, 182, 187, 188-190, 196, 198, 199, 200, 210, 211, 216, 220, 221, 223

Mullings, 92

Munich, 132, 133, 134, 178

Murray, Gilbert, 201

Music-camp, The, 19, 47, 48

Muzio, 76, 91

Nachtigall, Herr, 20

Naples, 74

New York, 37, 113, 166

Nissen, 185

Nichols, Robert, 175, 177

Nicolai, 203

Nicolini, 60

Nietzsche, 177

Nijinsky, 120, 169

Nikisch, 80, 134, 167, 200

Nillson, Christine, 21, 141

Nilsson, Birgit, 24, 88, 106, 152, 183

Nono, 30

Noorden, van, 114

Nordica, 58

Novotna, 190, 211

Oakey, 64

Offenbach, 128, 165,

Oistrakhs, The, 214

Old Vic, The, 92

Olczewska, 87, 88, 89, 135

Oliver, Vic, 84

O'Mara, 141

Onegin, 88, 116, 211

Osten, van der, 130

O'Sullivan, 23

Oved, Moshe, 181

Owen, Wilfred, 34, 35

Pacetti, 156
Pacher, 183
Pachmann, 64, 208, 209
Pacini, 45
Paderewski, 88, 208, 209
Paganini, 213
Palermo, 114
Palladium, The, 78
Pampanini, 156
Panzera, 39
Paris, 23, 39, 43, 45, 47, 51, 75, 94, 95, 116, 119, 128, 131, 137, 142, 144, 157, 158, 159, 163, 167, 170, 174, 187, 188, 197
Parry, 196
Pasta, 20
Patti, 20, 22, 23, 55, 58, 60, 66, 114
Patzak, 142
Pauly, 142
Pavlova, 170
Pears, 40
Peri, 100, 119, 122
Petersburg, St., 52, 92, 168
Pifferari, the, 173
Philharmonia, The, 47, 77, 147, 168, 198
Pilenko, Elizabeth, 202
Pinza, 157, 190, 197
Pitt, 141
Pitz, 47, 168
Plançon, 169, 204
Plato, 62, 77, 207
Plotinus, 63, 121
Ponselle, 23, 74, 95
Price, 198
Pro Arte Quartet, The, 221
Proch, 114
Proms, The, 199-202
Puccini, 22, 38, 108, 124, 126, 129, 136, 137, 138, 152, 153, 154, 156-160, 162, 170, 180
Pugno, 208, 212, 213, 214

Purcell, 196

Queen Mary, Her Majesty, 155, 156

Rabaud, 188
Radford, 71, 128
Rappe, von, 78
Raisa, 156
Rameau, 188
Rankl, 144
Ravel, 188
Ravoglis, The, 60, 113, 115
Reinhardt, 130, 131, 185, 189
Renaud, 165
Reszkes, The de, 58, 60, 141, 169
Rennert, 137
Rethberg, 23, 88, 93, 157, 211
Richter, Hans, 71, 80, 85, 116, 120, 183, 200
Richter, Sviatoslav, 65
Rimsky-Korsakoff, 170
Robinson, Bernard, 48
Rossellini, 18
Rome, 28, 41, 42, 114, 119, 157, 173
Ronald, 163
Rooper, Ralph Bonfoy, 52
Rooy, van, 24, 71, 80, 89
Rose, 125
Roselle, 93
Rosenthal, Harold, 144
Rosenthal, Moriz, 209
Rossini, 23, 44, 45, 53, 59, 60, 72, 158, 170, 179, 203
Rothenburg, 178
Roussel, 188
Royal Academy of Music, The, 115
Royal College of Music, The, 128
Royal Choral Society, The, 195
Rubinstein, Artur, 37
Rubinstein, Ida, 217
Ruffo, 45
Rumi, 63
Russell, Ella, 60

St. Pancras Town Hall, The, 45
Saint-Saëns, 89, 116
Saltzmann-Stevens, 71
Salzburg, 28, 116, 134, 144, 152, 173-190, 210, 217
Sammarco, 72, 73, 156
Sammons, 128
Sapelnikoff, 209
Sargent, 220
Sauer, 209
Savoy Hotel, The, 115, 171, 173, 175
Savoy Theatre, The, 115
Scacciata, 93, 157
Schalchi, 60
Schalk, 47, 72, 80, 142, 188
Schipper, 185
Schnabel, 30, 88, 148, 220, 221
Schönberg, 124
Schonberg, Harold, 208
Schöne, 142
Schorr, 88, 89, 185
Schröder-Devrient, 146
Schubert, 92, 105, 134, 182, 188, 199, 210, 211, 214, 220, 223
Schumann, Elisabeth, 23, 47, 87, 88, 89, 130, 131, 135, 185, 189, 202, 210, 211
Schumann, Robert, 200, 209, 220
Schumann-Heink, 88
Schwarz, 73
Scotti, 22, 27, 70, 76, 156, 189
Scotto, 43
Serafin, 119, 197
Serkin, 214
Shaftesbury Theatre, The, 116
Shakespeare, 34, 47, 103, 139, 213
Shaw, Bernard, 113, 117, 201
Shaw-Taylor, Desmond, 91
Shelley, 34, 60, 175
Siena, 93
Sibelius, 199
Silveri, 172
Simionato, 89
Simoneau, 152

Slezak, 75
Smith, Matthew, 116
Smyth, 128, 170
Solomon, John David, 48
Spender, Stephen, 182
Spinoza, 117
Stabile, 91, 95, 189
Staegemann, 135
Stahremberg, 184
Stear, 172
Stein, Gertrude, 166
Stignani, 89
Strachey, John, 52, 155
Strauss, Johann, 128, 130, 133-135, 159, 180, 188, 210, 211
Strauss, Richard, 21, 23, 34, 43, 49, 101, 102, 120, 124-133, 141, 161, 168, 169, 200, 210, 211
Stravinsky, 27, 28, 43, 49, 169, 170, 201, 207, 216, 217
Stuttgart, 19, 178
Sucher, Rosa, 88
Sukerkandel, 182
Sullivan, Sir Arthur, 128
Sutherland, 21, 45, 74, 88, 162
Swedenborg, 176

Tamagno, 21, 75, 90, 92
Tamberlik, 60
Tauber, 47
Tchaikowsky, 195, 199
Tchernicheva, 169
Tebaldi, 138
Tertis, 128
Tessmer, 135
Tetrazzini, 22, 66, 72, 74, 94, 114, 204
Teyte, 22, 121
Thibaud, 208, 214
Thill, 119
Thomas, Ambroise, 60, 114, 128, 204
Thomson, Virgil, 166
Thorborg, 116
Titch, Little, 194
Tivoli music-hall, The, 132

Toller, 39
Toscanini, 28, 37, 89, 91, 127, 174,
    185, 186, 188, 190, 198, 223
Tosti, 114
Toye, 45, 94
Tree, Viola, 115
Trebelli, 21
Tubb, 128
Turner, Eva, 157
Turner, W. J., 40

Ude, 133
Unwin, Sir Stanley, 29
Urlus, 217

Vaughan Williams, 196
Venice, 75, 93, 141, 152, 173, 203, 222
Verdi, Chapters V, VII, VIII, pp. 196-
    198, *et passim*
Verona, 28, 179
Veronese, 140
Viardot, 163
Vickers, 142, 154
Vienna, 29, 43, 47, 87, 93, 134, 144,
    146, 164, 182, 188, 197, 223
Vinay, 91
Vincent, Ruth, 115
Visconti, 17, 136
Vishnevskaya, 71
Vivaldi, 83

Wagner, Richard, Chapters V, VI,
    VII, VIII, *et passim.*
Wagner, Wieland, 19, 46, 47
Walker, Edyth, 71, 125

Walter, 71, 72, 87, 89, 95, 116, 125,
    127, 130, 135, 142, 144, 145, 174,
    175, 182, 185, 188, 189, 202, 210,
    217
Walton, 214
Weidemann, 71, 125
Weingartner, 28, 127, 147, 188, 211
Welitsch, 129
Welsh National Opera Company,
    The, 59
Westerhausen, von, 162
White City, The, 61, 180, 202-205,
    208
Whitehill, 71, 77, 128, 141
Wildbrunn, 142
Wilde, Oscar, 61
Wittgenstein, 32
Wolf-Ferrari, 162
Wolf, Hugo, 184, 200, 209
Wolff, Albert, 220
Wolfgang, St. 183
Wood, 36, 78, 127, 171, 201, 202,
    217
Woodland, 142, 152
Wordsworth, 30, 31, 32, 117, 121
Wörle, 135

Ysaÿe, 88, 208, 212, 214

Zanelli, 91
Zeffirelli, 17, 44, 95, 119, 126, 136,
    137, 139, 140, 162, 195
Zenatello, 22, 27, 75, 76, 91
Zeretelli, 170
Zucchi, 22